Approaches to Teaching the Works of Ralph Waldo Emerson

Approaches to Teaching the Works of Ralph Waldo Emerson

Edited by

Mark C. Long
and
Sean Ross Meehan

The Modern Language Association of America
New York   2018

MLA and the MODERN LANGUAGE ASSOCIATION are trademarks
owned by the Modern Language Association of America.
For information about obtaining permission to reprint material from
MLA book publications, send your request by mail (see address below)
or e-mail (permissions@mla.org).

Library of Congress Cataloging-in-Publication Data
is available from the Library of Congress.

ISBN 978-1-60329-373-0 (cloth)
ISBN 978-1-60329-374-7 (paper)
ISBN 978-1-60329-375-4 (EPUB)
ISBN 978-1-60329-376-1 (Kindle)

Approaches to Teaching World Literature 155
ISSN 1059-1133

Cover illustration of the paperback and electronic editions:
Watercolor sketch of *Juniperus virginiana L.* (1908) from *Water-color
Sketches of Plants of North America and Europe*, vol. 1, by Helen Sharp.
Image from the Biodiversity Heritage Library (www.biodiversitylibrary.org).
Digitized by Chicago Botanic Garden, Lenhardt Library.

Published by The Modern Language Association of America
85 Broad Street, suite 500, New York, New York 10004-2434
www.mla.org

CONTENTS

ACKNOWLEDGMENTS

We are grateful to the community of Emerson teachers and scholars who have supported this project from the inception of the idea of this book to its completion. Wes Mott has offered invaluable support ever since this volume began with a simple question posed to him: why isn't Emerson represented in the MLA's Approaches to Teaching series? Ed Folsom offered encouragement over lunch at the 2014 American Literature Association Conference in Washington, DC, as the volume began to take shape. The members of the Ralph Waldo Emerson Society have received the prospect of this collection with enthusiasm, participating in the survey that provided material for the preparation of this book as well as contributing their classroom experiences and research in the essays collected in this volume. We acknowledge each of the contributors to our survey who offered useful insights into Emerson's continued relevance in the classroom. We are also grateful to the editors and readers at the Modern Language Association for their instructive professional guidance.

In addition to recognizing the institutions in which we teach, Keene State College in New Hampshire and Washington College in Maryland, we would like to recognize our students, whose interest and engagement with Emerson demonstrate the relevance of his work in our classrooms today and the continuing place of Emerson's ideas in our lives.

Part One

MATERIALS

Editions and Texts

With the recent completion of the definitive, ten-volume scholarly edition of all of Emerson's works published in his lifetime and under his supervision, *The Collected Works of Ralph Waldo Emerson* marks the culmination of a half century of vigorous textual editing that has conveyed the full range of Emerson's writing and thinking with unprecedented accuracy and authority. The publication of this textual scholarship—along with *The Early Lectures of Ralph Waldo Emerson* and the sixteen volumes of *The Journals and Miscellaneous Notebooks*, extending to *The Complete Sermons*, *The Poetry Notebooks*, *The Topical Notebooks*, the four-volume supplement to *The Letters of Ralph Waldo Emerson* and *The Selected Letters*, *Emerson's Antislavery Writings*, *The Later Lectures*, and *The Selected Lectures*—has reintroduced to Emerson's readers, particularly students without access to these previously unpublished materials, the ways that Emerson worked and thought through his ideas in the medium of his writing. The Emerson scholar and biographer Lawrence Buell refers to Emerson as "a kind of performance artist" to characterize a fundamental paradox of his work, the ways he pursued a core idea by "forever reopening and reformulating it, looping away and back again, convinced that the spirit of the idea dictated that no final statement was possible" (*Emerson* 2). The scholarship represented in these definitive editions of Emerson's works brings the artistry of Emerson's performance center stage for the twenty-first-century study of this important author.

Replacing the Riverside Edition of *Emerson's Complete Works* (1883–93), edited by James Elliot Cabot, Emerson's literary executor, and the Centenary Edition of *The Complete Works of Ralph Waldo Emerson*, edited by Emerson's son Edward, *The Collected Works of Ralph Waldo Emerson* will guide the study of Emerson in its comprehensive attention to the authorship of Emerson's published work and to the contexts of its composition. This standard edition of Emerson's works provides in its first eight volumes the books of prose brought to press by Emerson: *Nature, Addresses, and Lectures* (1849), *Essays: First Series* (1841), *Essays: Second Series* (1844), *Representative Men* (1850), *English Traits* (1856), *The Conduct of Life* (1860), *Society and Solitude* (1870), and *Letters and Social Aims* (1875). A ninth volume offers a variorum edition of Emerson's poems, including the poetry originally published in *Poems* (1847) and *"May-Day" and Other Pieces* (1867). The tenth and final volume gathers all of Emerson's previously published prose writing left uncollected at the time of his death in 1882.

While students will certainly benefit, much as researchers continue to benefit, from consulting the extensive historical and textual introductions and the editorial apparatus provided in this edition, the significant cost of each volume limits its adoption as a classroom text. However, the Belknap Press of Harvard University Press published in 2015 two single volumes containing selections from these editions that will be valuable and feasible for classroom study, particularly in upper-level courses that seek to read Emerson at greater length: *Ralph Waldo Emerson: The Major Poetry* and *Ralph Waldo Emerson: The Major Prose.*

The selection of Emerson's major prose provides a particular example of how the significant textual scholarship pursued in Emerson studies over the past fifty years will shape and indeed change the ways Emerson will be read and taught in the classroom over the next fifty years. While selecting Emerson's most recognizable prose the editors, Ronald A. Bosco and Joel Myerson, also broaden our understanding of Emerson's authorship in offering "the only anthology of his writings that draws from the three predominant sources of his prose: the pulpit, the lecture hall, and print" (*Ralph Waldo Emerson: The Major Prose* xxix). Furthermore, this volume reedits texts drawn from the first three volumes of the *Collected Works* to correct inconsistencies that resulted from an "editorial policy of producing eclectic texts drawn from many sources over many decades" (xxxvii). These reedited texts include *Nature*, "The Divinity School Address," "Self-Reliance," "Circles," and "Experience." Ronald A. Bosco, who also serves as the general editor of *The Collected Works of Ralph Waldo Emerson*, will explore further lessons for teaching derived from the editing of Emerson in his contribution to this volume in part 2.[1] Bosco advances the concern that the Emerson canon has been shaped primarily by textbook anthology editors rather than teachers. He argues persuasively that introducing the scholarly, edited archive of Emerson's volumes into the classroom enlivens and broadens the Emerson canon in ways that would have made sense to Emerson and his "authorial mind at work." This archive, moreover, will guide our students toward the central question we continue to pose to them: where do we find Emerson? As a start, we recommend that teachers consult the bibliography of authoritative editions of Emerson's writings provided by the Ralph Waldo Emerson Society ("Writings by Emerson").

Our survey of scholars indicates a wide range in the texts teachers use to assign Emerson in the classroom, particularly in the case of books ordered for student purchase. For courses and seminars dedicating significant time to the study of Emerson, the Norton Critical Edition by Joel Porte and Saundra Morris, *Emerson's Prose and Poetry*, provides an attractive combination of primary and secondary texts, including as it does in one volume a broad selection of Emerson's major writing as well as a range of critical perspectives. Porte's Library of America edition, *Emerson: Essays and Lectures*, remains an option for assigning extensive reading of Emerson's prose beyond a selection of essays. This volume includes all the prose works published by Emerson through *The Conduct of Life*. The Library of America also offers a volume of Emerson's *Collected Poems and Translations* (edited by Harold Bloom and Paul Kane) and two volumes of extensive selections from his journals, *Selected Journals: 1820–1842* and *Selected Journals: 1841–1877* (both edited by Lawrence Rosenwald). A handy "College Edition" paperback of *Emerson: Essays and Poems* is no longer available from Library of America, though a paperback edition *Essays:*

First and Second Series (Porte) remains in print. Richard Poirier's 1990 edition *Ralph Waldo Emerson* for the Oxford Authors series is also now out of print. A new *Selected Writings of Ralph Waldo Emerson*, edited by Robert D. Habich, offers students a generous selection of Emerson's poetry and prose published in his lifetime, drawing from the more familiar earlier works but also, significantly, the work of the 1850s and beyond.

When less extensive selections of Emerson's most familiar works are needed, given a shorter time frame in the course, paperback editions that select from his essays, poetry, and some lectures include *The Essential Writings of Ralph Waldo Emerson* (Atkinson), which leads off with an engaging introduction by the poet Mary Oliver, and more recently an update of *The Portable Emerson*, edited by Jeffrey S. Cramer. David Mikics's *The Annotated Emerson* provides extensive and vivid annotations for a selection of Emerson's most well-known essays and poems. For the purpose of teaching Emerson within the constraints of an American literature survey course, literature anthologies remain a popular if also problematic option; the two most often used anthologies are *The Norton Anthology of American Literature* (Baym et al.) and *The Heath Anthology of American Literature* (Lauter et al.), both of which continue to reprint a familiar selection of texts, from *Nature* to "Experience."

For teachers wanting to cultivate Emerson's significant example in the legacy of nature writing in a course in environmental studies or environmental literature, the Beacon Press edition *Nature/Walking* provides an inviting option, pairing Emerson's *Nature* with Thoreau's essay "Walking" and offering an introduction by John Elder. A more extensive offering of Emerson's environmental writing that includes his early natural history lectures is available in *"The Best Read Naturalist": Nature Writings of Ralph Waldo Emerson*, edited by Michael P. Branch and Clinton Mohs. (Branch discusses these writings and their uses in teaching *Nature* in part 2.) Though many acknowledge Emerson's importance in the tradition of the essay genre, his presence in anthologies of the type that teachers might assign in courses on creative nonfiction and the essay is surprisingly limited. *The Oxford Book of Essays* (Gross) offers "The Conservative," Emerson's lecture from 1841, for its one selection. For those wanting to bring into a course on the essay something more representative of Emerson's rhetorical poetics, Patrick Madden's *Quotidiana*, a digital resource and compendium of classical essays, provides digital versions of four essays by Emerson, including "Experience" and "Illusions."

General Reference

As a general reference for further reading and study, both for instructors developing an Emerson curriculum and for students in reading Emerson, Tiffany K. Wayne's *Critical Companion to Ralph Waldo Emerson: A Literary Reference to His Life and Work* offers a useful starting point. Along with a bibliography of primary and secondary sources and a chronology of Emerson's life and times, Wayne offers a brief summary and critical commentary on nearly 140 sermons, lectures, and poems, as well as individual discussion of all the essays published in Emerson's books. Additional entries also provide reference to significant figures and topics associated with Emerson and transcendentalism. To guide course development and critical reading for students beyond summary of Emerson's texts, teachers should consult Wesley T. Mott's *Ralph Waldo Emerson in Context* (2013), which offers thirty-two accessible readings into core concepts and contexts for understanding Emerson's work and thought, produced by leading Emerson scholars. The topics covered include "Europe," "Democracy," "Race," "Publishers," and "Fame," among many others.

Biographical Resources

Emerson: The Mind on Fire (1995), by Robert D. Richardson, Jr., is arguably the most authoritative and engaging intellectual history of Emerson's reading and thinking. Richardson's work is a particularly effective companion for the study of Emerson's texts, an Emersonian reading into Emerson's life of the mind. It remains an invaluable starting point for conceiving of the study of Emerson and also, given Richardson's other biographies (on Thoreau and William James), for thinking through Emerson's intellectual relations and friendships. Ralph L. Rusk's *The Life of Ralph Waldo Emerson* (1949), Gay Wilson Allen's *Waldo Emerson: A Biography* (1981), and John McAleer's *Ralph Waldo Emerson: Days of Encounter* (1984) each provides readers extensive biographical details and are worthy of consultation. For classroom use, however, Lawrence Buell's *Emerson* (2003) is particularly effective in organizing its biographical focus around key elements and critical problems of Emerson's thought and writing (for example, "Emerson as a Philosopher?" and "Emerson as Anti-Mentor"). Buell makes a compelling case for understanding Emerson as a national icon, America's first public intellectual, as well as an author of world literature. Buell's study is useful for the teacher thinking through issues that an upper-level course might engage while also providing a critical discussion of Emerson that is accessible to students at both introductory and advanced levels.

For instructors interested in earlier biographies of Emerson, as well as the construction of the author by his earliest biographers, Robert D. Habich's *Building Their Own Waldos: Emerson's First Biographers and the Politics of Life-Writing in the Gilded Age* (2011) provides generative insights. Bosco and Myerson's *The Emerson Brothers: A Fraternal Biography in Letters* (2005) brings a unique approach to biography by way of Emerson's relationship with his brothers. For guidance in placing Emerson's life and work in the larger context of the nineteenth century, and most particularly the extensive lecturing that Emerson pursued across four decades, Albert J. von Frank's *An Emerson Chronology* is remarkably detailed and useful; a revised and enlarged second edition of the book (2016; originally published in 1994) is now available. James Elliot Cabot's two-volume *A Memoir of Ralph Waldo Emerson* also places Emerson's work in chronological context, while providing summaries of many of the lectures that Emerson gave throughout his career. Finally, Joel Myerson and Leslie Perrin Wilson's *Picturing Emerson: An Iconography* further illuminates Emerson's biography by reproducing all known images of the author created from life.

Critical Reception

Studying the critical reception of Ralph Waldo Emerson is an invaluable aid to instructors preparing a course. The ongoing critical dialogue about one of the most generative writers in literary and cultural history is enormously helpful to students as well.

The bibliography in the first edition of George Willis Cooke's *Ralph Waldo Emerson: His Life, Writings, and Philosophy* (1881) indicates both the historical and cultural interest in Emerson's reception. Just over one hundred years later, an astonishing volume of critical commentary on Emerson's writing is noted by Robert E. Burkholder and Joel Myerson in *Emerson: An Annotated Secondary Bibliography* (1985) and by Kenneth Walter Cameron in *The Emerson Tertiary Bibliography with Researcher's Index* (1986). The chapter "Emerson, Thoreau, Fuller, and Transcendentalism," in *American Literary Scholarship: An Annual* (Habich), provides insights for the continuing Emerson bibliography. The most current and comprehensive bibliography of writings about Emerson (more than 1,500 entries) is available on the Web site of the Ralph Waldo Emerson Society.

Sarah Ann Wider's excellent interpretive overview of the critical reception of Emerson across the nineteenth and twentieth centuries, *The Critical Reception of Emerson: Unsettling All Things*, begins with an acknowledgment that any account of the critical reception of Emerson (indeed any well-known author) will be "a study in exclusion" (2). Her introductory essay, "Emerson and His Audiences," surveys the early accounts of the critical reception of Emerson, including Bliss Perry's *Emerson Today* (1931), Frederic Ives Carpenter's *Emerson Handbook* (1953), and Milton R. Konvitz and Stephen E. Whicher's *Emerson: A Collection of Critical Essays* (1978). Instructors and students interested in a more narrowly focused account of the critical reception of Emerson in the nineteenth century will find useful *Emerson and Thoreau: The Contemporary Reviews* (1992), edited by Joel Myerson. In addition, a fascinating compendium of critical perspectives from Emerson's contemporaries is Bosco and Myerson's *Emerson in His Own Time: A Biographical Chronicle of His Life, Drawn from Recollections, Interviews, and Memoirs by Family, Friends, and Associates* (2003).

A useful survey of the critical conversation about Emerson, from his time to the present, can be found in David LaRocca's *Estimating Emerson: An*

Anthology of Criticism from Carlyle to Cavell (2013). For critical assessments of Emerson at the end of the twentieth century, Joel Porte and Saundra Morris's *The Cambridge Companion to Ralph Waldo Emerson* (1999) chronicles the renewed critical appreciation of Emerson since the 1970s. Teachers looking for representative critical approaches may also find useful Joel Myerson's *Emerson Centenary Essays* (1982), Lawrence Buell's *Ralph Waldo Emerson: A Collection of Critical Essays* (1993), Wesley T. Mott and Robert E. Burkholder's *Emersonian Circles: Essays in Honor of Joel Myerson* (1997), and Harold Bloom's *Ralph Waldo Emerson* (2006). Finally, those interested in Emerson's early reception in the anglophone world beyond the United States may consult William Sowder, *Emerson's Impact on the British Isles and Canada* (1966) and *Emerson's Reviewers and Commentators* (1968).

Critical Studies

Emerson helped to define a canon of literature in the United States and the field of American literary and cultural studies, and his writings continue to preoccupy and provoke critics, as well as critical theorists and philosophers, in the ongoing assessment of our literary and cultural heritage.

In this section we have chosen critical studies that will be most useful for teachers and that have proven to be most productive in the ongoing conversation between Emerson and his readers. There is no question that F. O. Matthiessen's *American Renaissance: Art and Expression in the Age of Emerson and Whitman* (1941) was a singular influence in the study of Emerson as a progenitor of the American literary tradition. Subsequent assessments of Emerson's place in the emergence of a distinctive literary tradition in the United States include Stephen E. Whicher's *Freedom and Fate: An Inner Life of Ralph Waldo Emerson* (1953), Charles Malloy's *A Study of Emerson's Major Poems* (1973), David T. Porter's *Emerson and Literary Change* (1978), Barbara L. Packer's *Emerson's Fall: A New Interpretation of the Major Essays* (1982), and Julie K. Ellison's *Emerson's Romantic Style* (1984). Each book-length study offers distinct and incisive commentaries on Emerson's writing. Emerson's literary and rhetorical practices are elaborated in David M. Robinson's *Apostle of Culture: Emerson as Preacher and Lecturer* (1982), Lawrence Rosenwald's *Emerson and the Art of the Diary* (1988), Wesley T. Mott's *"The Strains of Eloquence": Emerson and His Sermons* (1989), Susan L. Roberson's *Emerson in His Sermons: A Man-Made Self* (1995), and Roger Thompson's *Emerson and the History of Rhetoric* (2017). Other critical studies have considered Emerson's use of language, including David LaRocca's *Emerson's English Traits and the Natural History of Metaphor* (2013), as well as more broadly Emerson's contribution to the development of literary language and culture in the United States, notably Richard Poirier's *The Renewal of Literature: Emersonian Reflections* (1987).

The critical conversation about Emerson has, at least since Matthiessen, been concerned with Emerson's social, cultural, political, and philosophical significance. The essays in Branka Arsić and Cary Wolfe's *The Other Emerson* (2010) provide an illuminating introduction to reading Emerson on subjectivity, politics, and philosophy. Instructors interested in the literary and political resonances of Emerson's approach to the self should consider Quentin Anderson's assessment in *The Imperial Self: An Essay in American Literary and Cultural History* (1971), as well as the later critiques of Emerson's individualism. These critiques include David Marr's *American Worlds since Emerson* (1988) and Christopher Newfield's *The Emerson Effect: Individualism and Submission in America* (1996). In contrast, a generative elaboration of the cultural resource of democratic individualism—and of Emerson's contribution to the development of American political philosophy—is available in two studies by the political theorist George Kateb: *The Inner Ocean: Individualism and Democratic Culture* (1992) and *Emerson and Self-Reliance* (1995; reprinted with new preface and introduction 2002). The history of the critical debate over Emersonian individualism is the subject of Charles E. Mitchell's book-length study, *Individualism and Its Discontents: Appropriations of Emerson, 1880–1950* (1997), and a detailed study of the theory and practice of liberal culture in Emerson's thinking is Neal Dolan's *Emerson's Liberalism* (2009).

Emerson's political and ethical orientation is explored in Len Gougeon's *Virtue's Hero: Emerson, Antislavery, and Reform* (1990). Gougeon offers a corrective to earlier readings by turning to the materials that have become available in the new editions of Emerson's journals, notebooks, and early lectures. Readers interested in Emerson the social reformer will also find useful Eduardo Cadava's *Emerson and the Climates of History* (1997), Albert J. von Frank's *The Trials of Anthony Burns: Freedom and Slavery in Emerson's Boston* (1998), and *The Emerson Dilemma: Essays on Emerson and Social Reform* (2001), edited by T. Gregory Garvey. Alan M. Levine and Daniel S. Malachuk's *A Political Companion to Ralph Waldo Emerson* (2011) usefully gathers into one volume critical discussion of Emerson's politics.

Intellectual and Critical Contexts

There is no more reliable and rewarding resource for understanding Emerson's intellectual and critical contexts than the historical and textual introductions to each volume of *The Collected Works of Ralph Waldo Emerson* (1971–2013). The extended historical essays situate the primary documents included in each of the volumes among the biographical, social, and political events of nineteenth-century America and as such provide instructors with indispensable intellectual and critical contexts for the classroom. The textual introductions familiarize readers with the textual histories and variations that have preoccupied editors and scholars and suggest the pedagogical significance of Emerson's writing process, and textual variations, in the classroom.

Instructors and students interested in the relationship between Emerson and transcendentalism will find an enormous range of useful critical commentary and analysis. The most indispensable resources include Joel Myerson, Sandra Harbert Petrulionis, and Laura Dassow Walls's *The Oxford Handbook of Transcendentalism* (2010) and the extended discussion of the historical contexts that inform Emerson's work in Myerson's *A Historical Guide to Ralph Waldo Emerson* (2000).

Emerson is concerned with fundamental philosophical questions. It is therefore unsurprising that philosophers since William James and George Santayana have been engaged with Emerson's thinking. One of Emerson's most rigorous, sympathetic, and creative readers, Stanley Cavell, offers extended readings of Emerson's philosophical contributions in, among other writings, *Conditions Handsome and Unhandsome: The Constitution of Emersonian Perfectionism* (1990) and *Emerson's Transcendental Etudes* (2003). In addition, Branka Arsić discusses Emerson's emphasis on change and transformation in *On Leaving: A Reading in Emerson* (2010). Literary and cultural historians have also explored Emerson's philosophical orientation and influence in American intellectual history. These studies include Cornel West's *The American Evasion of Philosophy: A Genealogy of Pragmatism* (1989), Richard Poirier's *Poetry and Pragmatism* (1992), and Jonathan Levin's *The Poetics of Transition: Emerson, Pragmatism, and American Literary Modernism* (1999). More specialized studies of Emerson and philosophy are useful as well, including David Van Leer, *Emerson's Epistemology: The Argument of the Essays* (1986); John Michael, *Emerson and Skepticism: The Cipher of the World* (1988); David Jacobson, *Emerson's Pragmatic Vision: The Dance of the Eye* (1993); David M. Robinson's *Emerson and the Conduct of Life: Pragmatism and Ethical Purpose in the Later Work* (1993), which is a particularly valuable guide to Emerson's neglected later work; and Gustaaf Van Cromphout's *Emerson's Ethics* (1999).

Instructors and students interested in learning more about Emerson and nature, natural history, and science should consult Laura Dassow Walls's *Emerson's Life in Science: The Culture of Truth* (2003). Additional study of Emerson's engagement with natural history, and the fascination with the aims and methods of natural science that Emerson cultivated during his visit to the Jardin des Plantes in Paris, include Lee Rust Brown's *The Emerson Museum: Practical Romanticism and the Pursuit of the Whole* (1997). Earlier studies of Emerson's idea of nature include Sherman Paul's *Emerson's Angle of Vision: Man and Nature in American Experience* (1952) and the collection of essays *Emerson's*

Nature: *Origin, Growth, Meaning* (1969), edited by Merton M. Sealts, Jr., and Alfred R. Ferguson.

A welcome context for the critical evaluation of Emerson has grown from a global perspective on his literary and cultural work. Teachers and students interested in Emerson's transatlantic exchanges will benefit from *A Power to Translate the World: New Essays on Emerson and International Culture* (2015), edited by David LaRocca and Ricardo Miguel-Alfonso—a compelling collection of readings, in a wide range of geographical and cultural contexts, that elaborates the trajectories of Emersonian thinking among non-American writers and intellectuals. Readers may also consult *Emerson for the Twenty-First Century: Global Perspectives on an American Icon* (2010), edited by Barry Tharaud; *Emerson's Transatlantic Romanticism* (2012), by David Greenham; and *Transatlantic Transcendentalism: Coleridge, Emerson, and Nature* (2013), by Samantha C. Harvey. Emerson's cultural affiliations and literary influences beyond the United States may be further explored in Daniel Koch's *Ralph Waldo Emerson in Europe: Class, Race, and Revolution in the Making of an American Thinker* (2012) and *The Correspondence of Emerson and Carlyle* (1964), edited by Joseph Slater.

Digital Resources

Instructors and students of Emerson will find a range of primary material and secondary works on the Web. However, the varying quality of Web-based materials and accuracy of digital editions necessitate cautious use. Although there is as yet no comprehensive electronic research and teaching resource dedicated to Emerson on the order of *The Walt Whitman Archive*, sites developed by the Ralph Waldo Emerson Society and digital portals at several libraries and educational institutions provide access to an electronic Emerson that can supplement the study of his texts and contexts. We include here a selection of available Web sites, digital portals, and digital editions that teachers should find to be both productive and appropriate for use with students.

The Centenary Edition of Emerson's *Complete Works* (1903–04) is available in digital format at *The Works of Ralph Waldo Emerson* Web site, edited by Jim Manley, as well as at the University of Michigan Library (*The Complete Works*), where a variety of word searches can be conducted. *Project Gutenberg* provides access to digital editions of works by Emerson on its Emerson author page ("Books by Emerson"), and an edition of *Representative Men* has been digitized by the University of Virginia American Studies Program (*Representative Men*). Instructors and students interested in a searchable, digital version of Emerson's early poetry can consult the *American Verse Project* in the University of

Michigan Humanities Text Initiative (*American Verse*). Eugene F. Irey's concordance to the Centenary Edition of Emerson's *Complete Works* is available through the Concord Free Public Library Web site. And nine manuscript items are accessible through Lehigh University's *I Remain: A Digital Archive of Letters, Manuscripts, and Ephemera.*

The Ralph Waldo Emerson Society maintains a Web site that, in addition to providing extensive bibliographic references for the study of Emerson, curates a listing of digital resources available for the study of Emerson and his contemporaries ("Related Sites"); a series of drawings, engravings, and photographs of Emerson, following his development from a young man to old age ("Images of Emerson"); and access to *Emerson Society Papers* dating back to the first issue in 1990 ("Emerson Society Papers"). Other Web-based materials for instructors and students include the Emerson materials available at *The Web of American Transcendentalism* ("Ralph Waldo Emerson") and Paul P. Reuben's "Ralph Waldo Emerson" page on his Web site *Perspectives in American Literature.*

There is also an archive of video discussions about Emerson available in C-SPAN's *American Writers* series, including "Emerson and the Examined Life," featuring Robert Pinsky, Richard Geldard, and David M. Robinson. David A. Beardsley's video biography, *Emerson: The Ideal in America*, includes discussions with Robert D. Richardson, Jr., and Sarah Ann Wider, among other scholars. Finally, instructors and students will benefit from the comprehensive entry on Emerson as a philosopher by Russell Goodman in *The Stanford Encyclopedia of Philosophy*, accessible on the Web.

NOTE

[1]We would like to acknowledge the numerous editors who contributed to *The Collected Works of Ralph Waldo Emerson*: Alfred R. Ferguson, Robert E. Spiller, Joseph Slater, Douglas Emory Wilson, and Ronald A. Bosco (general editors); Robert E. Burkholder, Jean Ferguson Carr, Joel Myerson, Philip Nicoloff, Barbara L. Packer, Albert J. von Frank, Wallace E. Williams, and Thomas Wortham (editors).

Part Two

APPROACHES

Introduction:
Learning from Emerson

Mark C. Long and Sean Ross Meehan

Ralph Waldo Emerson's continuing presence in our literature and culture remains as vigorous and as varied as the works he produced. A leading figure of American transcendentalism and transatlantic Romanticism, a prominent nineteenth-century poet and literary mentor, and arguably America's greatest essayist, Emerson was also America's first public intellectual. His addresses, essays, and poems were deeply engaged with the social and political ferment of nineteenth-century America.

Ever since F. O. Matthiessen made him a founding figure of the "American Renaissance," Emerson has remained a staple of undergraduate surveys in American literature and seminars on the "Age of Emerson." More recently, in emphasizing the wide-ranging global, and not just national, "vitality of Emerson's writing," Lawrence Buell shows Emerson's intellectual presence extending across the Atlantic and around the world (*Emerson* 5). Students today encounter Emerson's works in courses focusing on transcendentalism, Romanticism, environmental literature, literary theory and philosophy, rhetoric and composition, media studies, and genre courses in poetry and the essay; moreover, in upper-level seminars, students read Emerson alongside writers and thinkers influenced by his example, including Henry David Thoreau, Walt Whitman, Emily Dickinson, Friedrich Nietzsche, William James, Wallace Stevens, Robert Frost, Ralph Ellison, Mary Oliver, and Annie Dillard. *Approaches to Teaching the Works of Ralph Waldo Emerson* recognizes Emerson's continuing presence in the curriculum and, for the first time, offers instructors a pedagogical resource to guide and inspire their teaching.

A working model for such pedagogical guidance derives from Emerson himself. Over a period of forty years, from the 1830s through the 1870s, Emerson delivered approximately 1,500 public lectures. These rhetorical and pedagogical performances engaged thoroughly the ideas and the topics of the times while moving toward the published writing for which he was, and still is, well known. In the 1840s, Emerson described the lecture hall of the lyceum as "the most elastic and capacious theater of eloquence," an educational forum where oratory emerges from "the depths of philosophy and poetry" to "agitate, convict, inspire, and possess us" (*Later Lectures* 1: 48). This is the forum where Emerson made a name for himself as America's first public intellectual. It is also the venue that served as the "laboratory of Emerson's composing process," as Ronald A. Bosco and Joel Myerson note in their introduction to *The Later Lectures of Ralph Waldo Emerson*. Bosco and Myerson conclude that to "understand Emerson's writings, one must first see him at work as a lecturer" (1: xx). Indeed, in the nineteenth century, with an eye to the pedagogical ethos of the lyceum,

Bronson Alcott characterizes Emerson's works as a version of continuing education, an Emersonian alternative school that took the place of the professorship in rhetoric in which he expressed interest, though it was never offered. "His works are studies," Alcott writes in 1865, "[a]nd any youth of free senses and fresh affections shall be spared years of tedious toil,—in which wisdom and fair learning are, for the most part, held at arm's length, planet's width, from his grasp,—by graduating from this college" (*Ralph Waldo Emerson* 22).

Alcott proposes Emerson's works as a tangible alternative to the abstraction he locates in conventional education. With Emerson, Alcott understands, the works of the author can be grasped by the work of learning. This is not to suggest that learning from Emerson has ever been easy. Richard Poirier, one of Emerson's most sympathetic readers, identifies the central complication of the literary and cultural history that Emerson inaugurates in the fact that Emerson "coveted the idea of popularity with a general audience," yet also believed that language necessitated "a saving uncertainty and vagueness" in order for it "to represent the flow of individual experience" (*Poetry and Pragmatism* 3–4). In *The Renewal of Literature*, Poirier describes the Emersonian challenge this way: "Why not erase every sentence just as soon as it is written and read? Wouldn't that be the purest form of action as Emerson imagines it?" (47). Something of this challenge and complication, this layering of rhetorical purpose with linguistic intransigence, follows Emerson into the classroom. And for good reason: for in the flow of their individual experiences, sometimes with excitement and sometimes in frustration, students will note the apparent lack of logical method in his essays (of the kind expected in *their* essays), or wrestle with the syntactical challenge of his aphoristic style. In this "gymnast's struggle," to borrow Whitman's apt description of reading, students are no more ambivalent than the literary critics. Matthiessen regrets the "indifference to the tools of the artist" (26) that limited Emerson's achievement of poetic form, yet he underscores the important oratorical sources of Emerson's "energy of thought and of action" (21) and his pursuit of a transcendental "form without boundaries" (24). Harold Bloom further celebrates that rhetorical energy in Emerson, locating within its dynamics a "map of misreading" that speaks to Emerson's influence and "peculiar relevance" in both literature and criticism (*Map* 171). More recently, Phillip Lopate takes up the challenging density of thought in Emerson's essays and makes a case for "Emerson's relevance today," not despite the challenge but in response to it. "Yes," Lopate concludes, "we can even revere him, as a model of how to overcome anxiety and despair, and eloquently wed uncertainty to equanimity" ("Foreword" xx–xxi).

In reckoning with the dynamic effects and effectiveness of Emerson's writings, critics and students are following the lead of Emerson himself. "I need hardly say to anyone acquainted with my thoughts that I have no System," Emerson observes in an 1839 journal, going on to refer to his writing as a "parabola whose arcs would never meet." Emerson, we learn, had set out in his journal to delineate "the great topics of human study, as, *Religion, Poetry, Politics, Love,* &c"

in encyclopedic form. But the topics, much like Emerson's thought and writing, wouldn't stay put under these discrete titles (*Journals* 7: 302). The topics from the journal continued to move, working their way into his lectures and essays and poems. This circulation of ideas, never systematically finished, as Emerson suggests, yields the achievement of his works. As Poirier argues, Emerson seeks to write "the *workings*" rather than "the *works* of genius" (*Renewal* 68).

Emerson scholarship has brought these cultural and rhetorical "workings" of Emerson's writing to the fore. Jonathan Bishop's insight from his *Emerson on the Soul* (1964) offers both a turning point and a template for the best in Emerson criticism that has emerged in the last fifty years. "What one wants, then, is not a criticism of Emerson," Bishop proposes, "but a continuation—or rather, a continuation that would make the criticism real" (220). That real criticism, Sarah Ann Wider notes in *The Critical Reception of Emerson: Unsettling All Things*, has been informed by the various editions of his journals, notebooks, lectures, and other previously unpublished writings that have helped more recent readers to reenvision Emerson's thought and achievement (146). Fifty years after Bishop, with the completion in 2013 of the Harvard University Press edition of *The Collected Works of Ralph Waldo Emerson*, it is now time to join the critical insights of Emerson's workings and the pedagogical lessons of scholars at work with Emerson in the classroom.

In bringing together these insights and lessons, the contributors to *Approaches to Teaching the Works of Ralph Waldo Emerson* offer experienced and prospective instructors an understanding of Emerson that reaches from his nineteenth-century contexts into the twenty-first-century classroom. We explore the cultural and intellectual contexts of Emerson's works, the creative and rhetorical conditions of his multi-genre writing, and the continuing influence of his reception in English and American literature, across academic disciplines and around the world. In these various approaches to teaching Emerson, the classroom emerges as another laboratory for Emerson's composing process, another venue for bringing scholars—students and teachers alike—into meaningful and relevant relation with Emerson's thought and writing, with works that continue to agitate, convict, inspire, possess, and, indeed, educate us all.

Emerson's Texts and Contexts

Emerson's works both advance and reiterate a series of productive tensions: relations between the singular and the plural, the familiar and the unfamiliar, the local and the global. In the first section, "Approaching Emerson as a Public Intellectual," the contributing writers present a series of literary and cultural contexts for reading Emerson in the classroom. These essays approach the singular figure of Emerson by turning our attention to his multiple intellectual roles and the variety of public engagements that shaped his works. In relating texts to contexts, teachers are introduced to the Emersonian logic of representativeness.

As Emerson writes in "Nominalist and Realist," published in *Essays: Second Series* (1844), "a man is only a relative and representative nature. Each is a hint of the truth, but far enough from being that truth, which yet he quite newly and inevitably suggests to us" (*Collected Works* 3: 133). These relative and representative characters—orator, essayist, poet, philosopher, reformer, educator, author—inform but also circulate throughout his works.

These intellectual and cultural contexts are embedded in the works discussed in the sections that follow. Teachers will likely return to these contexts for further thinking (and rethinking) after reading later approaches to an individual text in the classroom. For example, a discussion of "Circles" appears in the second section of approaches ("Teaching Emerson's Essays"), dedicated to Emerson's singular and most familiarly taught body of work, his essays. But "Circles" also appears in the first section in the context of Emerson's rhetoric of reform. And "Circles" necessarily reappears in later sections and discussions, including "'These Flames and Generosities of the Heart': Emerson in the Poetry Workshop" ("Emerson across the Curriculum") and "Emerson and Nietzsche" ("Emerson around the World"). As Emerson writes in "Circles" of the nonlinear method of thought that applies surely to his own writing, "every ultimate fact is only the first of a new series" (*Collected Works* 2: 181).

In the first contribution in "Approaching Emerson as a Public Intellectual," we learn from David M. Robinson of the Emerson who is an accomplished orator, whose sermons and lectures from the pulpit and the lectern drew audiences to hear what one of his biographers, Robert D. Richardson, Jr., has called a "mind on fire." As Ned Stuckey-French demonstrates, this rhetorical power extends to the Emerson who is also an essayist, whose experiments with creative nonfiction place him in the company of Montaigne and Bacon, as well as among contemporary essayists such as Lopate and John D'Agata. With Saundra Morris, we are reminded that Emerson is also a poet, one whose poems and "politically ethical aesthetics" were a wellspring for his nineteenth-century contemporaries, such as Dickinson, Whitman, Bryant, and Longfellow, and remain one for the contemporary classroom focused on diversity in the United States and including (as Morris demonstrates) multicultural literature written by American Indian, black, feminist, and LGBTQ authors. Susan L. Dunston encourages us to read Emerson as a philosopher as well, one whose intellect ranges across the arenas of metaphysics, epistemology, values, and spirituality; this philosophical Emerson returns in later discussions of the essays "Friendship" and "Experience" and the lecture series Natural History of Intellect, as well as in explorations of Emerson's interests in Asiatic thought and Friedrich Nietzsche's interest in Emerson.

Approaching the Emerson who is also a reformer, and not merely a "sage," one whose writings were inspired by and shaped nineteenth-century social and political reform movements, Todd H. Richardson shows that the conventional wisdom of Emerson's removal from his society is difficult to sustain. As Martin

Bickman demonstrates in his contribution, the same engagement can be credited to the Emerson who is also an educator, whose ideas shape an educational tradition of active learning that should be brought into the classroom with Emerson's texts. Ronald A. Bosco, general editor of the recently completed Harvard University Press edition of *The Collected Works of Ralph Waldo Emerson*, culminates this section by exploring the Emerson who is also an author, whose vast archive of personal and private as well as public writings, from the 1830s into the 1870s, greatly expands the circle of his literary and cultural inheritance.

This newly edited Emerson for the twenty-first-century classroom, as Bosco well knows, is a writer actively engaged in the process of composition. In describing his approach to Emerson's most well-known and challenging religious texts by way of the contexts of Emerson's oratorical culture, Robinson proposes that a more accessible, if now less familiar, Emerson can be recovered through the historical narratives and rhetorical techniques embedded in the texts. The storytelling Emerson, Robinson suggests, is the one who filled lecture halls in his own day and one to whom students and readers will respond today. This pedagogical recovery of a more lively and approachable Emerson, embedded but often forgotten in the form of his expression, is a continuing theme in the essays throughout this volume.

"Teaching Emerson's Essays" explores the literary and cultural contributions of Emerson in their most familiar form, his published essays and addresses. Experienced and new teachers will find here insightful discussions of the most widely read essays that have for generations found their place on the reading lists of American literature survey courses: *Nature* (1836), one of Emerson's earliest published works and a founding document of American transcendentalism; the important and provocative early addresses at Harvard, now known as "The American Scholar" (1837) and "The Divinity School Address" (1838); three of his most frequently anthologized essays from *Essays: First Series* (1841), "Self-Reliance," "Circles," and "Friendship"; and "Experience" (1844), considered to be among the greatest essays in the English language. While these texts are familiar in name and known certainly in parts, for they contain the sentences frequently quoted from Emerson, the contributors in this section explore ways to present to students the lessons of these important works that reach beyond and behind their most memorable lines.

Michael P. Branch initiates this exploration with an argument that returns students and teachers to Emerson's *Nature*, a crucial text that readers have pretended to understand and, as the survey of scholars conducted for this volume indicated, that teachers have stopped teaching entirely or reduced to an excerpt. For Branch, natural science provides a framework for reapproaching *Nature* since many of the core arguments in the text emerge from Emerson's intellectual faith in science as a means of revealing spiritual value. Reading *Nature*, students engage with Emerson's views of the immense potential, but also the potential risks, of science as a vital means to an understanding of the natural world and of the nature of life. This perspective on the importance of natural science in the teaching of Emerson will be expanded upon and complicated in later contributions on Emerson's scientific method and environmental relevance.

Much as Branch does in proposing strategies for rethinking a text that has become perhaps too familiar, contributors across this section propose productively unfamiliar approaches to Emerson's most widely anthologized and taught essays. Andrew Kopec describes his pedagogical strategy of returning "The American Scholar" to its rhetorical occasion, an 1837 commencement address set amid a financial panic. This recovery of the pedagogical circumstances of the address renders the greater relevance of this text to college students, themselves working toward commencement and debating the value of liberal education in the twenty-first century.

The purposes of education and the meaning of religion are at the center of Corinne E. Blackmer's discussion of "The Divinity School Address" and the relation between the teachings in Emerson's text and the pedagogical situation of her classroom. Nels Anchor Christensen responds directly to the challenge of teaching Emerson's aphoristic style and unsystematic logic by way of "Circles," using that essay to initiate a more experiential approach to Emerson's rhetorical style and intuitive logic. And, taking up "Self-Reliance," Wesley T. Mott describes his seven-week general education humanities seminar, Studies in American Self-Reliance. In exploring self-reliance as an ambiguous and contested concept at the heart of American identity, Mott's students deepen their understanding of the essay by reckoning with the broader and less familiar claims of the concept in American culture. In a similar vein, by exploring the rich philosophical and biographical sources of Emerson's "Friendship," Jennifer Gurley guides her students into a more complex reading of both the essay and the ideals embodied in the text. Finally, among Emerson's most challenging essays, "Experience" is taken up by Branka Arsić to illuminate further the philosophical contexts of Emerson's thinking; in rereading this significant essay and rethinking its assumed pessimism, Arsić offers an insightful and affirmative approach to the inevitable complications and challenges of teaching Emerson's philosophical writing. Those challenges, as the contributors in this section demonstrate, are best approached by rethinking common presumptions about the self-evidence of these texts.

"Teaching Emerson's Other Works" broadens the circle of Emerson's writing by placing into dialogue the canonical essays described in the previous section with previously unpublished or formerly noncanonical writing, now more accessible to the classroom. Although these contributions might be read in response to the discussion in the previous section, teachers can also find lessons here regarding new or less familiar works before reading through "Teaching Emerson's Essays." Or they might turn back to the initial section for further insights regarding Emerson's poetic, political, or philosophical contexts after first looking into one of these approaches to an individual text or genre in the Emerson canon, be it well-known or new.

Christoph Irmscher describes teaching Emerson in the development of nineteenth-century poetry, confronting the irony that Emerson is in a somewhat marginal position in the American poetry classroom. Len Gougeon offers an example of teaching Emerson as a social and political activist, using "The Emancipation of the Negroes in the British West Indies" (1844) and the connection between Emerson and Frederick Douglass to engage students with the politics of democracy and race in nineteenth-century America. In approaching Emerson by way of his antislavery writings, formerly neglected but now a significant part of the Emerson canon, Gougeon offers teachers an alternative to the longstanding cliché of the sage of Concord's aloofness, showing how Emerson's writing and speaking served as a powerful instrument of reform, challenging the racism, bigotry, and material corruption of his day. Expanding this revised understanding of Emerson's social engagement to include his early lectures and sermons, Carolyn R. Maibor offers an approach to what she calls "the practical Emerson" by drawing on the 1832 sermon known as "Find Your Calling" and the 1837 lectures "Trades and Professions" and "Doctrine of the Hands." Maibor describes how these less familiar texts meaningfully open students to broader, practical concerns, including social action and the moral obligation to others. As with lessons drawn from "The American Scholar" in the second section, Maibor proposes a way back to Emerson by bringing his voice into the current civic debates about the purpose and meaning of higher education.

In approaching Emerson and gender through his journals and other writings, as well as his influence on writers such as Louisa May Alcott and Charlotte Forten Grimké, Jean Ferguson Carr extends the discussion of the practical uses of the educational Emerson, as demonstrated by emerging women writers in the nineteenth century and other writers with little formal education or cultural capital. Finally, Meredith Farmer presents an approach to Emerson in an interdisciplinary undergraduate course, Literary and Scientific Methods, that focuses on Emerson's lecture project known and posthumously published as Natural History of Intellect. As Farmer shows, in reading the literary, philosophical, and scientific methods informing these later lectures, students gain a better grasp on the method of Emerson's broad-ranging, multidisciplinary interests that reach back to his earliest writings on nature and extend out to his transnational readings and writings in both literature and the sciences. In this way, the various texts and genres of Emerson's previously neglected "other" works are emerging in the classroom while also expanding the reception of his expression beyond the traditional American literature course.

Emerson across the Curriculum and around the World

"Emerson across the Curriculum" introduces teachers to the broader significance and expanding circulation of the multidisciplinary Emerson. The contributors demonstrate Emerson's persistent presence across the humanities and offer both new and experienced teachers ways to include Emerson in courses in creative writing, environmental studies, communication and media studies, and the digital humanities. The essays in this section offer teachers fresh ways to integrate the emerging relevance of this boundary-crossing Emerson in the literature classroom. While demonstrating the expansion of Emerson's ideas and influence beyond the literature classroom, both in exploring new texts and circling back to others, the final two sections of the volume also return to the classroom the Emerson whose works in natural history, philosophy, poetics, and rhetoric are already lenses on other disciplines and cultures.

Dan Beachy-Quick, for example, derives "an unspoken ethic" for his poetry workshop from essays such as "The Poet," "Circles," and "Experience," one that offers his creative writing students a release from the tired conventions of the creative writing classroom. We are reminded that in "The American Scholar," Emerson proposes that "there is then creative reading as well as creative writing" (*Collected Works* 1: 58), arguably coining both phrases, though the latter is the more familiar—and once again, perhaps too familiar, as Beachy-Quick suggests. T. S. McMillin extends the lessons of "creative reading" to the sciences, uncovering in Emerson's writings on nature a perspective of "transdisciplinarity" that highlights Emerson's relevance for both English and environmental studies students and also makes Emerson a valuable intellectual field guide for instructors working in the environmental humanities. Emerson's curricular circulation into the area of new media is evident in the ways that Emerson's engagement with the new communication media of his day has been brought into the classroom. David O. Dowling teaches Emerson as a nineteenth-century media critic and media star in his journalism and communication studies classes, an author whose active use of media circuits and knowledge networks animating the nineteenth-century media ecosystem can be used by teachers to link Emerson's insights from the antebellum print revolution to contemporary digital culture. Taking up Emerson's emerging presence within the digital humanities, Amy Earhart concludes this section by exploring the ways that some of the computational tools of literary scholarship in the digital age can deepen engagement with Emerson's works in turning student attention to the editing of Emerson materials and to questions of editorial practice in both new and old media.

In "Emerson around the World," the contributors continue this discussion of Emerson's reach beyond the traditional classroom by mapping Emerson's presence in wider hemispheric and transatlantic domains. As Wai Chee Dimock argues, the image of Emerson as the father of American literary nationalism is a critical "caricature" of Emerson's cosmopolitan literary transcendentalism ("Deep Time" 770). The essays in this section, following Dimock and Buell, challenge the parochialism often associated with Emerson and familiar works such as "The American Scholar" and "Self-Reliance," in part by turning attention to Emerson's practices as a reader and translator of European and Asian literatures. The transnational reception of Emerson, recognizing the Emerson who travels widely as a reader "through other continents," in Dimock's phrase

(*Through*), becomes in turn the necessary complement, not just the counter, to the Emerson who writes mainly from the study in his Concord home.

Leslie Elizabeth Eckel helps teachers to situate Emerson's alleged parochialism alongside his work as a translator, his attention to cosmopolitan engagement with the world evident in works such as *Representative Men* (1850) and *English Traits* (1856), and his intellectual networking with writers such as Goethe, Wordsworth, Carlyle, and Swedenborg, as well as his contemporary interlocutor and American transplant, Margaret Fuller. In making a case for Emerson in Latin American studies, Spanish American literature, and translation studies, Anne Fountain's essay considers Emerson's influence on the exiled Cuban writer José Martí, the figure who first introduced Emerson to Latin America and translated some of his poems into Spanish, and takes up the critical and pedagogical complications of translation. In a similar vein, in teaching Emerson's considerable influence on the German philosopher Friedrich Nietzsche, Herwig Friedl describes a course in which Emerson reemerges as a cosmopolitan thinker no longer constrained by the regional, intellectual environment of New England. These transnational approaches to Emerson, tracking the translation of cultural ideas in his works as well as the authors inspired by him, concludes with John Michael Corrigan's approach to teaching Emerson in an Asian classroom. As Corrigan suggests, Emerson's lifelong engagement with literature from around the world illuminates the Emerson who can be taught as world literature in any classroom.

Approaches to Teaching the Works of Ralph Waldo Emerson affirms the continuing presence of Emerson's thinking and writing in the classroom, wherever that classroom might be. As the contributors to this volume demonstrate, Emerson is more than a reliable guide to the literary, social, and political life of nineteenth-century America. Emerson's thinking, our contributors make clear, has, from his days lecturing and writing in the nineteenth century into the present moment, provoked generations of artists, intellectuals, and students to engage more deeply in the literary activities of reading and writing. Emerson's provocation, at the same time, opens up productive pedagogical explorations of philosophy and the humanities, communication and media studies, environmental studies and the natural sciences, as well as inspired experiments with learning beyond the classroom and the academy, both at home and abroad. Given the intellectual breadth of his interests and influence, we believe it is reasonable to view Emerson much as Bronson Alcott does, as a college of liberal arts and sciences unto himself. And, like Alcott before them, the educators in this volume know that what works best in the teaching of Emerson—what's necessary to understanding this necessary author in the range of discourses, disciplines, and demarcations where we continue to find him today—is to engage students with the Emerson already at work in the education of the scholar.

Emerson the Orator:
Teaching the Narratives of
"The Divinity School Address"

David M. Robinson

The words that Emerson used when he addressed the Harvard Divinity School on 15 July 1838 were important. But their importance was conditioned and magnified by the nature of the audience members and the occasion that had brought them to listen, as well as the reaction Emerson's remarks would later provoke. The words were a crucial part of a web of narratives that stretched before and after their delivery. To know "The Divinity School Address," a student must know these narratives as well. This series of interconnected events also included several key narratives within the address itself that dramatized the controversial religious positions that Emerson put forward. Emerson's instinctive sense for story as a powerful mode of religious communication was a key element of his craft. Locating the stories in Emerson's ostensibly abstract lectures and essays can illuminate what students may encounter as an impenetrable verbal mass. Recognizing these narratives, within the text and surrounding it, can also guide student readers in understanding how the address prepared the way for "The Over-Soul" (1841), an essay that signaled an important shift in nineteenth-century religious opinion.

"The Divinity School Address" is best known for the controversy it stirred among Boston Unitarians and the resulting schism between the "transcendental" wing of the denomination and the moderate Unitarians, who were well established in Boston's historic churches. The year before Emerson's address, the prominent Harvard biblical scholar Andrews Norton published the first volume of his massive study *The Evidences of the Genuineness of the Gospels*, a strong justification of the historical validity of the miraculous events recorded in the New Testament. After reading Emerson's audacious dismissal of miracles as irrelevant to religious faith in "The Divinity School Address"—"the very word Miracle, as pronounced by Christian churches, gives a false impression; it is Monster" (*Collected Works* 1: 81)—Norton condemned the speech, thus igniting the simmering tensions within Unitarianism into an open controversy and giving Emerson valuable publicity as a dangerous radical (Robinson, *Unitarians* 75–81).

The Emerson-Norton dispute offers students an accessible but somewhat reductive story of the valiant and progressive young rebel (Emerson) challenging the adverse forces of obsolete tradition (Norton). This narrative can, however, be greatly enlivened and intellectually enriched if students are introduced to a series of local events preceding the address. It is sometimes overlooked, for example, that the address was putatively student-oriented, "Delivered before the Senior Class in Divinity College" (*Collected Works* 1: 76), as its full title makes clear. In fact, the selection of the speaker for the occasion was made by a committee of three graduating divinity students finishing their studies for the ministry. In Emerson, they selected a man who had gained a reputation for eloquence because of his annual lectures in Boston and his oration "The American Scholar," given at Harvard in 1837. As Albert J. von Frank notes, when William Dexter Wilson made initial contact with Emerson on behalf of the divinity students, he requested a copy of Emerson's recent lecture "The Head," earlier delivered in Cambridge (*Emerson Chronology* 1: 265–66). The lectures that Emerson had been delivering for several years in Boston provide the instructor with an entry point into the phenomenon of the nineteenth-century lecture circuit, one of the era's most influential forms of public performance and educational culture. In choosing a budding lyceum celebrity for their graduation speaker, the students paradoxically selected a man who had essentially withdrawn from the Unitarian ministry. Emerson's resignation six years earlier from his pastorate of the Second Church of Boston was well known around Boston and Cambridge. Wilson's letter reached him some two weeks before he stepped down from his final ministerial connection with a small congregation in East Lexington. Why would Emerson have accepted the divinity students' invitation if he had firmly decided that he would "preach no more except from the Lyceum" (*Letters* 2: 120)?

Discussing the nature of the Harvard invitation and describing the cultural institution of the public lecture have the potential classroom advantage of presenting "The Divinity School Address" in an educational context. Students may know little about nineteenth-century religious groups or their doctrines, but they are surely cognizant of the institution of graduation addresses through their visiting speakers. Not to be missed in this story is the students' request for a meeting with Emerson before the public event. "The Divinity School youths wished to talk with me concerning theism," Emerson noted. "I went rather heavy-hearted for I always find that my views chill or shock people at the first opening" (*Journals* 5: 471). These "views" were his growing doubts about a personal God, ideas that apparently both interested and concerned the students. Emerson's insistence on a deity that "knows no persons" (*Collected Works* 1: 82) called the notion of a fatherly or parental God into question. We might say that the students worried that they had invited an atheist to address them on their divinity school graduation. Although we do not know the details of their conversation, Emerson apparently gave them some comfort when he met with them. "But the conversation went well & I came away cheered," he wrote in his journal (*Journals* 5: 471). The positive response from the students may also have reassured Emerson in his decision to use the blunt terminology in addressing the inflammatory questions on the natures of God and Jesus in his upcoming performance.

Emerson also previewed another volatile opinion when his conversation with the students moved to preaching and the church: "I told them that the preacher should be a poet smit with love of the harmonies of moral nature: and yet look at the Unitarian Association & see if its aspect is poetic. They all smiled No" (*Journals* 5: 471). Emerson's attack on the preaching of his day was perhaps more incendiary for many of his listeners than his toying with the accepted notion of a loving and caring God. Though he does not say it in the address, the audience would have understood that the preaching he attacked was Unitarian preaching. In fact, it was prompted by one Unitarian preacher in particular, Emerson's own pastor in Concord, Barzillai Frost. Conrad Wright's classic study of Emerson's barbed journal entries on Frost's deadly preaching distilled the satiric descriptions of preaching in "The Divinity School Address" to one man's resentful boredom in his Sunday morning pew ("Emerson").[1] If students can grasp the picture of Emerson indignantly looking out at the snowfall while the Reverend Frost drones on—"the snowstorm was real; the preacher merely spectral" (*Collected Works* 1: 85)—his whole idea of the preacher as a passionate poet of truth becomes much more tangible.

When the closely focused narratives of Emerson's meeting with the students, his recent withdrawal from the ministry, and his exasperation with the Reverend Frost are made part of the classroom analysis, the text of "The Divinity School Address" will yield engaging issues for discussion that would never surface if students faced the work cold. In a literature course, the central issue is Emerson's vision of the preacher as poet, in which Emerson blurs the line between preaching and poetry. He thus provides a theory of poetry and the role of the poet that can readily be compared with other views of both the role and importance of literature. Students may also recognize that Emerson essentially performed this "smitten poet" role in the opening section of "The Divinity School Address" with his exaltation of the "refulgent summer" and his declaration that "one is constrained to respect the perfection of this world, in which our senses converse" (*Collected Works* 1: 76). An alert student may ask whether "the harmonies of *moral* nature" are the same as those worldly perfections "in which our senses converse." Indeed they are, Emerson would respond, and this translation of natural beauty into moral harmony was the essential argument of the book *Nature* (1836), which he had published two years earlier. What may have seemed on first reading to be a flowery oratorical introduction for a formal occasion can thus be disclosed as a serious philosophical argument that transforms the observant poet of nature into the modern prophet of religious truth. Emerson's contention that "whilst a man seeks good ends he is strong by the whole strength of nature" merges the moral with the natural (1: 79); the truth of this merger is, in Emerson's view, the new gospel of the preacher-poet.

Obviously Emerson is attempting to make the young preachers in the audience reevaluate their profession, as he had been doing personally for more than a decade. In so doing Emerson was also offering a high-minded rationale for his own troubled relationship with both the ministry and the Unitarian movement. To strengthen his case in a dramatic—and highly controversial—way, he grounded this conception of the minister as ardent poet in a radically revisionist version of the origins of Christianity. Emerson's retelling of the narrative of Jesus is the heart of "The Divinity School Address," a bold claim of sacred authority for his vision of a reformed church and a revitalized ministry. "Jesus Christ belonged to the true race of prophets," he declared, one who "saw with open eye the mystery of the soul" (*Collected Works* 1: 181). Students need to recognize the importance of Emerson's portrayal of Jesus as one of a series of prophets, not a singular or unearthly figure. His power arose not from a divine or supernatural nature but from a force of intellectual discernment. Jesus was "open," or receptive, and attuned to the "soul," a term suggestive of both the divine and the deeply human. He came less as a prophet with settled answers and conclusions than a searcher, sensitive to "mystery" and thus to the process of intellectual exploration and discovery.

Emerson portrayed Jesus as human, but not "merely human." Jesus understood the fundamental truth "that God incarnates himself in man, and evermore goes forth anew to take possession of his world." This radically democratic reading of the long-standing Christian doctrine of the incarnation was, Emerson explained, the basis of Jesus's claim to divinity: "He said, in this jubilee of sublime emotion, 'I am divine. Through me, God acts; through me, speaks. Would you see God, see me; or see thee, when thou also thinkest as I now think'" (*Collected Works* 1: 81). The success and the shock value of "The Divinity School Address" resulted from Emerson's complete reimagining of a very familiar story, rather than his pronouncement of a new set of theological doctrines. Discussing this narrative reinvention can lead students to consider the power of narrative in shaping the understanding of contemporary events as well.

The cost of locating God within men and women was the loss of a conscious, caring God beyond the self. This was the concern of Wilson and his fellow students when they asked Emerson to meet with them to discuss theism. This question emerged again in the controversy that followed the address. For the teacher, Emerson's frank rejection of the idea of a personal God opens for the classroom an important discussion of the nineteenth-century crisis of faith in Western culture—a potentially sensitive topic, since for many students those questions are still alive. Emerson was called down on his treatment of theism by Henry Ware, Jr., one of the most prominent and respected members of the Unitarian clergy. Ware had preceded Emerson as minister in the Second Church of Boston pulpit, the pastorate that Emerson had resigned in 1832. Some two months after Emerson delivered "The Divinity School Address," Ware delivered a rebuttal (Robinson, "Poetry"). His argument, quite simply, was that the idea of an abstract or impersonalized God, lacking a human and especially a parental character, robbed religion of its capacity to provide comfort and inspire worship. An impersonal God meant the end of religious faith. That Emerson was repudiated by a man who might be thought of as one of his guides and professional exemplars adds a dimension of narrative tension to the study of this event and another layer of complexity to the developing portrait of Emerson's character. Some students may see in Emerson a hero resisting a dead establishment with fresh and liberating ideas, while others, a troublemaking egotist attempting to justify his uncooperative attitude. Most will have encountered versions of both these personalities in the course of their university studies.

Ware's critique of "The Divinity School Address" centered on this intentionally inflammatory indictment by Emerson: "Historical Christianity has fallen into the error that corrupts all attempts to communicate religion. As it appears to us, as it has appeared for ages, it is not the doctrine of the soul, but an exaggeration of the personal, the positive, the ritual. It has dwelt, it dwells, with noxious exaggeration about the *person* of Jesus. The soul knows no persons" (*Collected Works* 1: 82). Far beyond a lack of reverence for Jesus, Emerson's phrase "noxious exaggeration" ridiculed the entire sentimental culture of Jesus veneration in nineteenth-century American preaching and religious writing. In 1835 Emerson had privately fumed about such blind adoration: "I do not see in [Jesus] cheerfulness: I do not see in him the love of Natural Science: I see in him no kindness for Art; I see in him nothing of Socrates, of Laplace, of Shakespeare." Parrying with an unnamed devotee of the perfect Jesus, he continued. "Do you ask me if I would rather resemble Jesus than any other man? If I should say Yes, I should suspect myself of superstition" (*Journals* 5: 72). His views hardened over the next three years, and in "The Divinity School Address" he had found a terminology that he believed could displace that of Christianity: "the doctrine of the soul" (*Collected Works* 1: 82).[2]

When Emerson insisted that "the soul knows no persons," he was condemning the cult of one man that he believed Christianity had become. But his attack on the son was implicitly an attack on the father as well. Emerson's deity was not individuated in the sense that a person must be, and it did not recognize or interact with those persons who were thus individuated. This is what chilled Henry Ware. The "soul" that Emerson speaks of is better understood as an energy, a law, or, perhaps in Taoist terms, a way. The "divine bards," including Jesus, preach "the doctrine of the soul" by inspiring, even provoking, individuals to act: "Noble provocations go out from [the bards], inviting me also to emancipate myself; to resist evil; to subdue the world; and to Be. And thus by his holy thoughts, Jesus serves us, and thus only" (*Collected Works* 1: 83). Jesus may have been "divine" in Emerson's sense of the term, but he was not supernatural. The word *soul* served Emerson's purposes well because of its deeply ingrained place in Christian theology, which held that the soul was a uniquely immaterial and immortal aspect of human nature that provided access to the divine.

Emerson did not believe that his rejection of a personal God was the abandonment of religion. Indeed he saw it as the only path that religion could take in the modern world. Despite his severe critique of the "calamity of a decaying church and a wasting unbelief" (*Collected Works* 1: 88), it is important that students recognize that Emerson ultimately advocated for the revitalization of the church and its ministry rather than the abandonment of it. He believed that a reorientation to a religion of the soul could achieve that. Therein lay the purpose of the preacher—and of the poet. Students can trace Emerson's transition in tone from satirical attack to fervent exhortation as he brought the presentation to a close, urging the incipient preachers to see themselves as "newborn bard[s] of the Holy Ghost" whose single mission is to "acquaint men at first hand with Deity" (1: 90). The conclusion of the address thus took the form of a classical oratorical peroration, in which Emerson attempted to instill new energy and new purpose in his hearers.

Emerson therefore urged his audience to "let the breath of life be breathed by you through the forms already existing." How to impart such life? Emerson's answer is brief, somewhat hazy, but also exhilarating. The "remedy" to what he called the "deformity" of the religion of his age was "first, soul, and second, soul, and evermore soul. A whole popedom of forms, one pulsation of virtue can uplift and vivify" (*Collected Works* 1: 92). In the word *soul* he embedded a host of interconnected meanings that encompassed vision, purpose, vigor, sentiment, sincerity, devotion, empathy, and harmony. These were the traits that the new ministers must themselves embody and impart to others.

The religion of the "soul" was Emerson's alternative vision of the faith of his day, best articulated some three years later in "The Over-Soul." In this essay he redefined God in modern terms. Teachers can profitably link this essay to "The Divinity School Address" to illustrate the way Emerson sought to separate the idea of the deity from the realm of the supernatural. Although the Over-Soul was a force greater than the individual, it was not beyond or apart from the individual. "Man is a stream whose source is hidden," Emerson wrote. "Our being is descending into us from we know not whence" (*Collected Works* 2: 159). Emerson's use of the image of the flowing stream and its hidden source captured both the individual's intimate connection with deity and the ultimate mystery of human origins and foundations. Calling the Over-Soul a "Unity" or a "common heart" that both contains us and makes us "one with all other," Emerson attributed to it our capacity for "wisdom, and virtue, and power, and beauty" (2: 160). Students reading the essay may notice the wealth of God synonyms that mark the opening pages of this essay. While the term "Over-Soul" is the most prominent and perhaps the most expressive renaming of God, Emerson also speaks of the "Supreme Critic," "that great nature," "that Unity," "the wise silence," "the universal beauty," "the Eternal ONE," "this deep power," "that Wisdom," "the Highest Law," "a light," "this pure nature," "the soul," and "the deep, divine thought" (2: 160–62). As the essay continues, he seems to settle on the "soul" as the most common referent, a term with roots, as we have seen, in "The Divinity School Address." Emerson's search for a language with which to express the deep spiritual experience illustrated the crisis of belief that marked his era. The traditional language of religion no longer carried sufficient meaning. Emerson's search for new expression illustrates for students the close connections between religious belief and the language with which it is expressed and understood. They may come to see that this search for adequate expression, so apparent in Emerson's writings, is also a twenty-first-century problem.

NOTES

[1] See also Wright's recently published account of "The Divinity School Address," "Soul Is Good, but Body Is Good Too."

[2] For a detailed discussion of Emerson's development of this concept, see Robinson, "Poetry, Personality, and the Divinity School Address."

Emerson the Essayist in the American Essay Canon

Ned Stuckey-French

That good student, the one who is consistently engaged and always prepared, raises her hand and asks, without a hint of insolence, "Excuse me, but why are we reading Emerson?"

The question is real and showstopping. Other students nod in agreement. You'll have to attempt an answer before the class can return to *Essays*.

And to be honest, you feel some unity with her question yourself. Emerson is knotty, difficult, often exasperating. Why *are* we reading him?

This sticky question lies behind what Joel Porte called "the problem of Emerson." "Emerson," wrote Porte in 1973, "has become the least appreciated, least enjoyed, least understood—indeed, least read—of America's unarguably major writers" ("Problem" 85). Students sense this. They resist Emerson. How is he to be taught? Should he be taught?

The problem of Emerson is also the problem of the essay, for Emerson is not alone among essayists in being marginalized. According to Lynn Bloom, by 1900 the literary essay had already fallen "from canonical status to school genre" ("Once More" 25). Robert Connors argues the essay is still seen as a "service genre," used to write about the more literary genres: fiction, poetry, and drama. Essays, he points out, are taught in required introductory composition classes by teaching assistants and adjuncts, not in upper-level literature electives taught by professors. In her groundbreaking 1999 article "The Essay Canon," Lynn Bloom surveyed the most widely used essay anthologies to find which essays were being read and why. She concluded that the essay canon is fundamentally a teaching canon as opposed to a historical, critical, or national canon (401). The essays that are well known, she argued, are those that appear in freshman composition anthologies, where they serve largely to model a rhetorical mode and prompt a student essay.

Despite the fact that many, perhaps most, colleagues and students still see the essay as the "fourth genre," the form is undergoing a renaissance. Houghton Mifflin has published the *Best American Essays* series annually since 1986. Several important historical anthologies of essays have been published since 1993.[1] Editors have launched new magazines devoted exclusively to the essay.[2]

Emerson, however, has not factored in this renaissance. Our bias is still toward an essay made of familiar language, windowpane prose, a narrative or descriptive essay that is personal, direct, accessible, and untroubling. That is not Emerson. He does not appear in Bloom's list of the fifty most anthologized essayists of the last half of the twentieth century. Instructors did not use *Nature* to prompt a "what did you do on your summer vacation?" essay, and in any case, the first-year writing courses that Bloom studied are in decline. High school advanced placement classes are replacing English 101. Emerson even has a hard time elbowing his way into the few American literature survey courses still around in a time when traditional literary and American studies programs are giving way to media studies and digital humanities. The percentage of humanities majors limps along in the low single digits.[3]

So where might Emerson be taught? Where might the essay be taught? My answer would be in creative writing programs, which are on the ascension. Prior to World War II, there was one creative writing program in the United States. Now there are more than five hundred. The Association of Writers and Writing Programs (AWP) lists more than 360 graduate programs alone, 209 of which offer concentrations in creative nonfiction. Over the last thirty years these nonfiction programs have been the fastest growing of all graduate writing programs.[4] The study of the essay is now situated in these programs. We need to be teaching Emerson in advanced undergraduate and graduate writing classes devoted to the essay.

But how do we do it?

I think the process is threefold. First, we acknowledge Emerson's difficulty and student resistance to him. It does no good to try to paraphrase "Self-Reliance" as an example of bootstrap boosterism. It does no good to pretend he isn't difficult. Second, we use Emerson's journals to introduce Emerson the essayist, who is, I would argue, a Baconian who longs to be a Montaignian, a lecturer who longs to be a conversationalist. Let students see how hard it was for Emerson to write a new kind of essay. Third, having used the journals to place Emerson in the living tradition of the essay, we can better explain why Emerson's prose in the essays is so dense, difficult, and poetic. It is only then that they might accept the paradox that they must read Emerson as a poet in order to read him as an essayist.

There are many ways to let students know that they are not the first to find Emerson frustrating or obscure. One might, for instance, introduce them to Edgar Allan Poe's short 1842 takedown. Poe accuses "Mr. E" of belonging "to a class of gentlemen with whom we have no patience whatever—the mystics for mysticism's sake." Poe even posits a fancy version of our good student's earnest question when he asks, "*cui bono?*—to whom is it a benefit?" to which he promptly answers, "If not to Mr. Emerson individually, then surely to no man living" (qtd. in LaRocca, *Estimating* 45).

Poe was not alone among contemporaries in critiquing Emerson's distance and difficulty. In an oft-quoted letter, Emerson's good friend Thomas Carlyle told Emerson that his book of essays felt like "a *sermon* to me" and that his voice was that of "a *Soliloquizer* on the eternal mountain-tops only, in vast solitudes where men and their affairs lie all hushed in a very dim remoteness." Emerson's sentences were difficult for Carlyle, and they will be difficult for us and our students. They do not, said Carlyle, "always entirely cohere for me." They were "strong and simple" and possessed "of a clearness, of a beauty—But they did not, sometimes, rightly stick to their foregoers and their followers; the paragraph not as a beaten ingot, but as a beautiful square *bag of duck-shot* held together by canvas!" (*Correspondence* 371).

Contemporary critics such as Richard Poirier (*Poetry and Pragmatism*) and Stanley Cavell (*Emerson's Transcendental Etudes*) put Emerson's difficulty and disjunctiveness at the center of their readings of *Essays*, but I think for most students (whether graduate or undergraduate) Phillip Lopate is a better first guide. Advanced students of creative nonfiction will likely be familiar with Lopate's seminal 1994 anthology, *The Art of the Personal Essay*, though not with his long resistance—and recent conversion—to Emerson. Discussing his principles of selection in the introduction to his anthology, Lopate explains, "Though it nearly killed me to leave out Bacon and Emerson, I decided in the end that they were not really personal essayists but great formal essayists whose minds moved inexorably toward the expression of impersonal wisdom and authority, regardless of flickering references to an 'I'" (li). I suspect most students will share Lopate's 1994 bias toward the personal and against the formal, or to put it another way, they will favor Montaigne over Bacon. To confirm this, assign and discuss a representative essay by each of these two authors. Most students will prefer Montaigne's bawdiness, skepticism, honesty, digressions, and affection for narrative to Bacon's distance, abstraction, aphorisms, and propensity to offer counsel.

It may seem I am working against Emerson, discouraging the students by focusing on how hard he is, but there is a method to my madness. There is no believer more devout than a convert, and now it is time to introduce the students to a convert. It is time for them to read Lopate's 2011 essay "Between Insanity and Fat Dullness: How I Became an Emersonian," republished as "Foreword: The Undisguised Emerson" in David Mikics's 2012 *The Annotated Emerson*. Here Lopate testifies that he was won over by reading Emerson's journals. As Lopate puts it, "The journals show his vulnerable side" (x). Previously he had seen Emerson as Baconian, his sentences possessed of an "aphoristic compression" that too often leaves readers in "a fog," but reading the journals enabled him to recast Emerson as "the American Montaigne" (xii).[5]

The journals, especially those of the late 1830s and early 1840s, show Emerson struggling to become an essayist.[6] It is the period during which he asks himself, "When will you mend Montaigne? When will you take the hint of Nature? Where are your Essays?" (*Journals* 5: 40). Weary of the lecture circuit, he decided to focus on his essays instead. For models he turned to Bacon and Montaigne, but especially Montaigne, whose essays were for him "the language of conversation transferred to a book." In Montaigne's essays, he heard the ecstatic eloquence, the voice loosed by conversation, the ventriloquism of the divine speaking through the self that he had hoped for in his own lectures:

> One has the same pleasure in it [Montaigne's book of essays] that he feels
> in listening to the necessary speech of men about their work, when any
> unusual circumstance gives momentary importance to the dialogue. For
> blacksmiths and teamsters do not trip in their speech; it is a shower of bul-
> lets. It is Cambridge men who correct themselves and begin again at every
> half sentence, and, moreover, will pun, and refine too much, and swerve
> from the matter to the expression.   (*Collected Works* 4: 95)

But Emerson, who graduated from Harvard at the age of eighteen, was certainly more "Cambridge man" than blacksmith, and his writing did not simulate
conversation in the same way Montaigne's did.

As much as Emerson identified with Montaigne, they were different men and
different essayists. Consider, for example, the tag lines we often (and rightly) associate with them—a question in Montaigne's case, a declaration in Emerson's.
"Que sais-je?" is, on the one hand, invoked as signaling Montaigne's rigorous
skepticism, but when we think of him talking about his kidney stones or im-
potence, the question hints at an almost silly self-deprecation, as if he were a
Borscht Belt comedian tossing off "What do I know?" with a shoulder shrug.
Emerson, on the other hand, was nothing if not serious. In "Literary Ethics" he
wrote, "I also will essay to be" (*Collected Works* 1: 121). "Literary Ethics"—the
title itself is revealing, suggesting that ethics and aesthetics are one and the
same. His aphorism, like Montaigne's, can also be read two ways at once: on
the one hand, he is saying, *I will try to live fully and be somebody*, while on the
other hand, he is saying, *I will write essays in order to find myself.* Either way
writing and acting are one. He lives on the page.

Montaigne also lived on the page but in a more improvisational way. He was,
he said, writing "a book consubstantial with its author," but for him the self was
mutable and worldly in a way that it was not for Emerson (504). Emerson was in
search of the "genuine" self; Montaigne trailed after a worldly self that, he admit-
ted, "goes along befuddled and staggering, with a natural drunkenness" (610).

With Montaigne we are able to maintain the illusion that we are sitting down
to talk; but if we go "in search of the living Emerson," according to Porte, we
will find him not chatting at the fireside but in his lines on the page ("Problem"
108). "Emerson *is* a great writer," says Porte (114), but we must "focus our attention on his writing *as writing*," not as simulated speech (108). Here is Porte's
conclusion, with a suggestion for how we should read Emerson:

> My thesis then is simple: Emerson, as he himself frequently insisted, is
> fundamentally a poet whose meaning lies in his manipulations of language
> and figure. The best guide to change, or growth, or consistency in Emer-
> son's thought, is his poetic imagination and not his philosophic arguments
> or discursive logic. The alert reader can discover, and take much pleasure
> in discovering, remarkable verbal strategies, metaphoric patterns, repe-

titions and developments of sound, sense, and image throughout Emerson's writing.   (94)

William H. Gass agrees. He observes that even when Emerson begins "conversationally," as in the opening of "Self-Reliance" ("I read the other day some verses . . ."), "he is not beginning a talk or an address, although such a deliverance may lie in its past; he is opening an essay," which, like a poem, is "meant to be experienced, not simply heard." To experience prose as poetry, cautions Gass, "is not always easy for the reader to grasp" ("Emerson" 41).

Helping our students become "alert readers" may not be easy, but it can be done. First, we must slow them down and ask them to read Emerson's prose with the same attention they use when reading poetry. Assign them each a sentence and to come to the next class having written a page or two about it. Put them in small groups with others who have been assigned sentences from the same essay and ask the group to try to figure how their sentences speak to one another. Ask students to read their sentences aloud. If the sentences they've been assigned still feel opaque, Lopate provides an example in such reading. He admits having been pulled up short by this sentence from "Experience": "The only thing grief has taught me, is to know how shallow it is." Emerson offers the sentence, says Lopate, "without elaboration," leaving Lopate to elaborate, which he does for more than six hundred words: retrieving passages about grief from the journals, discussing the psychology of grief, gazing at photographs of Emerson, lauding Emerson's humility and honesty, sharing a joke Emerson cracked when he met Lincoln. Lopate praises Emerson's "non-dogmatic sanity" and calls him a "good egg," but he admits that Emerson was also "a bourgeois and wrote in the style of middle age." For this, asks Lopate, "Can we ever forgive him?" Yes, he says. He can, and more than that, he adds, "I can identify with him, having at last entered both categories" ("Foreword" xxi).

In all likelihood, our students are neither middle-aged nor bourgeois, and perhaps they are not yet ready to forgive Emerson (or Lopate) for being both. Nor perhaps are they ready to forgive us for asking them to read Emerson, but one day, like Lopate, they may return to Emerson's thorny sentences and be won over by this essayist who writes like a poet, and remember that it was we who introduced them to him.

NOTES

[1] See, for instance, Early; Lopate, *Art*; Oates and Atwan; D'Agata, *Making, Lost Origins*, and *Next American Essay*; Williford and Martone; and Klaus and Stuckey-French.

[2] These include *Creative Nonfiction*; *Fourth Genre: Explorations in Nonfiction*; *River Teeth: A Journal of Nonfiction Narrative*; and *Assay: A Journal of Nonfiction Studies*.

[3] See Jacobs; Chace; and Bérubé.

[4]On the rise of creative writing, see McGurl and the AWP's "Guide to Writing Programs." Regarding the rate at which nonfiction programs are growing, see Hesse (238).

[5]Carl Klaus and I shared a similar moment of conversion. Initially, like Lopate (and for similar reasons) we were not going to include Emerson in our anthology *Essayists on the Essay*, but at the urging of Robert Atwan we reconsidered. We returned to the journals, where we found a wonderful passage about Montaigne and the writing of essays that migrated almost intact from the journals into "Montaigne; or, The Skeptic." We included it in our book and I quote it later in this article.

[6]Porte's *Emerson in His Journals* still gives students their best introduction to the journals.

Politically Ethical Aesthetics: Teaching Emerson's Poetry in the Context of Diversity in the United States

Saundra Morris

Emerson's poetry remains underemphasized in classrooms. Yet during his New York lecture tour of March 1842, Emerson wrote to his wife, Lidian, "I am in all my theory, ethics, & politics a poet" (*Letters* 3: 18).[1] By "poet," Emerson didn't mean exclusively a writer of verse but instead a person whose energy was fundamentally both iconoclastic and, as he emphasizes in his lecture and essay "The Poet," affirmative, creative, and imaginative. For Emerson, the best preachers, the best scholars, and even the best social activists are all poets. In "The Divinity School Address," he calls for the minister to be "a newborn bard of the Holy Ghost" (*Collected Works* 1: 90); in "Literary Ethics," he speaks of "immortal bards of philosophy" (1: 103). In "The Method of Nature," whoever seeks to realize her "best insight" becomes one of the "higher poets" (1: 136); in "Heroism," the life of the great person is "natural and poetic" (*Collected Works* 2: 151); and the "Representative Man" Plato, although not literally a poet, is "clothed with the powers of a poet; stands upon the highest place of the poet" (*Collected Works* 4: 25). This inclusive terminology shows how important Emerson felt poetry to be and how closely he identified himself with it.

Emerson's poetry helps us appreciate the poetic nature of his prose and calls our attention to its constant preoccupation with the poetic impulse. While Emerson writes in his essay "The Poet" that "the Knower, Doer, and Sayer" (*Collected Works* 3: 5) are of equivalent value and in various texts that a person can do any vocation poetically (i.e., imaginatively and out of one's integrated being), he clearly attaches particular value to writers of verse. For Emerson, poetry is supposed to bring us cheer—to lift us from depression and self-doubt by showing us that beauty is the fundamental essence of the universe and of ourselves.

Indeed, for Emerson the idea of beauty carries resonance within it of the necessity for benevolence, goodness, and justice, and for their enactment in the world (including by writing poetry). He powerfully ends his "Divinity School Address" by calling us to see that "the Ought, that Duty, is one thing with Science [as science and as *scientia* 'knowledge'], with Beauty, and with Joy" (*Collected Works* 1: 93). Accordingly, I emphasize what I have termed a "politically ethical aesthetics" that calls us to imagine the poetically beautiful in terms of the just, the just in accordance with beauty, and how we read in accord with how we live (189). While few of Emerson's poems have direct political content, I also attend to their underlying concerns with personal and political justice in relation to democracy, human rights, progressive politics, and anticapitalism that I find throughout his verse and his aesthetic.

Emerson collected his poetry into two major volumes, *Poems* (1847) and *"May-Day" and Other Pieces* (1867), the latter of which includes a section of original poetic epigraphs to his own essays. With friends and family, he selected, revised, and expanded works for inclusion in *Selected Poems* (1876). Emerson wrote these poems over the span of almost fifty years, from 1824 to 1873. Nonetheless, modern readers and scholars have tended to view his poetry as secondary to the "essential" Emerson, and far too few of us teach Emerson's poetry, either on its own or with his prose. Yet not only was Emerson consistently referred to and thought of in his own time as a *poet*-essayist, but his verse has exerted a persistent influence on other poets, Emily Dickinson, Robert Frost, A. R. Ammons, and Mary Oliver among them.

Several preoccupations and qualities characterize Emerson's poetry as a whole. Among its major concerns are our relationship with the natural world, aesthetics, the vocation of the poet, inspiration and intuition, and the relationship between the poetic and how we enact our lives. Like Dickinson's verse, Emerson's is oblique and often directly riddling. He tends to write in rhymed iambic tetrameter, though he did produce some blank verse poems and others in a type of free, variable, or experimental verse.

I have taught Emerson's poetry for over twenty years. In this essay, I explain how I do so in three classes: American Poetry of Diversity and American Romanticism and Diversity, two mid-level courses of fifteen to thirty-five students, ranging from first-years to seniors and including majors and nonmajors, and Emerson, Whitman, and Dickinson, a seminar for mostly upper-class majors and a few English graduate students. I teach Emerson's poetry as American Romantic literature in all three classes and emphasize close reading within historical, political, and literary contexts. In the seminar and in the American Romanticism class, I foreground reading Emerson's prose along with his poetry. The mid-level classes serve to fulfill the university's graduation requirement of a course about diversity in the United States, so I represent Emerson's poetry in the context of an American literature of diversity. We read, alongside the texts by white, straight, male authors, the works of Phillis Wheatley, Anne Bradstreet, Frances Ellen Watkins Harper, Rose Terry Cooke, James M. Whitfield, Jesse Bushyhead (Cherokee), Walt Whitman, Dickinson, Frederick Douglass, Sojourner Truth, José Martí (who loved Emerson's poetry and translated at least five of his poems; Martí also wrote an essay, "Emerson," and at least one poem to him—a verse elegy), Louise Erdrich (Turtle Mountain Ojibwe), Joy Harjo (Creek), Langston Hughes, Claude McKay, Emma Lazarus, Audre Lorde, and others. I teach poems throughout the course with emphasis on the construction of ideologies, nationalism, selfhood, and social justice.

My pedagogy itself is also constituted by attention to what the African American feminist theorist bell hooks has called, as in the subtitle of her book *Teaching to Transgress*, "education as the practice of freedom." Influenced by Paulo Freire and his *Pedagogy of the Oppressed*, hooks requires a pedagogy that is self-consciously "interrogated" (6), so that students and teachers can practice "a revolutionary pedagogy of resistance" (2) to hegemonies. Objecting to "the banking system of education" (students' simple consumption of as much information as possible), "boredom and apathy" (5), and "obedience to authority" (4), she praises such values as "joy" (3), flexibility, spontaneity (7), collectivity (8), and "recognition of differences" (9), along with academic rigor. She writes that "the engaged voice must never be fixed and absolute but always changing, always evolving in dialogue with a world beyond itself" (11), so that students and teachers "can create new visions" in the classroom, "the most radical space of possibility in the academy," and a "teaching that enables transgressions—a movement against and beyond boundaries" (12).

The other major theoretical influence on my teaching is Emerson himself. Although without a twentieth- and twenty-first-century sensitivity to some aspects of difference, Emerson's pedagogical principles are strikingly similar to those of hooks. A number of her notions resonate with Emerson's: her belief in resistance to authority, tradition, and social dictates; her notions of dynamic becoming instead of static being; her belief in spontaneity; her connection of thought with action in the broader world. But their most direct correlation occurs in "The American Scholar," where Emerson was speaking to Harvard's Phi Beta Kappa students in 1837. It is a sentiment that I include in all my required self-statements and that I tell each of my classes:

> Colleges . . . have their indispensable office—to teach elements. But they can only highly serve us, when they aim not to drill, but to create; when they gather from far every ray of various genius to their hospitable halls, and, by the concentrated fires, set the hearts of their youth on flame.
> *(Collected Works* 1: 58)

The "ray[s] of various genius" are the students and the professors. That their hearts are set on flame is more important than that their minds are taught more facts—which priority is reflected in hooks's rejection of a pedagogic "banking system."

I have tried to construct my own pedagogy to accord with these feminist, collectivist, antiracist, queered, and nonoppressive values. All my classes (including the thirty-five-student ones) are conducted in a circle and are discussion-based. The students journal on each poem or piece of prose, bring the journals to class, and use the journals to participate. I guide discussion and contribute information, but the students play a major role. I teach them to address one another, for example, not me. Sometimes I remove myself from the circle and let them talk to one another. I foreground the importance of kindness and collaboration over competition, so that students volunteer to meet with class members who miss a class to talk and to share notes. At the 200 level (non-seminar), the classes help create their own syllabi after I have spoken with them about canon formation and we have together developed criteria for the creation of a good syllabus (one that involves various diversities, one that has content that is at once enjoyable and significant, one that includes both better-known and lesser-known authors). The exams are open-note, open-book, and take-home, and can be done in groups of two or three, but students do not perform well if they have not attended class and done their reading. (Students with excessive absences must work alone.) The exams are designed to get the students to learn more and to continue to discuss the material. While, of course, the power in the classroom is ultimately mine, I try to destabilize that allocation in as many ways as I can.

The title of my essay, "Politically Ethical Aesthetics," calls attention to the inevitably political inflections of poetry's pleasure and beauty—in the imagination of the author, the structure of the language and form, and the reading and political praxes of groups and individuals with their variously constructed subjectivities and specific concrete existences. I do not mean to position Emerson's aesthetics in terms of an easily circumscribed political agenda, or to reduce reading to such, or to limit political attention only to poems about political topics. Instead, I want to bring to the forefront the political resonances of poems, including Emerson's, and readings by which we participate in the creation of poetic pleasure and beauty and by which we foster ideas about, and enactments of, political justice that the study of poetics can all too often train us to erase. I thus emphasize how poems resonate in terms of politics and justice, whether or not they are explicitly about those issues.

"The Rhodora," for example, can be taught as a sonnet exclusively about beauty in general. Instead, we explore the relationship between the specific sort of beauty that Emerson praises and a sort of beautiful politics that, for Emerson, always has to do with justice and love. That beauty, in contradistinction to that of the rose and all things based on hierarchy, elitism, cultural hegemony, and wealth, has to do with democracy, freedom, antimaterialism, wildness, experimentation, revolution, and equally available power.

As we discuss other poems later in the poetry of diversity course, we also look for particular qualities poems associate with beauty and power. Notions of beauty are culturally constructed and inflected with difference of subject position. Thus, for example, we refer back to "The Rhodora" when we read such texts as Maya Angelou's "Phenomenal Woman," a poem also about a nonconventional and this time even potentially threatening beauty. The poem opens with an assertion of the speaker's unconventional appeal: "Pretty women wonder where my secret lies, / I'm not cute or built to suit a fashion model's size" (126). The poem then explores the qualities of this woman who proudly describes herself as "phenomenal" in ways that transgress traditional notions of beauty. The voice in the poem is threatening and arrogant, even more so because the speaker is a black woman whose tone might be seen as especially dangerous by white patriarchy. In another poem about female empowerment, "Still I Rise," Angelou asks, "Does my sassiness upset you?" "Does my haughtiness offend you?" "Does my sexiness upset you?" (159). The title and refrain of "Phenomenal Woman" imply a pun that inscribes two of Angelou's points: she is a phenomenal, amazing woman, and she is a phenomenal, real woman instead of a noumenal, idealized one. Similarly, the rhodora represents, for Emerson, a real-world beauty—in contrast to the rose's cultivated and idealized one.

While "The Rhodora" considers the issue of American identity in terms of aesthetics, "Concord Hymn" focuses on the American Revolution, as do many texts by writers of diverse identities throughout American literature, in prose and poetry. At heart is the question of what being American means. Emerson's answer in "Concord Hymn" is to represent the American Revolution as being in the service of freedom and equality (however horribly those concepts were applied in the founding of America). His topic may initially strike us as un-Emersonian because the poem praises the forefathers, but it praises them specifically for being revolutionary on behalf of liberty, so that the poem ultimately serves, as does the Declaration of Independence, to endorse ongoing change toward greater freedom and justice. Indeed, the revolution has become a topos for all sorts of demands for liberty and equality. Elizabeth Cady Stanton rewrites the Declaration of Independence for her statement "A Declaration of Sentiments" for the Women's Rights Convention in Seneca Falls, New York; Douglass invokes the text in his 1852 Independence Day speech "What to the Slave Is the Fourth of July"; and John Wannuaucon Quinney does the same on behalf of the Mahican displacement in his Fourth of July oration of 1854. In my classes, including the seminar, we discuss America as a land in need of ongoing change and greater liberty as we read a number of poems. Whitman's "Song of Myself" is essentially a series of hymns in praise of American diversity and freedom. Other examples include Hughes's "I, Too," Allen Ginsberg's "America" and "A Supermarket in California," and Angelou's "On the Pulse of Morning." We also read Wheatley's "To the Right Honourable William, Earl of Dartmouth, His Majesty's Principal Secretary of State for North-America, &c.," which implies a connection between America's freedom from England and the slaves' freedom, and Lazarus's "The New Colossus," a pro-immigration poem part of which is carved on the Statue of Liberty near Ellis Island, both of which resonate with "Concord Hymn." These texts raise vital concerns for the contemporary United States, not least in terms of immigration and self-definition.

Freedom—and politics, for Emerson—always originates in justice, and justice exists in conjunction with truth, goodness, beauty, and love. He writes in "The Divinity School Address," for example, "If a man is at heart just, then in so far is he God; the safety of God, the immortality of God, the majesty of God do enter into that man with justice" (*Collected Works* 1: 78–79). In his Salem speech on behalf of John Brown, he asserts that "the arch-abolitionist, older than Brown, and older than the Shenandoah Mountains, is Love, whose other name is Justice" (*Collected Works* 10: 393). And in "Politics," he worries that too much power in our legal system has "allowed the rich to encroach on the poor, and to keep them poor," and he laments that "[t]he power of love, as basis of a State, has never been tried" (*Collected Works* 3: 119, 128).

Emerson objects to extravagant accumulation of wealth in two of his more explicitly political poems, "Hamatreya" and "Boston Hymn." "Hamatreya" indicts the greed of rapacious Concord farmers, Emerson's ancestor Peter Bulkeley among them, who arrogantly think the earth is theirs for their own gain. Opening in a sort of garrulous blank verse from the farmers' point of view, the poem then explodes into the harsh dimeter and trimeter of the embedded "Earth Song," which asserts that nonhuman nature will overpower and prevail, as the chastised poet affirms in the final quatrain.

"Boston Hymn" associates moral concerns about accumulation of wealth with slavery. Strikingly and paradoxically, the twenty-two-stanza "Boston Hymn" is not so much a hymn *to* God as a hymn *from* God in all except its first quatrain. This rhetorical gesture functions to blend the voice of the poem with that of God, causing the poem to assume divine authority. Consistently, God and nature appear as enemies of concentrations of power and money:

> I will divide my goods;
> Call in the wretch and the slave:
> None shall rule but the humble,
> And none but Toil shall have.   (*Collected Works* 9: 382)

Such emphases inform the most forceful and moving quatrain of "Boston Hymn":

> Pay ransom to the owner,
> And fill the bag to the brim.
> Who is the owner? The slave is owner,
> And ever was. Pay him.   (9: 383)

"God" thus forcefully calls for a freedom based on racial equality and an ethic that cuts to the core of capitalism.

My classes address the issue of the maldistribution of wealth as a justice and diversity issue, as do many of the poems we consider. William Carlos Williams's "The Yachts" is essentially a critique of the economic injustice that, symbolically, enables yachts to destroy everything in their paths. Sarah Piatt's poems "The Palace-Burner" and "We Two" concern economic injustice among poor whites. In the former, a woman's son has seen a picture of a burning palace during the Paris Commune insurrection of 1871, and tells his mother he would have liked to have burned the palace himself. The mother realizes, with guilt, that she would not have been brave enough to participate. "We Two" functions as a theodicy about poverty in America in the same time period. This complicated poem, written in the voice of an impoverished woman, questions the will of God in condemning some people to be poor. At the end of the poem the woman asserts that her will and God's are the same, because she actually does God's will in refusing to accept that poverty is the will of God.

Concerns with race, an issue in a number of Emerson's poems and prose writings, also permeate our discussions in other ways. We read racially diverse poems and also consider white privilege and the role of whiteness in the construction of ideologies and the choices of subjects, tropes, and forms. Emerson wrote "Concord Hymn" at a time when blacks were still enslaved (and women were denied many freedoms). Dickinson wrote from a feminist perspective but also from that of a relatively wealthy white woman.

Racial considerations emerge most directly, of course, when we examine poems from points of view of racial diversity. For example, "Christmas Comes to Moccasin Flat," by Blackfeet / Gros Ventre author James Welch, associates issues of race and poverty in a somewhat different way from "Boston Hymn." Welch's poem exposes the irony of a Christmas amid American Indian poverty in the light of what Christmas should be and in the light of religious imperialism that represses social justice. Set in a section of the Blackfeet Reservation in Montana, the poem represents the current problems of the reservation—poverty, alcoholism, and lack of hope—by contrasting these circumstances with the Christmas nativity story. Wise men are "unhurried" because there is no birth of hope to celebrate, candles are "bought on credit," warriors are "face down in wine sleep," windows are plastic instead of glass or, as in churches, stained glass. Yet children still "beg a story" about "honor and passion, / warriors back with meat and song, / a peculiar evening star, quick vision of birth," of a new way of life on the reservation (26).

Emerson's insistence upon equality and freedom extends by application to all poems concerning social injustice and diversity in America. That connection also pertains to poems about gender and, often, gendered implications about conceptions of the poet. Emerson's "The Sphinx," for example, is problematic in that it involves the male poet who blesses the threatening female Sphinx. But the poem also rewrites the Sphinx myth to undercut its overall agonistic emphasis and the requirement of the death of the female figure. For at the end of "The Sphinx," the male and the female figure are mutually enabled. The male poet blesses the Sphinx as a part of himself, turning her into a figure of animation and metamorphosis and turning the creative spirit into a partially androgynous one.

We attend to various aspects of gender, sexual orientation, and cisnormativity throughout the classes. Sometimes we do so in terms of discussing the gendered nature of topics and tropes of male poets, as I demonstrate in my treatment of "The Sphinx" above, or in our reading of Whitman's and Dickinson's both gendered and queered sets of images and concerns. For example, Whitman represents his poetry as, among other things, a "barbaric yawp" (55), "howls" (18), and "drum-taps" (in his collection of the same name), while Dickinson represents hers as objects such as a letter (#519, line 1) and a well (#1433, line 1), yet both poets use the figure of the poet as a spider and as flowers. Dickinson sometimes writes of herself using a male pronoun, and Whitman associates his poetry with queerness in theme and representation. Other poems, such as "Phenomenal Woman" and Adrienne Rich's "Diving into the Wreck," treat feminism (and, in the case of Angelou, black feminism) explicitly.

Many of Dickinson's poems raise gender concerns both in their very existence and also thematically. "They shut me up in Prose—" (#445, line 1), for example, indicts society for trying to shut up, to silence, a woman's voice, specifically the voice of the female poet, and confine her to the realm of the prosaic—both as genre and as boring, commonplace existence. The poem defies the narrow confines of gender and poetic social mandates, insisting that she has "but to will" (line 9) using the standard poetic trope of the poet as bird, to soar out of a figural cage to the realm of freedom, as she does by nature of the poem's existence. The poem's companion piece is even more affirming of female imagination. It begins "I dwell in Possibility— / A fairer House than Prose," setting up poetry as the realm of dream, imagination, hope, and freedom and prose a realm of confinement (#466, lines 1–2). Dickinson repeats the word *fair* later in the poem—"Of Visitors—the fairest" (lines 9–10)—claiming that the fairest readers, images, and imaginations visit her in her house of possibility. In both cases, we can read "fair" to mean both just and beautiful. The double meaning reiterates the concern of this essay.

We also examine the impossibility of considering gender in any binarized way as we bring up transgender issues and also discuss poems by poets who don't fit comfortably into any gender category. One such poem is Stacey Waite's "At a Rest Stop in Central Pennsylvania, a Man Chokes Me for Talking to His Girlfriend but, Thankfully, Lets Me Go after Referring to Me as a 'Man-Dyke Freak of Nature,'" from her collection *Butch Geography*. The painful poem describes an actual incident in which a man assaults Waite when she walks out of a women's bathroom. As a consequence, Waite writes, "These days I fuel up before leaving, I piss on the shoulders / of highways," and when the urine spreads to her shoes, "Sometimes I can smell it in the floor mats all the way home" (54). In an interview with the poet Jennifer Perrine, Waite, who identifies as genderqueer, explains that "to read my gender in an either/or way is always to misread it. Then again, to read my gender more queerly, as something else entirely, something not able to be captured in man/woman terms would, to some, be its own kind of mis-reading."

My 200-level courses include both canonical and noncanonical authors and as large a diversity of texts as possible. I usually don't pair or group poems or texts, generally proceeding chronologically and by author, but sometimes I do. For example, I often teach the introduction to hooks's *Teaching to Transgress* with Emerson's "The American Scholar." I bring in John Donne's "A Valediction: Forbidding Mourning" in conjunction with Bradstreet's "A Letter to Her Husband, Absent upon Public Employment." Students immediately note the gendered implications of the poems' arguments: the male poet minimizes and justifies his absence, while the female poet laments separation.

We also read Percy Bysshe Shelley's "Ozymandias" with Claude McKay's "America." The second sonnet strongly echoes the first in form, in theme, in its call for justice, in diction, and in figuration. Hughes sought to create a new African American poetry in part by incorporating jazz and blues rhythms. Countee Cullen and Claude McKay, on the other hand, often employ variations on traditional white male forms (as do some women poets, such as Edna St. Vincent Millay) to demonstrate that they too can perform in culturally sanctioned ways. Both "Ozymandias" and "America" assert that all rulers or empires, no matter how long they dominate or how powerful they seem, are doomed to eventual extinction. McKay's poem, a critique of racist America, represents America as a vampiric tiger about whom he has deep ambivalence because it has offered both oppression and opportunity. Yet, he writes, he calmly resists this "king," because, in the end,

> Darkly I gaze into the days ahead,
> And see her [America's] might and granite wonders there,
> Beneath the touch of Time's unerring hand,
> Like priceless treasures sinking in the sand.   (153)

This essay has, of course, not been comprehensive. I have not, for example, written about the many other sorts of diversities of poetry that exist in the United States, such as Japanese internment camp, corridos, and various other immigrant poetry or such contemporary poets as Ai, Alberto Ríos, Li-Young Lee, and Mark Doty. Classes in American literature lend themselves especially well to diversity-oriented approaches. Indeed, because America is an increasingly diverse nation, and because it still remains far short of offering freedom and justice for all, I believe that we are ethically obliged to make all our classes more concerned with those issues. We thus can enact the mandate in "The American Scholar" to think and live as whole, uncompartmentalized human beings; furthermore, we can connect our reading and teaching with the perennial Emersonian questions: Where do we find ourselves? How shall I live?

NOTE

[1] All serious study of Emerson's poetry is fundamentally indebted to the scholarship in *The Poetry Notebooks of Ralph Waldo Emerson*, edited by Ralph H. Orth, Albert J. von Frank, Linda Allardt, and David W. Hill, and volume 9 of Emerson's *Collected Works*, *Poems: A Variorum Edition*, edited by Albert J. von Frank and Thomas Wortham, with historical and textual introductions and poem headnotes by von Frank. I am grateful to Harold Schweizer for his help with this essay.

Teaching Emerson's
Philosophical Inheritance

Susan L. Dunston

Although I came to Emerson through literary studies, I now teach him in philosophy classes to students who are exclusively science and engineering majors. As a Romantic and transcendentalist, Emerson interweaves literature and philosophy, but by temperament and analytic skills my students are much more prepared to take him up as a philosopher than as a poet or literary essayist. They are skeptical about the possibility of expressing truth (beyond the purely personal) in literary language, and most of them are not accustomed, or inclined, to sift through the play of words that seem to them "just" poetic.

Teaching Emerson as a philosopher entails a shift from the strategies and emphases of literary analysis to let students' awareness of and facility with Emerson's language emerge as a function of their engagement with his questions and the ideas he leaves them with. If I begin with the language in a framework of American literature, most of my students quickly lose their way in what strikes them as "innavigable" textual seas of "slippery sliding surfaces" (*Collected Works* 3: 29, 28). Emerson seems too dreamy, self-contradictory, and unscientific to bother with. They are likely to revert to a barely adequate strategy that utterly betrays Emerson: figuring out what the teacher wants them to say *about* Emerson in exchange for a grade. I try instead to orchestrate ways they will learn *from* Emerson by reading him as a "ray of relation" to other philosophers and to themselves (*Collected Works* 1: 19).

Approaching Emerson as a philosopher solidly positioned in a discipline with strong ties to mathematics and science simply makes him more useful, interesting, and accessible to many students. Every day, students encounter the "innavigable sea" between themselves and the objects they seek to know, but the metaphor is not what connects them to Emerson; his predicament does. Students share the epistemological quandary Emerson describes so clearly in "Experience" as the oceanic gap "between us and the things we aim at and converse with" (*Collected Works* 3: 29). Furthermore, in writing of his young son's death, Emerson explicitly connects epistemological and visceral uncertainty as the complex predicament students also experience as loss or failure. The teaching opportunity here to fill in the details of this personal loss and present them as integral to the philosophical investigations of "Experience" affords students richer ways to engage Emerson's writing. Students also experience the pleasures and terrors of "endless" seeking, the dizzying oscillations between feeling like a "God in nature" and "a weed by the wall" (*Collected Works* 2: 188, 182). They have urgent questions about how to weigh anchor without becoming weighed down, how to "skate well" on those sliding surfaces Emerson describes, how to cultivate what Emerson calls "the art of life," how to form their own "original relation to the world" (*Collected Works* 3: 35, 1: 7). Those seemingly personal concerns assume curricular status and academic worth when teaching Emerson as philosopher. Taking up Emerson as their philosophical inheritance, as a resource already present yet not fully understood or tapped, in their cultural genetics can help students catch a wave of his thought and use it to navigate contemporary uncertainties, both personal and collective. Bringing Emerson the philosopher into their view makes it possible for students to work with and from his experience and insight toward fluent, creative, and ethical relations of their own with the world.

Though Emerson's philosophical status has risen steadily since Stanley Cavell began writing about him in the 1980s, Cavell's contention that "denying . . . Emerson the title of philosopher" is "all but universal" still challenges us to reconsider how we teach Emerson (*This* 78). Since 1905 Emerson Hall has been home to Harvard's philosophy department and Frank Duveneck's statue of Emerson, but, as Cavell argues, Emerson has largely been rejected by the philosophical tradition he helped to found—a starry-eyed transcendentalist, a hugely influential public intellectual, an essayist given to poetic language, yes, but a philosopher, strictly speaking, who contributed to the fields of metaphysics, epistemology, or ethics, to the philosophy of science or activism-oriented philosophies such as feminism, no.

It is useful to consider what philosophy and Cavell's figuration of philosophy as a "mood" (one that engages rather than avoids the nexus of autobiography and the more sustained and far-ranging lives of culture and society) provide in teaching Emerson (*Emerson's Transcendental Etudes* 26). Locating Emerson in the context of philosophy and the philosophical mood in which one finds oneself—almost inexplicably compelling one to question assumptions, to "let . . . loose" one's thinking (*Collected Works* 2: 183)—reveals an Emerson who is distinctly related to the other philosophers in courses on ethics, nature writing and environmental ethics, Western and Eastern philosophy, and comparative religion; who contributes to the philosophical investigation of science and engineering as cultural practices; and who is a forerunner, as Cavell and Russell Goodman suggest, to strands of contemporary antifoundationalism, pragmatism, democracy, and feminism. It also reveals an Emerson who firmly yoked philosophy to the personal and political realities of his life, a thinking person with whom students can have a mutual relationship.

Though often remembered for jettisoning the past in the opening lines of *Nature*, in formulating his own metaphysics, epistemology, ethics, and aesthetics, Emerson drew heavily and quite openly on philosophical forebears both Western and Eastern. For example, the influence of the *Bhagavad Gita* and the Sufi poets Saadi and Hafiz is clear in Emerson's monistic metaphysics of the slayer and the slain, his affirmational stance toward "each and all," the ethical ecology of the universe he takes as a model for the conduct of life, and his philosophy of creativity (*Collected Works* 9: 14). Equally evident is his engagement with Plato's idealism, Kant's transcendental arguments, Hume's skepticism, and the Scottish common sense philosophers' moral sentiment. Besides the patent links between Emerson and subsequent pragmatist philosophers such as William James and John Dewey, there are clear, often direct links between "Circles" and the antifoundationalism of Richard Rorty, Stanley Fish, and Jacques Derrida; between "Self-Reliance's" rejection of covenants for proximities and Emerson's refusal to "break myself any longer for you, or you" and the feminist ethics of Nel Noddings and Carol Gilligan (*Collected Works* 2: 42); between Emerson's sense that "imitation is suicide" (2: 27) and the feminist Audre Lorde's formulation of difference as "that raw and powerful connection from which our personal power is forged" (112).

Nineteenth-century feminists took Emerson's advocacy of self-reliance and his ethics, based on relation, empathy, and the intrinsic value of "each and all" (*Collected Works* 9: 14), to heart and passed these core values forward to future feminists. Helping students discover these affinities affords opportunities to better understand Emerson as well as contemporary feminist philosophy, to appreciate the historical context and development of contemporary feminism, and to form a coherent narrative of American philosophy that integrates difference. For example, rich discussions of caring evolve from having students read Emerson's "Self-Reliance" and "Each and All" with selections from Nel Noddings's *Caring: A Feminine Approach to Ethics and Moral Education* and Carol Gilligan's "In a Different Voice: Women's Conceptions of Self and of Morality."[1] Considered together, these texts prompt interesting investigations of care that do not always arise when the texts and genres are considered apart from each other: care as a principle, concept, relation, or practice; caring and gender (historically and biologically); and the ethical status/import of caring. Reading Emerson's "The Poet" with Audre Lorde's "Poetry Is Not a Luxury" invites marvelous parallels to be drawn between the writers' takes on poetry and liberation. It is helpful to consider the various oppressions from which each sought liberation and to make students aware of Emerson's stance against slavery. A roundtable discussion in which several students each take the "voice" or position of one of the authors and field questions from the rest of the class usually clarifies some of the differences between Emerson and modern feminism. This exercise can form the basis of a written assignment in which students are asked to respond as Emerson would to a particular passage in Lorde's essay, for example.

Cavell uses the philosophical confluence of Emerson and Wittgenstein to tackle questions of peace and political justice. Contemporary questions of ethics and values in science and technology often echo Emerson's critiques from *Nature* to *The Conduct of Life* of the cold, sometimes predatory engagement with nature that science fell into as it disengaged from religious tradition, cultivated a detached objectivity, and entered the marketplace of information as commodity. Emerson's resolved obedience to nature's "tuition" and his skepticism about claims to grasp reality are central to the possibility of scientific understanding and the principle of falsifiability (*Collected Works* 1: 24). With connective threads to many philosophical trajectories, Emerson also remains his own philosopher with personal inflections of the big questions, the methods, and the uses of philosophy—a helpful lesson for students about the relationship between circumstances and ideas.

Cavell extends a second challenge to teachers of Emerson, one about philosophy's value that is especially relevant given Emerson's intense desire to be of use. Thinking of the possibility of building or approaching a new and better world, Cavell asks, "can mere philosophy *do* anything?" (*This* 94). Presumably Cavell thinks it can, but he is well aware, as was Emerson, not only that the question is fair but also that philosophy must either demonstrably count or risk being sidelined as something intellectuals used to do before the scientific age of Emerson's time, now digitized as the information age. Do Emerson's philosophical methods of wondering, reflecting, and calling into question translate into practical reform? And more to the point of teaching Emerson, can his philosophy transform students and their lives? Can it help them "mend the bad world" by "creat[ing] the right one" (*Collected Works* 6: 119)?

While much in the history of philosophy counsels thinking before acting and suggests that mind-thinking trumps body-being, Emerson sidesteps those temporal and conceptual hierarchies to make ethics—the conduct of life—the central business of philosophy. He takes philosophy as a practice, a walking conversation with the world, much as he walked with Thoreau or Margaret Fuller. The act of thinking has a material form and gait; how else could it literally, not figuratively, leave a trail, forge a path, or do anything? Notwithstanding his idealism, Emerson was convinced "life is not intellectual or critical, but sturdy"; he was after "the transformation of genius into practical power" (*Collected Works* 3: 35, 49). Of specific concern to him in nineteenth-century America was using philosophical practice to address the crippling injustice of slavery, the pervasive disenfranchisement of women, and the hollow formalism of religion.

Emerson's philosophical methods—skepticism, questioning, debunking, reflecting, writing sutras that thread together reality and our participatory understanding of it—are classic and also corrective to any disciplinary penchant for wise answers to big questions by the end of the workday. Cavell, for example, defines philosophy as "aversive thinking" that counters habits of thought (*Philosophical Passages* 13). He names Emerson and Thoreau as the philosophers who do him "the most good" because their aversive thinking changes him (*This* 83). In "Self-Reliance," Emerson urges the "aversion" of conformity in thought and moral conduct, disdaining conformity as "the virtue in most request" owing to its very mindlessness (*Collected Works* 2: 29). "Circles" intensifies this message, noting "the terror of reform" lies in realizing "the virtues of society are vices of the saint" (2: 187).

While "Self-Reliance" is often the first essay assigned for the sake of engaging students, or *Nature* for chronological sake, "Circles" offers an exciting introduction to Emerson's philosophical methods. The endless seeking and experimenting Emerson describes, whether actively sought or bewilderingly endured, is familiar to most students not just academically but also personally, socially, and politically. But in the main, students are not at all sure that either this experience or thinking with uncertainty is acceptably curricular, let alone that it will translate into an exam answer or academic essay. "Circles" affords an opportunity to make the methods and uncertainties of philosophical practice curricular by using class time and assignments to emphasize dynamic, transformational conversations with the text rather than to arrive at fixed answers about the essay. Every student deserves to learn, as Emerson notes in *Nature*, "that there are far more excellent qualities in the student than preciseness and infallibility" (*Collected Works* 1: 39). It is important to acknowledge that fact explicitly in the classroom, because honing the courage and ability to engage and navigate the complex problems posed by life's "series of surprises" (significantly, a phrase Emerson uses in both the exuberant "Circles" and the profound "Experience") requires some freedom from the incessant pressure to know the right answer (*Collected Works* 2: 189, 3: 39).

Settling on precision and infallibility invites despair and error: there is always another detail to note, another adjustment to make, and we are always as mistaken as we are certain. One way to help students develop some "more excellent qualities" (for example, the abilities to wonder and recollect, to tolerate ambiguity), as well as some perspective on precision and infallibility, is to assign selections from Emerson's journals, the writing in the rough, with concurrent writing assignments that require students to try out, as philosophical, methods of observing, reflecting, calling into question, and composing/creating. For example, teaching Emerson in the context of nature writing and environmental ethics, I have students read his journal entries as anthologized in *The Norton Book of Nature Writing* (Elder and Finch). These are mindful and attentive observations but not wrestled toward ends or answers. We talk about the vast scope and lifelong habit of Emerson's journals, how he returned to them, rethinking and recovering private experiences and ideas toward creating the more public forms of writing and behavior. They read Emerson beside other American nature writers with diverse professions—philosophers, explorers, scientists, environmentalists, poets, historians, local color writers—and diverse perspectives of race, sex, and ethnicity. Then they join the tide of conversation by writing.

The semester-long writing project asks them to keep a journal of their observations of a particular place on campus over time: a precise record of events, inhabitants, changes, and their own circumstances, observational methods, and interests. Several weeks after starting this journal, they begin a second log that mines the first (still ongoing) to notice, articulate, and call into question how and why they observe, to unearth and examine their assumptions. The third part of this project is a creative document they develop from the other two out of some philosophical necessity or mood, accompanied by an explication of the relationships among the three elements. Small assignments along the way can help foster the kind of mindfulness I hope to see in their work. For example, early in the semester they go outside, with sealed envelopes of instructions, to find an interesting place to sit still, observe, and record a bit of nature writing on their own (cell phone photos are not sufficient, but I do invite sketches and diagrams). They open the envelopes after they sit down to find my first question: "what did you notice on the way to your spot?" The response is overwhelmingly their surprise that they did not notice much at all, that they were texting or talking on the phone or focused on getting somewhere suitable to complete the assignment, and we all share a laugh at how we so often walk, cocooned in our heads, *through* the world rather than *with* it.

Emerson's literary methodologies are part and parcel of his philosophical ones, and dismissing his literary language as beside the point is not an option, even in a philosophy class for science and engineering students. After some successful experience with his philosophical methods, however, they are more interested in the possibilities of literary language and more respectful of how Emerson plays with language to maximize its "vehicular and transitive" capability (*Collected Works* 3: 20). They see the liberating consequences of his exploration of the fugitive nature of language as means of escaping being fixed in a word, grateful that, as Richard Poirier writes, "Emerson is forever trying to liberate himself and his readers from the consequences of his own writing" (*Poetry* 27). Emerson writes convinced that each generation must write its own books, knowing that his own books are not best used as ends but as means. His definition of a "work of genius" is one in which "we recognize our own rejected thoughts," so he writes to cloak his readers' thoughts in "a certain alienated majesty" that inspires their discovery (*Collected Works* 2: 27). He is concerned that readers might fall into orbit and be made satellites instead of systems (*Collected Works* 1: 56), an insight that shaped the generous way he mentored other writers and can mentor our students. Sustaining creativity is his guiding principle as a writer. Student access to Emerson's literary language is enhanced when they hear and complete appropriate responses to his call to write and build their own world. Then they have more reason to invest in thinking about language and writing, both Emerson's and their own.

Like philosophy, Emerson can do something only when he is taught as vehicular and transitive. He functions best as conditional to students' own work. If Emerson were to walk into your classroom and find himself unuseful, he would handily excuse himself and erase his name from your syllabus. As Lawrence Buell notes, "more than any other major writer, Emerson invites you to kill him off if you don't find him useful" (*Emerson* 292). Student access to Emerson is enhanced by teaching for the connections: among the personal, political, and environmental; between philosophy and practice; within the textual exchange recorded and continued in philosophy as a discipline; and between students' concerns and Emerson's mentorial interest in all his readers' development. Adapting his methods to one's own circumstances is not playing at Emerson but experiencing the challenge to be an articulate, literary philosopher. Leveling the power differential between each and all (philosopher, professor, student) is not an abdication of the professorial role but an invitation for students to step up to the invigorating culture of difference in which "we are all teachers and all students—talkers, hearers, overhearers, hearsayers, believers, explainers; we

learn and teach incessantly, indiscriminately" (Cavell, *This* 75). Student interest in Emerson is enhanced by assignments that provoke some emulation of his
desire for originality by tapping into the aspiration that many students have but
often find difficult to incorporate openly into academic assignments, an aspiration that their own insights and abilities be of use in making the right world.

NOTE

[1] I have used Noddings selections anthologized in the textbook *The Good Life*, edited
by Charles Guignon (316–25), and Gilligan's original article published in the *Harvard
Education Review*.

Emerson and the Reform Culture of
the Second Great Awakening

Todd H. Richardson

I love teaching Emerson. I would be hard-pressed to find another writer who better promotes the liberal arts ideal—that students would awaken to and grow confident in the creative power of their own minds as a means of purposefully experiencing and contributing to life. Yet approaching Emerson the enigmatic bomb thrower can hold very real challenges for uninitiated students (and teachers). Many stand to be pushed beyond their tolerance threshold when they read such lines from "Self-Reliance":

> If, therefore, a man claims to know and speak of God, and carries you backward to the phraseology of some old mouldered nation in another country, in another world, believe him not.   (*Collected Works* 2: 38)

> Let us affront and reprimand the smooth mediocrity and squalid contentment of the times. . . .   (2: 35)

> I shun father and mother and wife and brother, when my genius calls me.   (2: 30)

On more than one occasion, after reading these passages and others like them, students have returned to class calling Emerson a "hippie"—probably not a compliment at the small regional university in West Texas where I teach and where many are religiously conservative. So the task for me as an instructor is clear: how do I teach students the liberating power of this great thinker without alienating them with his more inflammatory or inscrutable pronouncements? My approach, in sum, is to contextualize Emerson in the reform culture of the Second Great Awakening, among the most profound religious upheavals in American history. Such an approach can help students understand their own convictions—religious or otherwise—in a new light and ultimately feel welcome in Emerson's program of self-culture.

In preparation, I introduce students to some basic reading strategies. I quote Robert D. Richardson's dictum that "Emerson's preferred unit of composition is the sentence, not the paragraph and certainly not the essay" (*First* 4). I explain that Emerson wrote in brief bursts of inspiration in his voluminous journals (perhaps after a walk to Walden Pond), and when it was time to deliver a lecture, he would stitch together, almost randomly, portions scattered over many months or longer. Therefore, the best way to read Emerson for the first time, I suggest, is to read for favorite sentences. For fun, I encourage students to post one or two on Facebook and to tell us how their friends respond. Students have singled out such gems as "My life is not an apology, but a life" (*Collected Works* 2: 31) and "But the heart refuses to be imprisoned" (2: 181) and have gotten into funny discussions about who had the most "likes" from their friends. The intention of this exercise is not only to help students become dexterous with the words of this mysterious writer but also to help them lay claim to those that are personally most meaningful.

After a class period or so of such exercises and discussions, many students' confusion or apprehension has been ameliorated, so they are ready for deeper exploration of Emerson's work in the context of the Second Great Awakening. I begin with some of the basics of the movement, offering handouts from Daniel Walker Howe's *What Hath God Wrought: The Transformation of America, 1815–1848* or Perry Miller's *The Life of the Mind in America, from the Revolution to the Civil War.* (Useful chapters might include "Awakenings of Religion" from Howe and "The Intellect of the Revival" from Miller.) There they learn that the democratization of culture that began with the Revolutionary War spread to American religious practice. According to Miller, the Awakening "was a spasm among the populace, a violent explosion of emotions which for long had been seeking release." Those emotions most fully found expression in massive revivals in the "burned-over district" of western New York, where participants, in their moment of spiritual liberation, displayed "an incredible array of exercises—falling, barking, catalepsy, rolling, running. There were shrieks, laughter, outcries, incantations" (7). In *Nature* Emerson relates his own spiritual experience—one that would seem similar to that of a revivalist: "Almost I fear to think how glad I am . . . all mean egotism vanishes. I become a transparent eye-ball. . . . The currents of the Universal Being circulate through me; I am part or particle of God" (*Collected Works* 1: 10). Indeed, as Howe and Miller show, the Awakening, with its passionate democratization of religious experience, served as the seedbed for much of the fervor that characterized Emerson's transcendentalism in its heady early years (Howe, *What* 619; Miller 60). Emerson's career as a lecturer, in fact, has something in common with that of the revival preacher. Writing of Emerson's engagements in Providence in the spring of 1840, Margaret Fuller exclaimed (with only a whiff of irony) that "you have really got up a revival there. . . . Daily they grow more vehement in their determination to become acquainted with God" (*Letters* 2: 135).

Students also learn that Emerson and the transcendentalists shared a point of origin in the Awakening with the Methodists and Baptists, two major denominations that blossomed during the movement. (Emerson once expressed approval for "the heat of the methodist, the nonconformity of the dissenter" [*Journals* 4: 87].) All yearned for immediate, intuitive, spiritual empowerment as opposed to worn-out religious forms, exemplified by the rationality and cool formalism of the Episcopalians and Unitarians. This alone has helped some students, many of whom are active Methodists and Baptists, connect their own desire for spiritual knowledge to Emerson.

When students make these connections, they are primed to associate the moral and spiritual reform project of the revivals and affiliated denominations with Emerson's "The Divinity School Address." At its core, the Awakening was, of course, a movement of religious reform, and we certainly see that impulse at work in Emerson's famous address. His central purpose was to awaken what he called the "religious sentiment" not only in the divinity school students but in all the congregations these young ministers would touch throughout their careers. As he states:

> Wonderful is [the religious sentiment's] power to charm and to command. It is a mountain air. It is the embalmer of the world. It is myrrh . . . and rosemary. It makes the sky and the hills sublime, and the silent song of the stars is it. . . . This sentiment is divine and deifying. It is the beatitude of man. It makes him illimitable. Through it, the soul first knows itself. . . . Then he can worship, and be enlarged by his worship; for he can never go behind this sentiment. In the sublimest flights of the soul, rectitude is never surmounted, love is never outgrown. (*Collected Works* 1: 79)

I read such passages of soaring prose not only to dramatize Emerson's intentions to inspire an awakening but to underscore a fundamental irony in the address: shouldn't these divinity students have already become acquainted with the divine? Clearly Emerson was not confident they had. I ask students to imagine attending their graduation and the honored speaker telling them, in effect, that their education had been a waste of time.

Emerson blamed the divinity students' misguided education on "two errors . . . which daily appear more gross" in conventional Unitarian theology (*Collected Works* 1: 81). Class discussion of these "errors" helps students understand more fully how Emerson participated in the Second Great Awakening's protest against the cool formalism of established denominations. The first error was, essentially, that the church was so bound up in "ritual" and dry "historical Christianity" that the miraculous nature of the human soul actualized by God in the present moment was no longer understood (1: 82). The second error was that the church ceased preaching living "revelations" or "God himself" as a means of introducing the soul to "greatness." It was "as if God were dead" (1: 84). Emerson's remedy, characteristic of a Second Great Awakening revivalist, lay in inspiring new passion and enthusiasm: "I wish you may feel your call in throbs of desire and hope. . . . Yourself a newborn bard of the Holy Ghost,—cast behind you all conformity, and acquaint men at first hand with Deity" (1: 84, 90).

To further help students grasp the "errors" Emerson identified and the solutions he offered in response, I ask them to respond to a passage from the essay that includes the declaration "it is not instruction, but provocation, that I can receive from another soul" (*Collected Works* 1: 80). Specifically, students reflect on the difference between instruction and provocation, on Emerson's conception of the human mind that enables provocation as educational practice, and on the extent to which our current educational conventions are successful in attaining Emerson's ideals. The responses have been fascinating. Most students feel challenged and even inspired by Emerson's concept of provocation; just as many are deeply critical of the current emphasis on assessment and "teaching [or 'instruction'] to the test." One student, comparing grades K–12 to a prison, asked, "Where is our modern Emerson? Where is he now?" Another insightful student responded, "'Provocation' is being better than one's past self. 'Instruction' is being better than the person next to you."

Emerson's desire to reform American religious education and practice did not end with "The Divinity School Address." It extended over much of his career, as is evident, for example, in his support in 1867 for the Free Religious Association, a group of radical and apostate Unitarians. With others in the Second Great Awakening, Emerson came to promote a host of other reforms, abolition prominent among them. This fact can serve as an excellent segue to a discussion of Emerson's antislavery writings and to other writers who are often taught in antebellum literature classes, such as Frederick Douglass, Harriet Jacobs, and Henry David Thoreau. As Miller argues, the "ecstasies" of the Awakening "had to assure, not only the conviction of innumerable individuals, but the welfare of the young country" (12). For those in the Awakening, nothing threatened the "welfare of the young country" like slavery. It ruined the lives of enslaved Africans, it enabled alcoholism on account of the liquor trade, and it promoted licentious behavior among slaveholders and therefore destroyed families. Slavery corrupted the nation's very soul.

A useful essay for illustrating Emerson's abolitionist activity is "The Fugitive Slave Law, 7 March 1854," perhaps best known for its excoriation of Daniel Webster. For this reason it works well in conjunction with Emerson's "The American Scholar." Emerson represents Webster as, in effect, the antithesis of the scholar ideal. Although Webster's "power, like that of all great masters, was not in excellent parts, but was total," whether through "corruption of politics" or "original infirmity," he betrayed fundamental virtue and "most unexpectedly threw his whole weight on the side of slavery, and caused . . . the passage of the Fugitive Slave Bill" (*Emerson's Antislavery Writings* 76–77). For the remainder of the address, Emerson strove to awaken his audience's innate divinity to rescue the nation, as Webster could not, from its collision course with pure evil. Much like a revivalist preacher, Emerson proclaimed that "divine sentiments . . . are breathed into us from on high and are a counterbalance to a universe of suffering and crime, . . . [and] self-reliance, the height and perfection of man, is reliance on God." In such passages, students recognize that the religious reform program outlined in "The Divinity School Address" had significant implications for real-world ethical decision-making; indeed, as Emerson continued: "It is not possible to extricate yourself from the questions in which your age is involved" (88). One *must* rely on the living "religious sentiment" as opposed to dead institutions for the good of all humanity in the here and now. That point is wonderfully borne out in his clarification of "self-reliance"—it is not sublime egotism and self-seeking, as many of my students have feared after reading Emerson's essay by that name; it is, as Emerson states unambiguously, "reliance on God." In true revivalist fashion, it is this reliance on the divine that Emerson hoped to inspire in his audience. He concluded, "I hope we have come to an end of our unbelief, have come to a belief that there is a Divine Providence in the world which will not save us but through our own co-operation" (89). Defeat of slavery was possible, even imminent, but only when inspired men and women recognized the evil and, more important, recognized the power they could access to overcome it. Underscoring Emerson's fight for abolition in this fashion can go a very long way in demonstrating for students the long and rich tradition of American religious practice in progressive reform movements.

In the final analysis, what is the effect of teaching this approach to Emerson? In my experience, Emerson's faith in the "infinitude of the private man" is contagious—that in the face of racial oppression and entrenched but broken religious ideology, there is hope in any one of us for a solution (*Journals* 7: 342). And if the divine working from within can generate solutions to such profound social, cultural, and political problems, certainly our students will feel empowered to tackle a host of other challenges they face. One ESL student from China, on learning that she earned a B in my class, told me with tears in her eyes that she had failed her required sophomore survey three times before she took it with me. She explained that Emerson helped her believe she had the resources necessary to overcome her perceived language limitations and do well. Another student, experiencing enough provocation in Emerson's teaching to nurture her inner "Genius," related that she and her husband had begun playing drums—their true passion—after setting them aside for "more important" career-oriented activity. Some need something other than encouragement to succeed. As we all know, many of our students experience very real personal problems: divorce, childhood trauma, addictions, and financial difficulty. Emerson can speak to these as well. As one student wrote in a note to me:

> I believe I have shared with you some of the trauma that I have overcome in my life, and I have found hope [and] peace . . . in Emerson's work. His perspective on self-reliance and nature resonate with my soul. I continue to read and enjoy Emerson. Whenever I am faced with the inevitable changes and challenges of life I re-immerse myself in Emerson's writings. . . . I am able to feel grounded and am often able to adjust my perspective.

At a time when we read much about the need to forewarn those who may have sensitivities to this or that literary text, it can be refreshing to consider an author who inspires, emboldens, and even heals. As student comments would suggest, the inspiration that Emerson was so famous for dispensing in his

own lifetime continues today. All English programs aim to teach students critical thinking, reading, and writing skills, yet with Emerson they get something
more. One way to ensure this "something more" in the classroom is to teach that
Emerson's fiery emotional appeal participated in the remarkable conflagration
that was the Second Great Awakening.

The Turbulent Embrace of Thinking: Teaching Emerson the Educator

Martin Bickman

> Emerson's American Scholar is "man thinking," but so
> too are good scholars everywhere. In controversies about
> language since Plato the argument has always been made
> that it is incumbent upon us to release words from the
> posturing embrace of Thought so that they may enter the
> turbulent embrace of Thinking.
>   —Richard Poirier, *The Renewal of Literature*

The challenge for us as teachers is not so much to demonumentalize Emerson—
the diversification of syllabi and the sidelining of the essay as a literary genre
have diminished Emerson's relevance in curricula—but to unformulate him for
our students and ourselves, to embody his work in our very activities of mind.
This is difficult because his radicalism is often masked by a mellifluousness and
stylistic grace that led Oliver Wendell Holmes to remark, "He was an iconoclast
without a hammer, who took down our idols from their pedestals so tenderly it
seemed like an act of worship" (qtd. in Boller 4). We need to substitute for the
Emerson of statement and wisdom the Emerson of continual process and discovery through the very act of writing; we must show him—or catch him—in
the creation of meanings through our own active, dynamic constructions, in the
making of it happen.

I try to engage my students, then, in reading Emerson through their own and
their classmates' writing, an approach inflected through the lenses of reader
response theory and practice and constructivism. Even more relevantly, the approach is deeply rooted in what I have delineated as an American tradition,
or antitradition, of a strain in American intellectual and literary life that has
flowed as an underground stream in our educational history, rarely noticed and
never enacted on a large scale, a stream I trace in my book *Minding American
Education: Reclaiming the Tradition of Active Learning* (2003). Although its
central philosopher is John Dewey, the tradition has its roots in the practice
of Bronson Alcott and the two assistants in his Temple School, Elizabeth Peabody and Margaret Fuller, as well as Henry and John Thoreau in their Concord
Academy, and its great keynote address is Emerson's "The American Scholar."
This tradition views knowledge as provisionally constructed by the mind in per-
petual interaction with the world. The outcomes of this process are generally
cultural artifacts such as ideas, classifications, formulae—basically a body of
knowledge that has been organized and divided as the curriculum. The mistake
of conventional education is to overvalue these end products, handing them
over ready-made instead of involving students in the process of reconstructing

the world for themselves, of engaging in dialectical movements between experiencing and conceptualizing, acting and thinking, practice and theory. In trying to recuperate this tradition we would accompany Emerson toward a more student-centered, more metacognitive pedagogy. As a passage in "The American Scholar" proclaims, colleges "can only serve us when they aim not to drill, but to create; when they gather from far every ray of various genius to their hospitable halls, and by the concentrated fires, set the hearts of their youth on flame" (*Collected Works* 1: 58). The college is not merely to pass along the rays of knowledge but to stimulate its students to bring them to bear on some Promethean act of fiery creation, as a lens converges sunbeams. In other words, colleges should be places not just where culture is transmitted but where it is created and transformed, personally inflected and negotiated.

In line with this tradition, I avoid teacher-centered formats such as lecture or even discussions not prepared for by the students' own writing. I have found a huge disparity—in cognitive process, in depth of ideas, in student engagement—between classes where students have just "done the reading" and those where they have prepared by constructing their own thoughts through writing. For writing is not merely the setting down of thoughts we already had but itself our main method of discovery. As we push our vague, fuzzy thoughts to clarity, we discover along with Emerson that the very act of writing makes us articulate things we didn't know we knew. Before it is written, our knowledge remains locked in our own subjectivity, shadowy and inert. As we shape it into words and sentences, it becomes more objective, something external that we ourselves can scrutinize, analyze, reshape. As W. H. Auden said, "How can I know what I think till I see what I say" (345).

The mechanics of having my students participate in this process has changed with changing technology. I began decades ago using Ann E. Berthoff's method of the dialectical notebook (41–47), where students write down their initial thoughts and then at regular intervals reread their entries, respond to them in wide margins, and eventually hammer these fragmentary ideas into coherence in more formal "essays," in the sense of "attempts," used by Montaigne and Emerson (Bickman, "Seeing"). Now I use electronic bulletin boards so the students can read not only their own but their peers' writing before class and continue the dialogue both in and after class. In doing so the students are, indeed, reenacting Emerson's own procedures in hewing their finished papers from jottings and short passages. As Emerson said of his own journal, which he then went on to construct and reassemble into lectures and essay collections, "This book is my Savings Bank. I grow richer because I have somewhere to deposit my earnings; and fractions are worth more to me because corresponding fractions are waiting here that shall be made integers by their addition" (*Journals* 4: 250). Emerson returned, categorized, and indexed his journals in ways that our students can now do more easily, if not as brilliantly, using word processors. Thoreau discovered the power of this approach early in his own writing under Emerson's mentorship: "Thoughts, accidentally thrown together become a frame in which more may be developed and exhibited. Having by chance recorded a few disconnected thoughts and then brought them into juxtaposition, they suggest a whole new field in which it was possible to labor and to think" (4: 277–78). Without making these processes explicit, except through studying actual examples following Emerson's inchoate thoughts from notes to sentences to essays, the students learn from their own experiences how writing generates more writing, how it becomes a cognitive process and a window into Emerson's mind and their own.

Having said this, it may come as a surprise that I generally do not give my students the open field suggested by Thoreau for the students to ramble in. I usually focus their journal entries through prompts that ask them to relate a specific act of close textual analysis to more general ideas. I coax them toward the zone where the best learning is, in the dialogue between the concrete and the conceptual, and I try to formulate structures to help them engage in this area, as in the following assignment prompt:

> Tony Tanner, a British critic of American literature, has written:
>
>> It is my contention that many recent American writers are unusually aware of this quite fundamental and inescapable paradox: that to exist, a book, a vision, a system, like a person, has to have an outline—there can be no identity without contour. But contours signify arrest, they involve restraint and the acceptance of limits. . . . Between the nonidentity of pure fluidity and the fixity involved in all definitions—in words or in life—the American writer moves, and knows he moves. (17–18)
>
> Do a close analysis of these sentences from Emerson's "Circles" to suggest how they not only explore the same themes but embody them in the very texture and movement of their language, in the syntax, rhythms, diction, sound patterns. How does Emerson bring the tensions Tanner articulates into the act of writing and you into the acts of reading, analyzing, and doing your own writing?
>
>> For it is the inert effort of each thought, having formed itself into a circular wave of circumstance,—as, for instance, an empire, rules of an art, a local usage, a religious rite,—to heap itself on that ridge, and to solidify and hem in the life. But if the soul is quick and strong, it bursts over that boundary on all sides and expands another orbit, on the great deep, which also runs up into a high wave, with attempt again to stop and to bind. But the heart refuses to be imprisoned; in its first and narrowest pulses, it already tends outward with a vast force, and to immense and innumerable expansions. (*Collected Works* 2: 180–81)

When I read through the responses to prompts like this one, I often note with some humility that virtually anything I would have said in a lecture has already been suggested by at least one student and that taken as a whole their writings suggest a fuller and richer analysis than anything I could have done alone.

I have combined these insights into a composite form that incorporates many of their separate insights. They noted that each of these sentences, but especially the second, seems to run on beyond the point at which our syntactic ear expects it to stop, piling phrase upon clause upon phrase, until we finally reach some kind of closure, both semantic and grammatical, such as "to stop and to bind," a wonderfully appropriate way for that sentence to end. These five monosyllabic words reinforce the sense of closure implied by their meaning. Further, the initial sound of *bind* alliterates effectively with the powerful verb *burst* and with what is being burst, *boundary*. The accretion of words in the passage, like *and*, *also*, and *again*, along with the anomaly of two consecutive sentences beginning with *but*, signal and foreground the mind's reflecting and turning upon itself. The sentence beginning with the second *but* returns to the sense of an outward push with a vengeance, with *vast*, *immense*, and *innumerable*, each adjective stretching out with more syllables. True to the title of the essay and its themes, it solves some of the problems it articulates by using its language to draw a wider circle around statements that seem initially definitive and authoritative.

Some of the students used terms specifically about the mind's "turning" upon itself and, in doing so, unknowingly echoed a sentence of Emerson's crucial to this entire enterprise: "If he have not found his home in God, his manners, his forms of speech, the turns of his sentences, the build, I say, of all his opinions will involuntarily confess it" (*Collected Works* 2: 169). I pair this sentence with a passage from William Gass to emphasize that any general statement about Emerson's "philosophy" or his place in literary history must be anchored in a discussion of his language itself: the language is the philosophy and vice versa: "Every sentence, in short, takes metaphysical dictation, and it is the sum of these dictations, involving the whole range of the work in which the sentences appear, which accounts for its philosophical quality, and the form of the life in the thing that has been made" (*Fiction* 14). I also return to Emerson's use of the word *turn* to move into a discussion of his longer forms like the essay, using the term as inflected by Richard Poirier: "The word suggests an active, not merely reflective, response to the given, and it is synonymous with 'trope.' . . . The turning or troping of words is in itself an act of power over meanings already in place. . . . It promises after all to save us from being caught or fixed in a meaning or in that state of conformity which Emerson famously loathed" (*Renewal* 17). The turns do not so much deconstruct or self-consume the text as allow it to stand while permitting further writing and reading in new and often opposed directions. They prevent the hardening of imaginative play into creed, doctrine, or fixed belief, allowing the text to create a structure, but one with enough spaces for breath and for escape.

In Emerson specifically, such turns can occur in every sentence and paragraph, but they appear most explicitly in short paragraphs about three-fourths through each essay. They often begin with *yet* or *but* and call attention to the act of expression with verbs like *speak* or *write*. I frequently ask the students to find such turns themselves, but sometimes I point the students toward them and ask for an examination of their relation to the entire essay:

> Is there somewhat overweening in this claim? Then I reject all I have written, for what is the use of pretending to know what we know not? But it is the fault of our rhetoric that we cannot strongly state one fact without seeming to belie some other.   ("History," *Collected Works* 2: 22)

> The circle of the green earth he must measure with his shoes, to find the man who can yield him truth. . . . The waters of the great deep have ingress and egress to the soul. But if I speak, I define, I confine, and am less.   ("Intellect," 2: 202)

I should mention that I present this notion of Emerson's turns not as a proven truth but as a hypothesis that they have to measure against their own reading of the texts. If the course is at the graduate level, I sometimes assign the entire volume of *Essays: First Series* and have them nominate their own choices for this turn in each essay. I then have the students defend their choices in class as a way of fostering a discussion at once rooted in the text but related to theory, and, in a metacognitive turn, I ask them whether the theory is of any use to them.

But—and here comes the turn in my own essay—as a former director of service learning at my university, I take to heart Thoreau's definition of a good book: "I must lay it down and commence living on its truth. What I began by reading I must finish by acting" (*Journal* 1: 281). Just as I ask my students to read and write in the zone where the specific meets the general, I also ask them to make their course of study the place where the academic meets the realm of personal experience and inner life, to embrace Emerson's notion that life consists of what a person is thinking all day. I return to Tanner's observation and note that our education has not negotiated the tension with the honesty or success of our best literary artists; in education, the contest between fluidity and stasis, between vitality and formalism, has been repeatedly and heartbreakingly decided by an overemphasis on the latter. I ask my students to become more reflective and transformative about our class activities: What is the function of grading, and how should we handle it in our own situation? What kinds of reading and writing will best get us where we want to go? How do we move what we say and write into the larger academic community and then the community beyond the university? These questions cannot be answered with abstract formulae but must be negotiated every day, in every class.

We can be inspired, but not immediately directed, by words like the following from George Dennison, one of the foremost twentieth-century figures in the tradition of active learning, who says that our teaching

> requires, first, that the educator be modest toward experience, modest toward the endless opening-outward and going-onward of life, for this

going-onward is the experience of the young. Precisely this fact of life, however, evokes anxiety, sorrow, regret, and envy in the hearts of adults. It is not easy to give oneself wholeheartedly to the flow of life that leaves one, literally, in the dust. If we often scant the differences between the young and ourselves, and prefer the old way, the old prerogatives, the old necessities, it is because at bottom, we are turning at all times from the fact of death.   (257–58)

We must face this challenge by bringing our students in as collaborators and coconspirators, to help them become radicals in their own right.

Emerson the Author:
Introducing *The Collected Works of Ralph Waldo Emerson* into the Classroom

Ronald A. Bosco

Students often assume that Ralph Waldo Emerson was a popular author based on his presumed chosen profession and the durability of his reputation into the twenty-first century. Given the readings included in anthologies of American literature over the past century, the assumption is natural enough for students to make. In those anthologies, where the canonical Emerson reigns, *Nature*, "The American Scholar," "The Divinity School Address," "Self-Reliance," "Circles," "The Poet," "Experience," "Fate," and occasionally "Thoreau" are complemented by poems such as "Each and All," "The Rhodora," "The Sphinx," "The Snow-Storm," "Bacchus," "Threnody," "Days," and "Brahma." These works, especially *Nature* and the essays, have long been the source of students' lifelong knowledge of Emerson and his place in the American literary tradition emerging in the nineteenth century.

Without lessening the hold such works exert on Americans' historical sense of Emerson's aesthetic and intellectual service to those coming of age after the American Revolution, it is significant that at the outset of his public career Emerson never considered himself a professional author. Rather, his career toward authorship progressed by stages: as a Boston-area teacher (1818–26), a Unitarian minister at Boston's prestigious Second Church (1829–32), and then, after traveling through Europe in 1833, a lecturer. Having left the traditional "call" of the pulpit, Emerson never looked back, preferring the professional opportunities the lyceum movement afforded him. He wrote at the time, "The call of our calling is the loudest call" (*Journals* 4: 252), and within a month of returning home from Europe he lectured on "The Uses of Natural History" before Boston's Natural History Society.[1] Confident of his ability as a lecturer and the timeliness of his ideas, in 1835 he delivered two substantial lecture series in Boston and later characterized the lecture hall as the "true Church of the coming time," where everything will be admissible, from "philosophy, ethics, divinity, criticism, poetry, humor, anecdote . . . [to] the most liberal conversation"—all "combined in one speech" (*Later Lectures* 1: 48).[2]

During the stages leading to his career as a lecturer, Emerson developed a compositional method that served him in the preparation of the 1,500 lectures he would deliver by the 1870s and facilitated his emergence as an author. His initial level of composition occurred in the privacy of his journals and notebooks, where he recorded his waking thoughts, excerpts copied from his extensive readings, prose and verse he translated out of foreign editions, and snippets of conversations he engaged in with friends. There, Emerson also created modest drafts that were either original or elaborate syntheses drawn from one or more of the foregoing sources for delivery.[3] Although Emerson could be cavalier about his journals, once writing to Carlyle that they were a miscellany of "disjointed dreams, audacities, unsystematic irresponsible lampoons of systems, and all manner of rambling reveries" (*Correspondence* 272), they served as the "savings bank" into which he deposited ideas, the best of which he withdrew and enlarged upon in discourses (Perry, "Emerson's Savings Bank"). Drawing from these private papers, Emerson assembled lecture prose sentence by sentence. This second stage of composition yielded lectures that grew in length and sharpened in thesis with each delivery and proved invaluable when he moved to his third and final stage of composition: the revision of finished lectures for publication as essays. "The American Scholar" and "The Divinity School Address" were delivered as discourses before appearing as pamphlets, while *Representative Men* (1850), *English Traits* (1856), and *The Conduct of Life* (1860) each began as a lecture series developed over several years, and major essays of Emerson's later career such as "Fate" (1860) were subjected to close revision or rethinking of authorial thesis—all from the lectern.

Throughout *Approaches to Teaching the Works of Ralph Waldo Emerson* authors collectively identify an archive of more than fifty volumes of his journals and notebooks, lectures, letters, published poetry and prose, and sermons. Edited according to the highest standards of modern textual scholarship, these collectively provide readers with an archive of Emerson's oratorical and authorial practices throughout his career; they also provide those willing to probe deeply into their accompanying apparatuses with an archaeology of his private intellectual and imaginative life and his engagement in lectures and print with contemporary issues of conscience and social justice, such as abolitionism and women's rights. Citations from this accessible archive throughout *Approaches* introduce teachers to the rich preprint gestational contexts of Emerson's writings through reference to each edition's apparatuses and invite their development of practical applications for bringing together in the classroom his canonical and noncanonical writings through reference to those contexts.

A question Emerson variously put before lecture and essay audiences was "Where do we find ourselves?" The question I would foreground is "Where do we find Emerson?" My answer is that, while we find him on the printed pages of his public writings, Emerson's authorial mind at work is more directly visible by reading those pages against the annotations and manuscript or print copy-text alteration and parallel passage apparatuses contained in definitive editions of his works. Annotations inform readers about Emerson's meaning in a particular line or passage and identify his sources from a staggering array of writers (classical, foreign, premodern, and modern), from whom he drew upon for ideas; the language and substance of philosophical or scientific systems; and the historical markers embedded in his writings. By contrast, tables of copy-text alterations and parallel passages demonstrate Emerson's compositional practices. Alterations account for his changes in the written and printed form of works he published and demonstrate his repeated searches for the right word, transitional sentence, and paragraph or entire organizational structure to make his meaning clear; parallel passages locate the origin of those writings in his private writings and lectures. Copy-text alterations and parallel passages constitute the evidentiary heart of modern editions of Emerson's lectures (*Early Lectures*; *Later Lectures*), prose (*Collected Works*), poetry (*Collected Works*, vol. 9; *Poetry Notebooks*), and sermons (*Complete Sermons*).[4] The three case studies of Emerson's writings that follow reveal that the canonical prose and poetry with which students associate him today stand to be enlivened in the classroom by reference to his private writings, out of which those works were drawn, and to noncanonical prose or verse he published contemporaneously with the canonical.

Teaching Nature *(1836) alongside* An Historical Discourse, Delivered before the Citizens of Concord . . . *(1835)*

An admirable display of interpretive commentary on *Nature*'s origin and meaning occurs in essays throughout *Approaches*. The text through which most students first encounter Emerson in the classroom, *Nature* strikes new readers as an impressionistic rhetorical tour de force in which he announces "the laws of the First Philosophy" and asserts that, as "their enunciation awakens the feeling of the moral sublime," "they astonish the understanding"; the organizing principle of Emerson's "First Philosophy" is that all in the universe is related, and through its relatedness, everything in the universe enlarges "the limits of the possible" (*Journals* 5: 50–51; 4: 198–200). A forward-looking manifesto, *Nature* emerged out of Emerson's reliance on a type of naturalism that anticipated the observer of nature's intuitive capacity and the observer's ability to move from the factual to the metaphoric significance of objects, persons, and ideas encountered in nature; intuition also enabled the observer to see beyond the remoteness or ambiguity of words and things to thought. In its appeal to intuition and the senses, its conviction that language is symbolic of a higher spiritual reality that governs the universe, and its song of the "Orphic poet," which reminds modern man that he is the "dwarf" of a figure who "was [once] permeated and dissolved by spirit" and "filled nature with his overflowing currents" (*Collected Works* 1: 42), *Nature* impressed contemporaries such as Bronson Alcott, Margaret Fuller, Theodore Parker, and Henry David Thoreau as a progressive and idealistic text. Embracing *Nature*'s extravagant style as consistent with Emerson's message, in their respective professions these writers adapted his description of himself as a "transparent eye-ball" in whom all egotism has vanished and the currents of "Universal Being" circulate (1: 10) to transformations they aspired to effect in themselves and human culture.

Emerson intended *Nature* to serve as an empowering principle for thought and action in the still nascent American Republic. Yet even as he rejected historicization of the past as erecting "sepulchres of the fathers" and counseled readers to "Build . . . your own world" in *Nature* (*Collected Works* 1: 7, 45), in the contemporaneously composed *An Historical Discourse* (*Collected Works* 10: 17–54, 549–82), Emerson offered a vigorous defense of New England's and his own Puritan past. Reprinted serially in 1838 in the *American Historical Magazine*, the discourse resonated well beyond Concord. Introducing its serial publication, William Storer said the discourse "will not fail to meet the approbation of every[one] . . . who searches for truth, and tires not until he arrives at the fountain" (qtd. in 10: 551).

Reading *An Historical Discourse* alongside *Nature* confirms Ralph Rusk's assessment that the former work, ignored in biographical and critical treatments of Emerson, represents "the greatest effort [he] ever made" at researching and executing his subject "in the manner of a scholar" (221). Whereas *Nature*'s copy-text and parallel passage apparatuses document Emerson's compositional effort on that work, those for *An Historical Discourse* report three times more authorial effort.[5] Citing information drawn from church and town records, histories of Concord's founding, assessments of its political and economic importance during Massachusetts Bay's settlement, and testimonies by Concord's early settlers and participants in the revolution, Emerson described the "planting" of Concord as "the effect of religious principle" (*Collected Works* 10: 40).

Emerson's rhetorical approach to the American Revolution reflects the nationalistic hyperbole dominating nineteenth-century narratives of the event; however, his approach to Concord's history prior to the revolution defies the expectations of all who believe they know Emerson. Writing out of a style adapted from John Josselyn (*An Account of Two Voyages to New-England*), Peter Bulkeley (*The Gospel-Covenant*), Edward Johnson (*Wonder-Working Providence of Sions Saviour in New England*), Daniel Neal (*History of New-England*), and Thomas Hutchinson (*The History of the Province of Massachusetts Bay*), and quoting liberally from their writings, Emerson reprises the dominant historical narrative of Concord's and New England's founding. Traversing the twenty miles from Massachusetts Bay to what would become Concord, the first settlers undertook "a painful and dangerous journey through an uninterrupted wilderness," followed American Indian trading paths barely a foot wide, fell into hidden stagnant swamps, and plunged into thickets with axes to cut a road for teams drawing carts laden with meager provisions. Paraphrasing from Johnson, Emerson describes these people attacked by "ragged bushes" that "scratch their [bodies] foully" and draw blood "at every step." After sleeping on rocks wherever night found them, they reached Grassy Brook's meadows, to which they held a grant from Massachusetts' General Court. Once there, they burrowed "in the earth . . . under a hill-side" and built "a fire against the earth," neither of which provided durable relief from the harsh elements. Weakened from their journey, they became dispirited by "the sickening of their cattle" from "wild fodder" and the "loss of their sheep and swine, by wolves"; the suffering endured "in the great snows and cold soon following"; and their "fear of the Pequots." Emerson observes that these "poor servants of Christ" came to the New World with "an armed mind, better than any hardihood of body," yet "the rough welcome . . . the new land gave them was a fit introduction to the life they must lead in it" (*Collected Works* 10: 19–21). Introducing an air of romance into his narrative, he writes, "I seem to see them . . . addressing themselves to the work of clearing the land. Natives of another hemisphere, they beheld, with curiosity . . . the American forest. The landscape before them was fair," though "strange and rude," but they had "freedom, and the wailing of the tempest in the woods sounded kindlier . . . than the smooth voice of the prelates" in England (10: 23).

Using imagery he intended as a positive expression of their settlement practices, Emerson set out the founders' priorities. Along with establishing a school, promoting religion, and instituting democratic governance structures, "The wolf was to be killed; the Indian to be watched and resisted"; "the forest to be felled; pastures to be cleared"; "roads to be cut [and] town and farm lines to be run" (*Collected Works* 10: 26). Throughout its first century, Concord was the prowling ground for wildlife that included bears, wolves, foxes, and lynx and other wildcats; initially, farmers patrolled their lands, killing such animals when they came in sight, but as late as 1735 bounties of twenty shillings were paid to American Indian and white hunters for the animals' heads (10: 39). By contrast, the American Indians presented a different but complementary challenge, since they "inspire[d] such a feeling as the wild beast inspires in the people near his den" (10: 37). Ten years into settlement, efforts began to "civilize" the American Indians by winning them "to the knowledge of the true God." From the white perspective, those efforts seemed futile from the start. On the one hand, Emerson wrote, "The man of the woods might well draw on himself the compassion of the planters" through his "erect and perfect form"; on the other hand, that "form," which identified the American Indian as a natural part of the landscape, disclosed "irregular virtues, was found joined to a dwindled soul," and mirrored the "fierce instincts of the beasts he slew." Invoking the settlers' belief that American Indians descended from the lost tribes of Israel, Emerson accepts the characterization of them as "the ruins of mankind" and never questions their ultimate destruction (10: 29–30).[6]

In "Circles" Emerson wrote, "I unsettle all things. No facts are to me sacred; none are profane; I simply experiment, an endless seeker, with no Past at my back" (*Collected Works* 2: 188). Unsettling "all things" was one of Emerson's pedagogical specialties that contributed to his fame as a "university to our people" (B. Alcott, "Fuller" 2). However, students who read *Nature* alongside *An Historical Discourse* echo such estimates in the negative: in *Nature* they hear the voice of "an endless seeker" who upends claims the past holds over a culture's rising generation, while in *An Historical Discourse* they hear in Emerson's reprisal of inherited myths about Concord's founding a political brief that elevates the past at the expense of the future.

Ex oriente lux: Emerson's "Orientalist" (1850s–1870s) and "Persian Poetry" (1858, 1875)

Another way Emerson unsettles students, particularly those instructed to read him as an "original" American author, occurs when they encounter the "Eastern" sound of his expressions and sources. Along with images such as *Nature's* "transparent eye-ball" and the prophecy offered by its "Orphic poet," Emerson's invocation of Hindu philosophy in "Fate" and inclusion of verses he translated from the Sufi poet Hafiz and passages from *The Hĕĕtōpădēs of Vĕĕshnŏŏ-Sărmā*, Edward Davies's *The Mythology and Rites of the British Druids*, and "The Oracles of Zoroaster" prompt students to ask, "What is he thinking?" Even Emerson's contemporaries struggled to answer this question, but not Calcutta native Protap Chunder Mozoomdar, who, in addressing Concord's School of Philosophy in 1885, declared Emerson "a geographical mistake" (365): "His writings recall . . . Hindoo philosophy,—that all the universe is a divine dream passing away; but in passing it reminds us of the meaning, glory, presence, and life which it reveals and conceals at the same time[:] Creation rests on the bosom of man, and man rests on the bosom of the Infinite" (369–70).

In addition to providing accessible answers to students' questions, "Orientalist" (*Topical Notebooks* 2: 37–141) and "Persian Poetry" (*Collected Works* 8: 124–49) facilitate their inquiry into Emerson's intellectual investment in the aesthetics, religion, and philosophy of the East and are invaluable in courses that emphasize postcolonial, transnational, and translation studies. In the notebook "Orientalist," Emerson recorded his impressions while assimilating Persian and Eastern culture through a wide range of texts, most of which he came to own (Harding); there, he also drafted several versions of "Brahma" (*Topical Notebooks* 2: 96, 104, 131) and other poems and translated into English a substantial body of Persian poetry from the tenth through fifteenth centuries out of Joseph von Hammer's *Der Diwan von Mohammed Schemsed-din Hafis* and *Geschichte der schönen redekünste Persiens*, German translations of the lyrics of Hafiz, Firdousi, Omar Chiam, Enweri, Nisami, Saadi, and Kermani, among others.[7] "Orientalist" stands as Emerson's summary testimony to Eastern intellectual and imaginative influences on his idealism and the Eastern origin of values he had assimilated.

Emerson also drew on von Hammer's *Diwan* and *Geschichte* for "Persian Poetry," an essay in which he introduced the American public to early Persian aesthetics and culture. Celebrating the Persians as "exquisitely sensible to the pleasures of poetry" (*Collected Works* 8: 125), he wrestles with, but never reconciles, tensions he found between Eastern and Western experience: "Oriental life and society . . . stand in violent contrast with the multitudinous detail, the secular stability, and the vast average comfort of Western nations. Life in the East is fierce, short, hazardous, and in extremes. Its elements are few and simple, not exhibiting the long range and undulation of European existence" (8: 124).

The importance of the essay is in its display of occasional primitivism, imaginative freedom, wonder at nature's prospect, and comprehensive unity of Brahman faith illustrated by the panegyrics, epics, and sensual lyrics of Emerson's favorite Persian poets; what most excites Emerson in his recovery of their lyrics through translation is the antidote they provide to the brutality and vulgarity visible in nineteenth-century material culture. In the essay, he printed his own translations of numerous poems, including Hafiz's "The Phoenix," Kermani's "The Exile," Omar Chiam's quatrain "Each spot where tulips prank their state," a twenty-line excerpt from Nisami, and Enweri's "Body and Soul."[8]

"Persian Poetry" and related excerpts from "Orientalist" resonate positively with students when they recognize in the works Emerson's conviction that, as concepts, nature and fate transcend temporal and national expression. They report that "Persian Poetry," which moves between modest expository prose and generous poetic illustration, clarifies the "denseness" with which they struggle in *Nature* and "Fate" and establishes a new context for appreciating Emerson's "The Sphinx" (*Collected Works* 9: 3–12), "Saadi" (9: 242–50), and "Brahma" (9: 363–66). Students also respond positively to a portfolio of poems drawn from "Orientalist," where they discover that his initial and revisionary translations are creative acts themselves and have no difficulty grasping Emerson's reworking of Hafiz's intoxicating rhythms, his pleasure in re-creating Enweri's exoticism and spontaneity in verses of his own, or his embracing of Eastern mysticism as his formal homage to Eastern "Light."

Extending the Trajectory of Emerson's Canon in the Classroom

At the outset, I mentioned works that students accept as the canonical Emerson, largely bolstered by their inclusion in assigned anthologies. In his magisterial review of the ten-volume *Collected Works*, Robert N. Hudspeth praises the edition for providing a comprehensive view of Emerson's prose and verse canon in print; for me, that wider canon is most valuable in the classroom, where it challenges the artificial distinction between canonical and noncanonical Emerson as well as the unstated but nonetheless operative assumption that absence relegates certain texts to the noncanonical. With the exception of "Thoreau" (1862), all the anthologized works cited earlier create the impression that Emerson's career ended around 1860, when "Fate" appeared in print, but his career and positive reception by contemporaries had an extensive foreground, accessible through works such as *An Historical Discourse*, "Michael Angelo" (1837), "War" (1849), and "Persian Poetry," that continued uninterrupted into his later years with "American Civilization" (1862), "Saadi" (1864), "Character" (1866), "Introduction" to *Plutarch's Morals* (1870), and "Immortality" (1876).[9] My interest is not to announce an early or late Emerson canon but to recognize that the noncanonical Emerson merits reconsideration in the classroom.

The pairing of *Nature* with *An Historical Discourse* and of "Persian Poetry" with "Orientalist" models two ways of enlarging the inherited Emerson canon in the classroom. For teachers who find themselves fielding questions about Emerson's ruminations on what constitutes the practice of genuine religion, "Character" (*Collected Works* 10: 447–64, 810–36) offers a valuable classroom extension of his canon. The essay, which Hudspeth aptly describes as "a spirited, often acerbic attack on organized and formal religion, a credo of sorts by a man who hated creeds" (73), reprises career-spanning themes that Emerson engaged from the pulpit and lectern and in print.

Among Emerson's contemporaries, neither "Character" nor its advocacy of individuals' "moral sentiment" as the center of genuine religion would have come as a surprise. As a subject, character dominated his discourses on human conduct; in addition to making it the fundamental theme of "The Divinity School Address," character is central to his estimate of the worth of figures he treated in *Representative Men* and topics he developed in *The Conduct of Life*. And just as Emerson argued in "Uses of Great Men," "Once you saw phoenixes: they are gone: the world is not therefore disenchanted," despite America's immense political and social challenges at midcentury, he treated character as "the genius of humanity" (*Collected Works* 4: 19) and made its relation to "moral sentiment" his subject in lectures on "Morals" (1859), "Natural Religion" (1861–69), and "Truth" (1861–67).[10] Delivering "Morals" after John Brown's execution, Emerson insisted, "Character—not feats but forces, not set days, or public occasions, but at all hours, . . . can't be disposed of. . . . I like those who did not choose to defend this or that, but who were appointed by God Almighty, before they came into this world, to stand for that thing" (*Later Lectures* 2: 136).

In tone, intellectual elevation, and diminution of Christian orthodoxy's authority over an individual or society acting on the basis of "moral sentiment," "Character" is a powerful and radical statement. In the classroom, "The Divinity School Address" and "Character" are ideal as bookend treatments of Emerson's ideas on individual freedom, the nature of conscience, and their relation to religion; when read this way early in a course's treatment of Emerson's writings, students find "Character" essential to their understanding of "Experience" and "Fate." Hearing Emerson deliver an early version of "Character," James T. Fields asked him to revise the lecture for the *Atlantic Monthly*, but after paying him $200 for the finished essay, Fields canceled publication; according to Annie Fields, her husband had little choice: "Ordinary readers would not understand [Emerson] and would consider ['Character'] blasphemous" (qtd. in *Collected Works* 10: 813). "Character" finally appeared in the *North American Review*, edited by James Russell Lowell and Charles Eliot Norton. For the very reasons Fields had rejected the essay, they put it into print, eagerly anticipating the rage of clergy and the religious press that would follow publication. Calling it "the *religio Emersonii*," Norton wrote that "Character" "is the most unflinching assertion of the supreme right of private judgment; of the wrong done to human nature by 'authority' in matters of religion; of the temporariness of all the forms of religion, [and] the everlasting freshness of . . . religious spirit" (qtd. in 10: 814).

NOTES

I am grateful to Professors Joseph C. Henderson (State University of New York at Albany) and Jillmarie Murphy (Union College, Schenectady, NY) for their thoughtful comments on an early draft of my essay. Here, I disclose for the record that I edited from manuscript or, in one instance, print copy-text and wrote headnotes to and prepared textual apparatuses for these works by Emerson cited in my essay: *An Historical Discourse*, "American Civilization," "Character," "Introduction" to *Plutarch's Morals*, "Michael Angelo," "Morals," "Natural Religion," "Orientalist," "Saadi," "Truth," and "War."

[1] Delivered on 5 November 1833 and first printed in *Early Lectures* (1: 5–26), "The Uses of Natural History" was edited anew by Ronald A. Bosco and Joel Myerson (*Selected Lectures* 1–17) and is reprinted in their *Ralph Waldo Emerson: The Major Prose* (1–17); for their rationale governing the reediting of texts printed in *Early Lectures*, see *Selected Lectures* xxxi. *Major Prose* is the first anthology to print from the completed archive selections from three predominant sources of Emerson's prose: the pulpit, the lecture hall, and print.

[2] Emerson's first series consisted of six lectures on biography, while his second offered eight lectures on English literature; see *Early Lectures* 1: 93–216, 217–385, respectively.

[3] Emerson's synthetic or assimilative practices followed from a long-held belief he articulated in "Quotation and Originality": "If an author give us just distinctions, inspiring lessons, or imaginative poetry,—it is not so important to us whose they are. If we are fired and guided by these, we know him as a benefactor. . . . They fit all our facts, like a charm" (*Collected Works* 8: 100).

[4] With the exception of *Later Lectures*, editorial apparatus such as manuscript or copy-text alterations are printed in volumes of *Collected Works*, *Complete Sermons*, *Early Lectures*, and *Poetry Notebooks*.

[5] For the differences, cf. the apparatus for *Nature* (*Collected Works* 1: 270–73, 285–88) with that for *An Historical Discourse* (*Collected Works* 10: 572–82); Sealts and Ferguson slightly expand the number of journal and lecture passages referenced in *Collected Works* for *Nature* (46–65). Bosco and Myerson edited *Nature* anew in *Ralph Waldo Emerson: The Major Prose* (34–73) and explain their rationale for doing so (xxxv–xxxvi).

[6] What Emerson elevates here as the colonists' mission invites classroom attention to Thoreau's lamentation of the same throughout his life (Bosco, Introduction).

[7] This essay follows Emerson's spelling of the names of these Persian poets: Firdousi, or Ferdowsi: Abū Ol-qāsem Mansūr (c. 935–c. 1020); Omar Chiam, or Khayyám: Ghiyāth al-Dīn Abu al-Fath 'Umār ibn Ibrāhīm al-Nisābūri (1048–1131); Enweri, or Anvari: Awhad ad-Dīn 'Ali ibn Vāhid ad-Dīn Muhammad Khāvarānī (c. 1126–c. 1189); Nisami, or Nezāmī: Elyās Yūsof Nezāmī Ganjavi (c. 1141–1203/17); Saadi, or Sa'di: Musharrif al-Dīn ibn Muslih al-Dīn (c. 1213–1292); Chodschu, or Khwaju Kermani: Abu'l-'Atā Kamāl-al-Din Mahmud (1280–1352); and Hafiz, or Hafez: Mahammad Shams od-Dīn Hāfez (c. 1325–c. 1389). Translated by Emerson from the German, a variety of their poems appear in "Persian Poetry," with their sources identified below.

[8] This note, which identifies *Collected Works, Journals, Poetry Notebooks,* or *Topical Notebooks* sources for poems cited here from "Persian Poetry," is easily extended by reference to the notes and parallel passage apparatus in *Collected Works,* vol. 8, for numerous poems translated by Emerson but not cited in this essay. For Hafiz's poems, see *Collected Works* 8: 129–39, 271–74, 360–62; for Hafiz's "The Phoenix," see *Collected Works* 8: 137–38, 274, 362; 9: 631–34; *Poetry Notebooks* 221–22, 249, 272–73, 462; *Topical Notebooks* 2: 49–50. For Kermani's "The Exile," see *Collected Works* 8: 144, 275, 363; 9: 554–56; *Poetry Notebooks* 460; *Topical Notebooks* 2: 79, 86–87, 92, 97–98, 265. For Omar Chiam's quatrain, see *Collected Works* 8: 140, 274, 362; for "From Omar Chaim," see *Collected Works* 9: 565–66; *Topical Notebooks* 2: 52, 53, 87. For the excerpt from Nisami, see *Collected Works* 8: 145, 276, 363; *Journals* 11: 208–09; *Topical Notebooks* 2: 52. For "Enweri. Body and Soul," as titled by Emerson, see *Collected Works* 8: 145–46, 276, 362; *Topical Notebooks* 2: 56–57.

[9] For "Michael Angelo," see *Collected Works* 10: 58–74, 583–98; for "War," see 10: 351–64, 712–16; for "American Civilization," see 10: 394–410, 741–64; for "Saadi," see 10: 439–45, 801–9; for "Introduction" to *Plutarch's Morals,* see 10: 490–509, 857–77; and for "Immortality," see *Collected Works* 8: 179–94, 293–99, 369–71.

[10] For their sources, see *Later Lectures,* vol. 2: "Morals" (130–42), "Natural Religion" (177–95), and "Truth" (253–65).

Once More into the Breach:
Teaching Emerson's *Nature*

Michael P. Branch

There are many reasons Emerson's *Nature* is notoriously difficult to teach. To begin with, this text is unimaginably ambitious, attempting nothing more modest than an articulation of the value of nature in all its dimensions. The prose is often highly abstract, and the engagement of such topics as language theory and philosophical idealism compounds this problem. Then there is the troubled compositional history of the piece. Emerson had intended to write a book called *Nature*, to be followed by a sequel entitled *Spirit*. Instead, he made a late decision to integrate the two projects, a move that resulted in a text rife with seams and gaps. The book must also be understood as a product of the crisis of orthodox religious faith that drove Emerson to resign his ministry of Boston's Second Church in 1832. And his struggles in the years preceding the publication of *Nature* in 1836 were not strictly vocational, but also deeply personal. His wife, Ellen, had died in 1831, and he lost his brothers Edward and Charles in 1834 and 1836, respectively. *Nature* also emerged from the intellectual experimentation of a vibrant transcendentalist milieu that is not quickly explained in a literature survey course.

One happy upshot of these many challenges for teachers is that there are also many different ways of coming at this difficult text. Among these, I have found none as helpful as understanding *Nature* to be the result of Emerson's deep engagement with natural science. So useful is this contextualization of Emerson's magnum opus that I have, along with my colleague Clinton Mohs, edited a volume of Emerson's natural history sermons, lectures, addresses, and essays.

At the heart of *"The Best Read Naturalist": Nature Writings of Ralph Waldo Emerson* we have placed the old sphinx, *Nature*. We hope that presenting this difficult gem within the broadened context of Emerson's natural science writing will allow teachers and students a clearer path into *Nature*—one traced briefly in this essay.

After resigning the ministry in October 1832, Emerson made immediate preparations for a trip to Europe. He sailed on Christmas Day and remained abroad until early October 1833. Less than a month after his return from Europe, Emerson gave the first of his four early natural history lectures. Delivered in Boston between November 1833 and May 1834, those four lectures are "The Uses of Natural History," "The Relation of Man to the Globe," "Water," and "The Naturalist." While all four are helpful in understanding *Nature*, the first and last of these are of special value in teaching *Nature*, which would be published soon after, in September 1836.

To understand the radical new ideas that led to *Nature*, it is helpful for students to consider the most important experience Emerson had during his trip to Europe. Although his time abroad included visits to renowned museums and architectural monuments—as well as meetings with literary luminaries including Samuel Taylor Coleridge, William Wordsworth, and Thomas Carlyle—the experience he most treasured was an unexpected moment of clarity that occurred at the Jardin des Plantes and adjacent Cabinet d'Histoire in Paris. This important moment, which he recorded in his journals, is also recounted in his lecture "The Uses of Natural History":

> Moving along these pleasant walks, you come to the botanical cabinet, an inclosed garden plot, where grows a grammar of botany—where the plants rise, each in its class, its order, and its genus. . . . If you have read [the work of the botanist] Decandolle with engravings, or with a *hortus siccus* [an herbarium], conceive how much more exciting and intelligible is this natural alphabet, this green and yellow and crimson dictionary, on which the sun shines and the winds blow.   (*Early Lectures* 1: 8)

Emerson found the garden transformative because it triggered in him the sudden realization of a deep interrelationship among the plants as he observed them organized by the French botanist Antoine-Laurent de Jussieu. Emerson's heightened awareness of natural interrelationship set the stage for an even more powerful epiphany in the nearby zoological cabinet, where he reflected upon the dizzying variety of animal species he observed there:

> You are impressed with the inexhaustible gigantic riches of nature. The limits of the possible are enlarged, and the real is stranger than the imaginary. The universe is a more amazing puzzle than ever, as you look along this bewildering series of animated forms, the hazy butterflies, the carved

shells, the birds, beasts, insects, snakes, fish, and the upheaving principle of life everywhere incipient, in the very rock aping organized forms.
Whilst I stand there I am impressed with a singular conviction that not
a form so grotesque, so savage, or so beautiful, but is an expression of
something in man the observer. We feel that there is an occult relation
between the very worm, the crawling scorpions, and man. I am moved
by strange sympathies. I say I will listen to this invitation. I will be a
naturalist.   (*Early Lectures* 1: 10)

The botanical and zoological cabinets were inspirational to Emerson because
they led him to a profound awareness that all things in nature are intimately
related, both to one another and to the human observer. This core idea inspired
his belief that there exists throughout nature a grand unity that would, once revealed, explain how a wild diversity of heterogeneous natural facts actually com-
poses a great, unified whole. For Emerson the search for this all-encompassing
natural law was the highest goal of science.

Emerson further postulated that the unity throughout nature was a corollary of the human spirit and an expression of divinity. This leap of imagination,
which is difficult for both teachers and students to fully comprehend, is critical
to understanding *Nature*. The key for teachers is to emphasize how thoroughly
Emerson's view of science differs from the secular science that dominates our
own age, for Emerson's enthusiasm for science was inspired by his earnest belief
that the scientific search for a deep, hidden connection (the "occult relation")
uniting all of nature was ultimately a *spiritual* pursuit. As he later put it in
the lecture "The Relation of Intellect to Natural Science" (1848), which also
refers to the epiphanic moment in the Paris cabinet, "This singular exactness
of analogy between all the parts of nature,—this copula or tie between all the
sciences,—has been and remains the highest problem which men have to solve"
(*Later Lectures* 1: 159). Emerson even used the term "the natural history of
the soul" to refer to the ambitious project of pursuing science as a means to the
revelation of spiritual truth (*Collected Works* 1: 130).

Because Emerson understood natural science to be a spiritual pursuit, he
was enamored of the scientists whose work revealed the expansive laws that he
hoped would ultimately explain the hidden unity he intuited was at the heart of
the natural world. Emerson celebrated these "heroes of science" (*Early Lectures*
1: 22), among whom he included Pythagoras, Galileo, Johannes Kepler, Isaac
Newton, Pierre-Simon Laplace, Georges Cuvier, and Alexander von Humboldt.
These men had in common a passionate search for larger principles of relation;
they did not function simply as compilers of dry facts. Like Emerson in the
Cabinet d'Histoire, each of these "heroes" experienced a powerful moment of
insight that revealed a new understanding of natural relationships. Much like
students who have a breakthrough moment when they are at last able to see
the connections among the things they are studying in very different kinds of
classes, Emerson's heroic scientists are able to connect the dots, showing how

disparate parts of the natural world are intimately related to one another. In his 1834 lecture "The Naturalist," for example, Emerson articulated his fervent belief that the work of the many gifted scientists of his own day might ultimately reveal the grand unity of nature:

> We are born in an age which to its immense inheritance of natural knowledge has added great discoveries of its own. We should not be citizens of our own time, not faithful to our trust, if we neglected to avail ourselves of their light. . . . No truth can be more self evident than that the highest state of man, physical, intellectual, and moral, can only coexist with a perfect Theory of Animated Nature.   *(Early Lectures* 1: 83)

And yet, for all his faith in the existence of this grand law or theory whose revelation would make obvious the spiritual power of science, Emerson saw around him a culture that employed science to produce profit rather than generate insight. In the second half of "The Naturalist," Emerson pivots significantly to a discussion of the *disadvantages* of studying natural science. Chief among these, he warns, is the risk that the pursuit of science may blind us to the higher purpose of the endeavor:

> The necessity of nomenclature, of minute physiological research, of the retort, the scalpel, and the scales, is incontestable. But there is no danger of its being underestimated. We only wish to insist upon their being considered as *Means*. We only wish to give equal and habitual prominence to the Love and Faith from which these should flow. This passion, the enthusiasm for nature, the love of the Whole, has burned in the breasts of the Fathers of Science. It was the ever present aim of Newton, of Linnaeus, of Davy, of Cuvier, to ascend from nomenclature to classification; from arbitrary to natural classes; from natural classes, to primary laws; from these, in an ever narrowing circle, to approach the elemental law, the *causa causans*, the supernatural force.   (1: 80)

Even as Emerson asserted that science had the power to reveal truths of the soul, he cautioned that it should never become an end in itself, but only a means to the higher end of spiritual growth. As he put it in "Humanity of Science," a lecture given in 1836, the same year *Nature* was published, "[that] science is bankrupt which attempts to cut the knot which always spirit must untie" (*Early Lectures* 2: 30).

I have devoted much of this essay to the early natural history lectures because, having taught Emerson for thirty years, I find the core insights of those lectures the most effective way to help students grasp the expansive, complex literary performance that is *Nature*. Although I would encourage teachers of *Nature* to approach the text by first teaching a few of the natural history lectures, even instructors who choose not to do so can improve the effectiveness of their teaching of *Nature* by familiarizing themselves with the key ideas from those lectures. It is useful for teachers to remember not only that *Nature* developed from the natural history lectures but also that the text is laced with important ideas and even borrowed material from such antecedent works as "The Uses of Natural History" and "The Naturalist."

One practical way for teachers to help their students understand the influence of Emerson's natural history studies on the larger argument of *Nature* is to ask students to identify passages in the text that seem to be inspired by Emerson's hope that science might reveal a grand unity throughout nature. For example, students coming to the text for the first time are likely to notice that in the introductory section of *Nature* Emerson declares that "[a]ll science has one aim, namely to find a theory of nature." "Whenever a true theory appears, it will be its own evidence," he writes. "Its test is, that it will explain all phenomena" (*Collected Works* 1: 8). Emerson here refers to the quest of natural science to reveal the foundational laws unifying all of nature.

Attention to the "uses of natural history" (as Emerson put it in the title of an early lecture) will also help students to comprehend the challenging environmental aesthetics of the "Beauty" chapter of *Nature*, which argues that beauty may be fully appreciated only when it is understood as a spiritual phenomenon. Reflections on aesthetics offered in the natural history lectures make clear that Emerson values natural beauty primarily as an enticement to us to seek in nature the corollary "laws" of our souls. This is why in *Nature* he offers the otherwise perplexing assertion that "this beauty of Nature which is seen and felt as beauty, is the least part" (*Collected Works* 1: 14). If students are encouraged to consider how Emerson's idea of beauty extends beyond perceived visual beauty to the "beauty" of the universal laws he hoped would be revealed by an emergent natural science, they will better understand why a chapter on aesthetics is so devoted to the intellect and, ultimately, to the soul.

Teachers and students who approach *Nature* through the lens of natural history will discover that even the elusive "Language" chapter of the book is illuminated by Emerson's insistence, in his earlier natural history lectures, upon the foundational mirroring of the physical and spiritual worlds—what he calls in *Nature* "this radical correspondence between visible things and human thoughts." Emerson called upon natural science to forge a "language" of correspondence that would reveal the relationship of the world to the soul and thus confirm his belief that "all spiritual facts are represented by natural symbols" (*Collected Works* 1: 19). Likewise, the philosophical idealism of the "Idealism" chapter, which can feel nearly impossible to teach effectively, is clarified when understood as an assertion of Emerson's core belief that nature cannot exist independently of the human observer. The central principles of the natural history lectures make clear to students Emerson's view that nature's grand laws exist in intimate relationship to the human soul. This is why, in "Idealism," he concludes that "even in physics, the material is ever degraded before the spiritual"

(1: 34). This insight can also lead students to better grasp the core assertion of the "Spirit" chapter, in which Emerson claims that God "does not build up nature around us, but puts it forth through us, as the life of the tree puts forth new branches and leaves through the pores of the old" (1: 38). Understood as an expression of the sentiment that animates the natural history lectures, this lyrical, organic metaphor may be seen as a reaffirmation of Emerson's deep belief that nature is never other than or outside of us; in studying the natural world, Emerson felt, we necessarily study ourselves in relation to it.

I have found that, for teachers and students alike, the most baffling part of *Nature* is its inspiring but ambiguous and elliptical final chapter, "Prospects." Key to understanding this difficult and important concluding chapter is recognizing the figure to whom we are introduced in its opening paragraph:

> Empirical science is apt to cloud the sight, and, by the very knowledge of functions and processes, to bereave the student of the manly contemplation of the whole. The savant becomes unpoetic. But the best read naturalist who lends an entire and devout attention to truth, will see that there remains much to learn of his relation to the world, and that it is not to be learned by any addition or subtraction or other comparison of known quantities, but is arrived at by untaught sallies of the spirit, by a continual self-recovery, and by entire humility.   (*Collected Works* 1: 39)

While students at first find the character of this "best read naturalist" to be mysterious, exposure to the early natural history writing helps them to see that this key figure is clearly patterned after Emerson's "heroes of science." Unlike secular scientists, however, Emerson's idealized best read naturalist is distinguished by his disciplined recognition of the spiritual significance of his studies.

A clear identification of this iconic best read naturalist is crucial to students' understanding of "Prospects," because this figure is the heroic embodiment of Emerson's faith that natural science would discover foundational principles affirming the wholeness of nature and thus reveal the unity of material and human natures. "It is not so pertinent to man to know all the individuals of the animal kingdom, as it is to know whence and whereto is this tyrannizing unity in his constitution, which evermore separates and classifies things, endeavoring to reduce the most diverse to one form," writes Emerson. "I cannot greatly honor minuteness in details, so long as there is no hint to explain the relation between things and thoughts," he continues, "no ray upon the *metaphysics* of conchology, of botany, of the arts, to show the relation of the forms of flowers, shells, animals, architecture, to the mind, and build science upon ideas" (*Collected Works* 1: 40). Students are likely to feel empowered when they realize that a locution as opaque as the "the *metaphysics* of conchology" means simply that every scientific pursuit, even one as specialized as the study of mollusk shells, should be in service to spiritual aims.

Teachers and students who come to *Nature* along the path of the early natural history writing will not be surprised to discover that here, in the apotheosis of the book, Emerson returns to the site of his inspiration. "In a cabinet of natural history," he writes, "we become sensible of a certain occult recognition and sympathy in regard to the most unwieldy and eccentric forms of beast, fish, and insect" (*Collected Works* 1: 40). This profound awareness of the powerful relationship between nature and the human spirit, which emerged from Emerson's early study of natural history and his transformative experience in the Parisian cabinet, is the central idea around which the chapters of *Nature* are organized. Just before launching the soaring peroration with which he concludes *Nature*, Emerson offers a summary diagnosis of the cause of our regrettable alienation from nature and from ourselves. It is one that students of Emerson's spiritualized brand of natural history will recognize and understand. "The reason why the world lacks unity, and lies broken and in heaps," explains Emerson, "is, because man is disunited with himself. He cannot be a naturalist, until he satisfies all the demands of the spirit" (1: 43).

"The American Scholar" as Commencement Address

Andrew Kopec

Emerson's iconoclastic "The American Scholar," delivered before the Phi Beta Kappa Society at Harvard College on 31 August 1837, has achieved iconic status: "This grand Oration," as Oliver Wendell Holmes argues, "was our intellectual Declaration of Independence" (115). For Kenneth Sacks, Emerson's address represents more specifically "the most famous [speech] in American academic history" (5). For their part, students at the two public institutions (one flagship, one regional) at which I have taught Emerson's address generally presume its "grand" status. Yet, because of its reputation as a touchstone event of cultural history, the text's humbler status as a commencement address remains largely invisible. Here I'd like to suggest presenting to students "The American Scholar" precisely along these lines in order, ultimately, to understand one of its chief themes: how a new college graduate ought to conceive of the value of his or her work on entering a precarious labor market. Doing so, I believe, not only encourages students to reflect on American literary history but also challenges us to see the relation between the university—that is, the students', faculty's, and Emerson's shared institutional space—and the world of work. This is to recognize, in other words, that the work of "The American Scholar" is indeed very much about the scholar's work.

Emerson's "Secular Pulpit"

To apprehend Emerson's oration as a commencement address, at the outset of class I ask students to define the genre. In general, a few ideas emerge, especially in regards to why a speaker receives the honor of making the commencement address in the first place. (Most agree that it *is* an honor to be invited to offer such a speech.) These reasons, each of which relates to the speaker's ethos, include but are not limited to the speaker's status as an alumnus; the speaker's standing in and contributions to the various institutions that shape public life (business, politics, entertainment, the arts and sciences, and so on); the speaker's experiences, which put him or her in a position to share advice to new graduates, thereby providing a model that will shape the student's life course. Building on this student-generated definition, I find it useful to introduce key biographical material that frames Emerson's ethos in the 1830s. First of all, there is the basic fact of Emerson's status as an alumnus. More particularly, Emerson was "[e]lected as one of the first graduate initiates" of the college's Phi Beta Kappa chapter (Sacks 10), making him a member of the very group sponsoring the address. Then there is Emerson's standing in and contributions to important public institutions. Here, I mention Emerson's work in and eventual turn away from

Unitarian preaching, in addition to his public speaking engagements on the lyceum circuit—what one scholar terms Emerson's "secular pulpit" (Ljungquist 338). And, finally, there is Emerson's publication of his treatise *Nature* in 1836, which signaled his affiliation with the Transcendental Club then gaining notoriety as the "New Thought" challenging the theological and philosophical orthodoxies of Harvard, Unitarianism and empiricism, respectively.

Yet if *Nature* adds to Emerson's ethos by pursuing that great question—"to what end is nature?" (*Collected Works* 1: 7)—"The American Scholar," I suggest to students, pursues a seemingly humbler one: to what end is academic study? Using this question as a way to transition from the biographical to the rhetorical invites analyses that consider "The American Scholar" as an address offered to students at the outset (commencement) of public life. This is a defamiliarizing tactic that encourages reader response as a way into Emerson's potentially abstruse text. In a reaction I've now come to expect, indeed, students express sympathetic dismay over the idea of having to *listen* to this address, as many have been subjected to a "boring" commencement address at prior events. ("Boring," by the way, often emerges as a common descriptor of the genre!)

A quick discussion of an audience for "The American Scholar" returns me to presentation slides, some of which sample first-person accounts from Emerson's auditors. I first emphasize the negative responses, a move that can validate students' initial confusion over Emerson's address. John Pierce, a Harvard student and eventual Unitarian minister, for instance, expressed his frustration over the address being "in the misty, dreamy, unintelligible style of Swedenborg, Coleridge, and Carlyle" (qtd. in Sealts 109). (Pierce here not only humanizes the event but also points to some of the historical-intellectual contexts I sketch for students and which scholars like Barbara L. Packer and Philip Gura have so thoroughly explored.) In addition, although William Henry Channing, writing in the newly formed *Boston Quarterly Review*, treated the print version of the oration favorably, he likewise "freely express[ed] our regret that Mr. Emerson's style is so little a transparent one" (75).

To move from the style to the content of the address, I next note the enthusiasm it likewise generated. For Bronson Alcott the address certainly resulted in "[m]ixed confusion, [and] consternation," but there was also "surprise and wonder with which the audience listened to it" (qtd. in Sacks 17). James Russell Lowell perhaps is most useful here in demonstrating Emerson's rhetorical power. In his review of Henry David Thoreau's posthumous *Letters to Various Persons* (1865), which Emerson edited, Lowell lauds Emerson's "genetic power"—his ability to influence a "generation" of readers. For Lowell, "No man young enough to have felt it can forget the mental and moral *nudge* which he received from the writings of his high-minded and brave-spirited countryman." "The American Scholar," in particular, exemplified for Lowell Emerson's affective power: it "was an event without any former parallel in our literary annals, a scene to be always treasured in the memory for its . . . inspiration" (600). Lowell's retrospective account not only conveys the impact that the address had for the younger generation, but it also gestures toward this impact's transtemporality. In other words, "The American Scholar" was, and remains, an address that ignited both the college students who heard it in 1837 and those who reflected on it long after the fact.

"Not Enough of Labor": Success and the Panic of 1837

Lowell's writing prompts us to consider how Emerson's address is intended to *"nudge"* students toward achievement in its own time and in ours. Of course, a problem with Emerson's text—a consequence perhaps of the fact that its "style is so little a transparent one"—arises from the instability over the very definition of achievement. I emphasize to students how transcendentalism in general and "The American Scholar" in particular contest the equation of success in the market with money. Economic themes, indeed, inform the oration from its outset, as Emerson immediately muses that "[o]ur anniversary is one of hope, and perhaps, not enough of labor" (*Collected Works* 1: 52). To make this mild lament resonate with students, I turn to the broader context of economic history, in particular the Panic of 1837, a devastating financial crisis that had occurred in the spring prior to Emerson's address. If most commencement addresses anticipate how graduates will make future contributions to public life, Emerson's speech had to acknowledge the hard times and their "barriers for the career" (1: 69).

Students are sometimes surprised to find, given Emerson's seeming abstractions from reality, that those "barriers" in 1837 were material. "[B]etween February and June 1837," as one historian writes, the economic boom of the mid-1830s "fell to pieces" (Larson 92). At the same time, as land and securities values fell precipitously and employment rates plummeted, writing about economics skyrocketed (Fabian). I project a sampling of this writing on a slide. For instance, the transcendentalist Orestes Brownson, who was critical of Emerson's later oration "Literary Ethics" (1838) at Dartmouth College, published in May 1837 his sermon *The Spirit of Gain; or, The Fall of Babylon, a Discourse on the Times*, polemicizing against "the evil propensities" that the modern "commercial system" has nurtured (4). Brownson's point is that the "embarrassment in the commercial world . . . is no temporary" one; instead, "[i]t proceeds from causes which lie deep": the penetration of commercial values in everyday life (5).

Passages from Emerson's journal illustrate how he likewise dwelled on the panic before delivering his commencement address. In a passage I share with students from May 1837, Emerson laments, "Young men have no hope. Adults stand like daylaborers in the streets. None calleth us to labor" (*Journals* 5: 331–32). In an August journal passage he bemoans that we have become "money chest[s]" (5: 332), allowing what he calls in "The American Scholar" "the 'spoils,' so called, 'of office'" to dictate our lives (*Collected Works* 1: 65).[1] These passages work especially well to raise the issue of what *changed* for Emerson from the spring to the summer: how Emerson in May sees "no hope" and no one "labor[ing]," yet in August he imagines the possibility for a return to labor.

What gave Emerson hope in August, despite a grim economic outlook as the business cycle turned toward a prolonged depression? The hard times, indeed, put the Cambridge scholars at risk of becoming what a 2013 article in *The Wall Street Journal* (*WSJ*) termed a "lost generation" of college graduates: "young people [who] have come of age amid the most prolonged period of economic distress since the Great Depression" (Casselman and Walker). Yet in "The American Scholar," Emerson articulates a hard-earned "remedy" for the very hopelessness that he imagines "the suicides" to emblematize (*Collected Works* 1: 69), imagining economic depression as an opportunity to probe the very logic that has turned us into money chests in the first place.

In order to challenge further the perception of Emerson's aloofness from his culture—and, moreover, to forge connections between Emerson's age and our own—I distribute copies of the *WSJ* article for students to read together in small groups. (The activity provides a break from the software-assisted lecture and discussion sketched above.) I prompt them to scan for thematic overlaps between address and article and to discuss similarities and differences among themselves before regrouping as a class. Unlike the "The American Scholar," the *WSJ* article includes harrowing labor statistics for recent college graduates. Similarities between the two texts quickly emerge, though, as both Emerson and the *WSJ* examine the linkage among education, career, and hope. Indeed, as this compare-and-contrast activity plays out, I am eager to add to the fray one of my favorite journal passages from May 1837, in which Emerson describes his transition from abject despair to postpanic hope. Where the *WSJ* article likens the economy to a "sinkhole," Emerson sees an "earthquake": "I learn geology the morning after the earthquake. . . . The Artificial is Rent from the eternal" (*Journals* 5: 332–33). The panic is a revelation to Emerson, leading him to question the extent to which success is material rather than ideal ("eternal"). And, in the wake of this insight, the rhetorical task of "The American Scholar" becomes to advocate to college students that one can labor successfully in the face of diminished labor opportunities. As he urges, "Success treads on every right step" (*Collected Works* 1: 64).

The Value of the Liberal Arts?

Reading "The American Scholar" as a commencement address that speaks to college students about their labor prospects ultimately emphasizes certain passages from the oration that tend to go overlooked. If they haven't come up already in class discussion or during the *WSJ* reading activity, I highlight moments where Emerson debates the value of the liberal arts. His attempts to combat the biases against "speculative men" and for "[t]he so-called 'practical men'" hit this note (*Collected Works* 1: 61). He also tries to establish values that, in their permanency, counter "some ephemeral trade, or war, . . . [that] is cried up by half mankind and cried down by the other half." "In silence, in steadiness, in severe abstraction," the scholar will labor not for money but in order to "see something truly" (1: 64).

Emerson's rhetoric seems far from practical here, but it challenges students to imagine their education as decidedly not "transparent"—the way in which many students might imagine a STEM education to be—but valuable never-theless. The stakes are high for Emerson, just as I believe they are for educators today: "Young men of the fairest promise . . . are hindered from action by the disgust which the principles on which business is managed inspire, and turn drudges, or die of disgust—some of them suicides." As a "remedy," he counsels self-reliance of course and, above all, patience (*Collected Works* 1: 68–69). He wants college students to believe what seems to him (and, I assume, to those of us drawn to Emerson's address in the first place) so obvious: that there is a value to a liberal education that need not only be defined through the market.

The financial press has sought to define the value of a liberal education pre-cisely by way of the market. A 2015 headline in *Forbes* reads: "That 'Useless' Liberal Arts Degree Has Become Tech's Hottest Ticket" (Anders). To conclude the session, I pose the question to students about what is lost when we define a liberal education as merely a competitive advantage in the labor market. In his 1838 address "Ethics," which previews the claims of the essay "Self-Reliance" (1841), Emerson likens the self to a "workyard" (*Early Lectures* 2: 151). What is gained and what is lost when the site of a scholar's labor changes from the self to the twenty-first-century office, from transcendental self-culture to corpo-rate culture? These are hard, necessary questions that "The American Scholar" poses. Moreover, they are questions that, as we search for answers, require us to work to overcome "barriers" both material and ideal. It is this monumental task toward which he "*nudges*" us still in his "grand" oration from that day in Cambridge in August 1837.

NOTE

[1] Emerson repeats the phrase "money chest" in his "Address on Education" from June 1837. For a perceptive account of this address as a critique of privatized education, see Meehan.

The Divine Sublime: Educating Spiritual Teachers in "The Divinity School Address"

Corinne E. Blackmer

Deciding what to teach from among the dense thickets of significant details that characterize a "typical" Emerson essay is an imposing task, especially since, as Barbara Packer points out, Emerson "eliminates the connections between one sentence and another, one paragraph and another, or between the essay and anything in the world outside it" (*Emerson's Fall* 7). However, for me, there are five major ideas articulated in "The Divinity School Address" that rise, powerful and indispensable, above other matters. In advance of delving into more substantive pedagogical methods for teaching this address, I briefly outline these major ideas to help my classes on Emerson—whether courses on transcendentalism, nineteenth-century American literature, or religious studies—to start out, so to speak, on the same page:

> The substantial costs but also the inestimable blessings arising from the exercise of intellectual and moral courage;
> The teachings of the mortal man Jesus, which alone—and not the churches built around him—have the power to instruct and whose "idioms" and "figures" have "usurped his truth" (*Collected Works* 1: 81);
> The discrepancy between meaningful religious sentiment—based on nature, intuition, and reason—and historical Christianity;
> The dispiriting ordeal of witnessing failed "formalist" preaching; and
> The "new Teacher," whose advent "shall show that the Ought, that Duty, is one thing with Science, with Beauty, and with Joy" (1: 93).

Ultimately, from investigation of these topics and consideration of the qualities of this new teacher, who can illuminate the relations among moral, aesthetic, and physical law more than Jesus in his ancient era could, emerges the overarching question of the address: should educators be traditional authoritative figures whose instruction to students centers on historical models of imitation, or, in contrast, innovative equal partners who inspire others to create original knowledge and spiritual intuitions? In this pedagogically revolutionary essay, Emerson argues strenuously for egalitarian relations between aspiring teachers and learners. He insists, "It is not instruction, but provocation, I can receive from another soul" (1: 80).

Intellectual and Moral Courage

Embarking on this issue provides a larger context for the essay and an empathetic understanding of Emerson's psychology and moral vision with which students can identify. Moreover, creating connections between Emerson and the students in the beginning helps overcome the alienation and sense of anachronism that the topic of nineteenth-century religious controversies can elicit in courses on American or transcendentalist literature. "The Divinity School Address"—a sublime instance of his earlier philosophical transcendentalism—was a watershed event in his life. It caused such uproar, spearheaded by Andrews Norton's scathing review in the *Boston Daily Advertiser* (22 Aug. 1838), that Harvard barred Emerson from speaking there for a generation. Norton attacked Emerson's putative insult to religion, failure to reason logically, poor taste, distortion of ideas, and assumptions that historical traditions should be superseded by private spiritual intuition. Prior to this time, Emerson had been considering becoming a professor at Cambridge after he resigned his post as junior minister at the Second Church of Boston in 1832 over his refusal to administer the Lord's Supper. As Susan L. Roberson points out, Emerson used the controversy over the Lord's Supper to "formalize his religious thought and to actualize the separation from organized religion toward which he had been moving for some time" (194). However, he started his permanent career as a public lyceum speaker and author in the wake of "The Divinity School Address." It required courage and faith for Emerson to quit established and potential seats in the clergy and professoriate and, instead, pursue an uncertain, arduous pathway whose taxations eventually had a deleterious effect on his health. Emerson thus proved himself willing to pay the price for his moral and intellectual convictions—a point that should be emphasized with students. Doing so enables them to apprehend the stakes involved in showing intellectual bravery and in delivering the address. Following up on themes he explored in relation to creative vision in *Nature* and literature in "The American Scholar," Emerson told the students that "the preacher should be a poet" (*Journals* 5: 471). His surprise at the antagonism he generated shows that Emerson had already collapsed the distinction between sublime literature and sacred texts, for his opponents thought it was one thing to call upon scholars to distinguish between man thinking and mere thinking, or parroting of others' thoughts, but quite another to assert that Jesus was only an exemplary mortal man who should not inspire supine imitative worship, or that even the Bible (which Emerson never quotes), albeit an inspired work, had no "epical integrity" (*Collected Works* 1: 92) and could be improved upon.

Jesus

The gravitational center of "The Divinity School Address" concerns the status and place of Jesus as a teacher—not a savior, since, according to Emerson, we are responsible for our own "saving," and salvation is a doctrinal concept. Institutional Christianity had long cherished the belief that Jesus was the Christ, the Son of God. And Trinitarian Christians believed him to be Logos, a temporarily sinless human who became God during his ascension to Heaven. However, according to Emerson, Jesus was a man who taught against pure reverence for tradition. He had come to preach, much like the divinity students Emerson addressed. The gospel of Jesus was not final and Jesus had not intended any such finality or canonization of his teaching. While liberal Christians such as the Unitarians believed reflexively in Christian supersessionism, they were not prepared for the supersession of Jesus or institutional Christianity. For them, Jesus was the savior, and no "mere modern man" could replace him, even though Unitarianism regarded him as mortal, not divine, and believed that each person had an obligation to reject the customary and search Scripture independently. As Peter S. Field asserts, "Emerson urged these novices to follow him by following their own inner path toward enlightenment and spiritual truth" (12). Jesus, according to this view, was not so much an inimitable exemplar, but one example among others who desired posterity to supersede him.

Historical Christianity

Emerson means, by this term of art, the merely customary, traditional, and social vision of Christian faith that accepts miracles, as well as the rites, rituals, dogmas, and doctrines of some particular incarnation of institutional Christianity. This encompasses all forms of religion that have closed sacred books and that regard revelation as something that has occurred in the past, neither possible nor conscionable in the present. Emerson learned, in contrast to his education, of the philosophical skeptic David Hume's conclusion that miracles violated the laws of nature. Emerson concluded logically that Hume had destroyed the grounds of traditional Christian belief in miracles. Emerson, like Kant and Coleridge, grounds the truth of religion on inner spiritual essence, reason, and intuition, rather than on tradition, social norms, or empirical-style "proofs" of Christian doctrine.

Formalist Preaching

This section illustrates what happens when the dead verbal formulas and venerations of historical Christianity are put into real practice as preaching. Emerson's thundering, eloquent condemnation of this failed teaching practice remains unequally his oeuvre and proves the inimitable importance Emerson gives to preaching. Such oratorical spiritual teaching is a "holy office which is coeval with the world," which "the spirit only can teach" (*Collected Works* 1: 83), and which entails "the expression of the moral sentiment in appellation to the duties of life" (1: 84). Emerson recollects going into a church and feeling "defrauded and disconsolate" by an abject man who had, as a formalist, "usurped" the pulpit. Nothing of the doctrine had this unfortunate man passed through his real "historical experience" or "the fire of thought." Emerson wants the preacher to address his audience of worshippers through his life experience to counteract the traditional preaching that "comes out of the memory, and not out of the soul." In brief, "historical Christianity destroys the power of preaching" (1: 86). As everyone in the classroom, both teacher and students, shall recollect experiences of such insupportable teaching, devoid of soul, faith, and spirit, all shall be able to relate to this section of "The Divinity School Address."

After providing this overview in a lecture-discussion format, I change the pedagogical methods that I use to impart Emerson's transcendentalist philosophical ideas, which, in keeping with his dominant ideas about teaching explored in "The Divinity School Address," transfer interpretive knowledge of this work to my students. As the subject matter, diction, tropes, aphorisms, and style in his essays remain formidable for most students, I have recourse to the ancient Jewish practice of *havruta*, or "fellowship," which was originally designed for instruction in the Talmud and other demanding Jewish religious texts.[1] Students are paired together (either for the duration of the address's study or, better, the semester) as fellows. No longer isolated, *havruta* partners engage in making meaning around difficult passages, topics, and phrases: they complete short research assignments (around, for instance, the controversy over miracles, the Lord's Supper, reason versus understanding, the "new Teacher," or historical Christianity), participate in and lead class discussions over the meanings of signal phrases or words in the address ("not virtuous, but virtue," "divine laws," "intuition of the moral sentiment," "Good is positive. Evil is merely privative," "the religious sentiment," "Cultus," "Mythus," "miracle is monster," "Moral Nature," "Law of laws," "formalist," "newborn bard of the Holy Ghost," "Self of the Nation," "epical integrity," and "Imperial Guard of Virtue," among others), converse about the text, and write about the relation of the address to life and to their lives as students in particular. Through these means, they are, most important, equipped to correct the biases and limitations in each other's visions and to learn to appreciate the divergent pedagogical and philosophical viewpoints expressed by their *havruta* partners and other pairs of fellows in the classroom.

Vigorous expression of the diverse viewpoints generated by *havruta* is aided by taking a dialectical approach to the text that at once encourages an enthusiastic embrace and sharp questioning of Emerson's beliefs regarding spiritual instruction, practice, and belief. Teachers can achieve such a perspective on "The Divinity School Address" through various means, but I like to have the *havruta* partners research and come to class prepared to engage in debate over the views expressed by Emerson's nemesis, Andrews Norton. I provide them with relevant excerpts from *A Discourse on the Latest Form of Infidelity* (1838), where Norton lambastes self-reliant religious thinking as a disaster, argues that Christianity must rely on reason and the testimony of others through history, and denies that elevating Jesus above other humans removes the possibilities of holiness in others.

That student responses to Emerson tend to sort themselves along certain fault lines composed of the yea-sayers, the apprehensive, and the naysayers assists materially in taking the dialectical approach elicited by reading Norton's withering article. Like the committee of three who asked Emerson to address their graduating class at Harvard Divinity School in 1838, there are always those students who find in Emerson a revelation that inspires new consciousness, enthusiastic aspiration, and creative ambition. For these students, Emerson and the self-reliance he represents stand as an invigorating invitation that "comes graceful and beloved as a bride" (*Collected Works* 1: 91). Like all talented, passionate students in every place and time, they choose someone who would affirm their desire to think, write, create, and, in this case, preach without the constraints of preset topics, tedious doctrine, or anxious concerns over what professors "really wanted to hear."

Other students, on substantive or rhetorical levels, experience awed apprehension as the "default setting" in response to his vaulting high oratorical style, with its signature gravitas and insouciance, pithy and quixotic maxims, common admixed with obscure terms, personifications, metaphors, enigmas, paradoxes, aphorisms, and, above all, parrhesia, the trope of speaking bold, muscular truth to those with greater power for the public good, which grounds the daring, majestic conception of religion in "The Divinity School Address." While teaching the address, probably toward the end of the initial overview section, students should be acquainted (or reacquainted) with the meaning of the above rhetorical terms, which appear regularly in Emerson. I provide the *havruta* partners with examples and ask them to find one or two others in the address, which gives them practice looking at rather than through the oration. More important, as a trope of thought that Emerson uses throughout his work, and might be said to constitute the spine of his philosophical practice, parrhesia deserves special attention. Michel Foucault has a particularly significant and informative discussion of parrhesia from *Fearless Speech* that one should share with students (19–20).

Finally, a number of students end by agreeing in part or whole with Norton. They take objection to the Emerson evinced in the address: tradition is invigorating; imitation is requisite; pure reason and intuition as the path to authentic spirituality, without institutional safeguards and memory, is an invitation to religious bigotry and narcissism; the author's fervent, romantic concerns with personal religion are naive, irrelevant, and embarrassing. As these debates segue back to the address and the imposing importance Emerson gives to the office of preaching, his conceptions implicate both teacher and student—for both are actual or potential educators—in socially essential responsibilities not to become mere formalists or imitators.

These divergent viewpoints, which manifest as often in strong as in weaker students, establish the framework for wide-ranging, animated, and sometimes heated debates over students' relations to differing meanings, methods, and purposes of education; the role of educators; and, finally, the definition of religion, which Emerson describes as belief in God, Sabbath observance, and the "institution of preaching—the speech of man to men" (*Collected Works* 1: 92). The implication here is that while we can agree on broad interpretive paradigms for this oration, student readers, as I believe Emerson intended, should culminate their learning of the text by producing their own unique interpretation of the address. Instead of an analytical or research-based paper, I have students, particularly (although not exclusively) in religious studies courses, write a five- to six-page sermon or spiritual address that avoids the pitfalls Emerson discusses in his section on formalist preaching and that draws on the students' personal experience as well as comprehension of Emerson's ideas. In this quite popular and inspiring assignment, students not only translate Emerson into their own language but also take personal ownership of and responsibility for the address.

As Barbara Packer argues in *Emerson's Fall*, Emerson found that women and men had come to believe in the myth of the fall of mankind, and his purpose in the address is to dispel this illusory myth—to "speak the very truth, as your life and conscience teach it" (*Collected Works* 1: 92). If taken in this fashion, the final, relevant point of educating inspirational teachers in "The Divinity School Address" involves restoring that "Imperial" spiritual and rhetorical self-confidence that leads to educational passion, eloquence, and achievement.

NOTE

For Barbara Packer, Emerson scholar and teacher of blessed memory.

[1] For an invaluable discussion of the pedagogical practice of *havruta*, which has, until recently, been confined to Jewish contexts, see Holzer, *A Philosophy of Havruta*; and Kent, "A Theory of *Havruta* Learning."

Experimenting with "Circles"

Nels Anchor Christensen

A major challenge in teaching Emerson's essays concerns the unique and often vexing relationship between his ideas and his form. Students find themselves attracted to isolated epigrammatic ideas, even to the point of being emotionally and intellectually moved by them, but they also tend to reject the essays on the whole as logically contradictory. The reason for the attraction is clear. Aphoristic sentences articulate powerfully inviting ideas. The reason for the rejection, however, is less clear but more pedagogically significant. Though students will find an idea in any Emerson essay that feels relevant and right, something that sounds personally or intellectually true, those students will also find in that very same essay ideas that don't seem to fit logically with—or, in fact, actually contradict—the ideas coming before or after. Much to students' discomfort, Emerson's sense of intuition guides and shapes his form, not the logic of discursive argumentation they have been trained to expect and emulate in the English classroom. So while students reach eagerly for individual Emersonian ideas, articulated appealingly in aphoristic sentences, the overall argument they assume exists slips their grip.

Not surprisingly, Emerson's enticing slipperiness can be even more vexing for teachers than for students. Students and teachers alike have been trained to doubt the intuitive in favor of the discursive. And for good reason: a scholarly essay based exclusively, or even significantly, on how "I feel" about a literary text, cultural artifact, or intellectual idea is of questionable value. I take this regard for rational objectivity as the reason so many teachers—from grade school to college—continue to insist that students avoid the first-person pronoun "I" in their academic writing, especially when it's linked with an emotive verb. Emerson would be appalled. For him, objective fact lies in the perception and expression of the individual I/eye. Our "highest behavior," Emerson writes in his journal, "consist[s] in identification of the Ego with the universe" (*Journals* 11: 203). To avoid speaking from the vantage of the "I" is, for Emerson, to blind our eyes to the reality of what is.

The essay "Circles" offers an effective starting point for teaching Emerson precisely because it provides an accessible but intellectually rigorous platform for innovative, experiential classroom activities to help students understand Emerson by asking them to do what he does in "Circles." More than any of his other essays, "Circles" provides a clear, concrete, and familiar organizational principle: the circle as literal geometric shape, literary metaphor, and philosophical idea. In "Circles," the very thing that tends to trip students up when reading Emerson's essays—the seeming lack of consistency—poses less of a problem given the clarity and concreteness of the circle as a controlling idea and metaphor. So when the challenges of Emerson's form arise, when individual metaphors and moods and ideas pull students in while the overarching point threatens to slip by, the clean coherence of the circle provides a firm handle.

Take, for example, one characteristic sentence from "Circles": "Our life is an apprenticeship to the truth that around every circle another can be drawn; that there is no end in nature, but every end is a beginning; that there is always another dawn risen on midnoon, and under every deep a lower deep opens." Philosophically, the sentence expresses the controlling idea Emerson pursues in "Circles"—that, as he puts it later, "there are no fixtures in nature." The sentence also demonstrates Emerson's tendency to enact his ideas rhetorically: it contains at least four different metaphors presented in a spiraling series of increasing abstraction. It's almost as if, given the absence of fixtures in nature, Emerson lets us know we shouldn't expect to find them in his sentences. At the same time, though, even as the sentence itself performs Emerson's claim "that every action admits of being outdone" (*Collected Works* 2: 179), the simple and concrete image of a circle drawn around another circle does, in fact, seem to offer something fixed on which students might hang their critical analysis.

In the remainder of this essay, I offer two pedagogical experiments inspired by specific passages from "Circles." Each is designed to introduce students experientially to Emerson's intuitive logic as it plays out in his sentences and paragraphs. The motivation behind each experiment is the attempt to enact, in one way or another, Emerson's claim that "conversation is a game of circles" (*Collected Works* 2: 184). As such, the experiments are designed playfully to disorient students, to force them out of conventional expectations of academic discourse, in order to reorient them to Emerson's particular way of thinking and writing. My purpose in offering these experiments is not to supply cut-and-paste assignments but rather to present a few examples of classroom activities—built on the assumption that understanding Emerson requires enacting Emerson— and to explain why these experiments achieve certain goals.

Experiment 1: "Our life is an apprenticeship to the truth that around every circle another can be drawn. . . ."

This is a short writing activity that works effectively as a preparation for class-room discussions of "Circles." It attempts literally to enact an idea Emerson asserts, thesis-like, at the end of the opening paragraph of "Circles"—"that around every circle another can be drawn."

Ask students to get out a journal, notebook, or a few loose sheets of paper. Then read aloud the opening three paragraphs of "Circles." It's a good idea to have students themselves share the task of reading aloud rather than you doing it for them. If you've already got the students situated in a circle, start with one student and go around the circle having each read just one sentence aloud. Do-ing it this way provides another point of entry for experiencing Emerson's ideas and form physically: each individual reading one sentence at a time in a circular fashion emphasizes the strange way Emerson's discrete sentences fit and don't fit together.

Tell them they will be freewriting for a total of ten to fifteen minutes about the passage—but with a twist. Before the students begin writing, tell them you will interrupt them from time to time by saying "circle." At that point, students must immediately stop writing (often in midsentence), draw a circle around what they have written, and then begin again. Once the students understand the basics of the experiment—when you say "circle," they stop, circle their writing, and start over—read the passage one more time and then offer an open-ended prompt to start the freewriting, such as "what specific idea or detail did you find most interesting and why?" Then, as they write, say "circle" from time to time to trigger the experiment.

The interruption is the most important element of this writing activity. The point is to enact—in a simple, easily identifiable way—Emerson's central claim that "our life is an apprenticeship to the truth that around every circle another can be drawn." It forces students to stop in the midst of their thinking and writing and literally draw a circle around their sentences on the page, before continuing on with what will be in some sense a new thought. Drawing these circles is, in a way, a sleight of hand that performs on the page one of Emerson's easiest ideas to swallow but hardest rhetorically and stylistically to digest: "every end is a beginning."

Students tend to react in one of two ways to this activity. After being forced abruptly to stop midsentence and draw a circle around their writing, they either attempt to continue writing from where they were before the interruption, or they take the opportunity to change tack in their thinking. But even those students who try to carry on after the circle often find it difficult, if not impossible. The interruption changes things, and they can see that change on the page.

What makes this experiment intellectually interesting and complicated, rather than merely playful, is the conversation it can produce when you ask students about their thought process during the activity. They often notice the disruptive and generative consequences of stopping and starting, which helps them think about the disruptive and generative qualities within Emerson's prose.

Experiment 2: "Our moods do not believe in each other."

Just as with the first, this experiment takes inspiration from an epigrammatic sentence in "Circles" that captures the interplay of Emerson's ideas and form. When Emerson declares, "Our moods do not believe in each other" (*Collected Works* 2: 182), he provides an apt description of "Circles" itself, an essay seemingly motivated by Emerson's mercurial moods rather than by the step-by-step connectivity of discursive logic. This experiment draws attention to the capriciousness of Emerson's style by way of a writing exercise based not on language (student prose) but rather on visual impressions of rhetorical structures. The point is to help students understand Emerson more fully by making visible and comparing the formal qualities of his writing and their own assumptions about academic discourse.

Introduce the experiment by addressing how and why it will feel strange and potentially uncomfortable. Students have been taught to articulate analytical ideas using the spoken and written word in English classrooms. But in this exercise, they will be asked to express analytical ideas visually, using shapes, arrows, and other schematic shorthands to express their thoughts. So before you actually ask them to do that different kind of work, talk a bit about what's coming and why it's going to feel strange. Be sure to offer some specific examples of models they likely are familiar with, such as flowcharts or the standard high school composition technique of imagining the structure of five-paragraph essays as an inverted triangle.

The students' task here is to represent visually the shape of the essays they tend to write in English classrooms, so give them a few minutes to sit and think about the academic essays they have been taught to write, about what their teachers and professors have taught them to value and emulate in their academic prose. Recalling a specific essay they have written and revised can be very helpful here. Then ask them to *represent visually* the shape of the essays they typically write (or strive to write) in English classrooms. Tell them to draw the shape of the essay. Give students lots of freedom, bound only by one very strict rule: no words allowed, only lines, geometric shapes, and arrows.

Spend a few minutes identifying and discussing any interesting patterns. In a small class, you can simply ask students to hold up their drawings while everyone looks around. In larger classes (with desks already formed in a discussion circle), you can ask students to orient their sketches on their desks facing the inside of the classroom, and then you and the class walk around the inner circle, observing each person's sketch in turn. The basic point here is to identify any interesting patterns among the drawings and to explore what those patterns have to say about your assumptions regarding what you value and strive for in your academic prose in terms of formal organization and presentation of ideas.

Now repeat the experiment, with one key difference: this time ask students to represent visually the shape of Emerson's "Circles." Again, you're asking them to draw the shape of the essay. No words are allowed, only lines, shapes, arrows, etc. Again, identify and discuss patterns, then move into a discussion of the significance of what you've just done and discovered. This is the time to ask students to compare the visual representations of their own writing with that of "Circles" and, in turn, to compare their assumptions guiding what they have been taught to value and strive for in academic writing with Emerson's own assumptions. These comparisons help them understand why Emerson might have crafted "Circles" in this particular way.

Robert D. Richardson usefully points out that "[i]f Emerson's writing does not always, or even usually, proceed in a straightforward, logical manner, it is not because he couldn't write that way, but because he didn't want to, and was after something different" (*First* 35). The ultimate goal of this experiment is to shepherd students through an activity that requires them to grapple with the motivations behind Emerson's choices as a writer as well as their own. The motivation behind Emerson's choice to write the way he does seems to be un-flinching belief and conviction. It's interesting, and potentially unsettling, to then wonder what role belief and conviction play in our own assumptions as academic writers.

Keep in mind that both of these experiments are intended to initiate discussion, to lay the groundwork for a rich and rewarding collective engagement with "Circles." But they don't ensure it. Pedagogical experiments of this kind require a striking tolerance for not knowing where the conversation is headed. They expose and unsettle the expectations that we and our students have about what discussions look like, asking us to think about how ideas actually evolve and about the sometimes rich productivity of intuitive leaps and the contradictions they produce. As such, these experiments seek to create the possibility of a classroom experience that, as much as possible, mimics key qualities of Emerson's particular genius.

Emerson insists in his essays that writing is the true path to understanding himself and his place in the world. At its best, as in "Circles," his writing is honest, curious, specific, and overflowing with his own glorious, contradictory self. It reminds us that all good writing is personal. And it asks us to consider that our approaches to teaching literature and writing, with our understandable emphasis on rational argumentation, just might be missing something important—which Emerson would likely describe as conviction, as belief.

NOTE

My understanding of Emerson and my approach to teaching "Circles" have been profoundly shaped by the staff and students of the University of Michigan's New England Literature Program (NELP). I am especially indebted to Rachael Cohen, Nick Harp, Aric Knuth, Ryan Walsh, and Becky Wright.

Beyond "Mendicant and Sycophantic" Reading: Teaching the Seminar Studies in American Self-Reliance

Wesley T. Mott

Teachers encounter two stubborn challenges with Emerson's "Self-Reliance," whether in classes for English majors or—as at Worcester Polytechnic Institute (WPI)—for students who major primarily in engineering and the life sciences: Emerson's most famous concept seems, on its face, self-explanatory, yet his prose is notoriously nonlinear and elusive (and allusive). In a seven-week quarter, the seminar Studies in American Self-Reliance seeks to unfold a more complex yet also more accessible and pertinent Emerson. Exploring competing meanings and historical contexts of individualism and self-reliance in American culture, the seminar moves from Emerson's essay into contemporary culture, pursuing, by way of Emerson's inspiration, a variety of topics and interdisciplinary approaches.

The very title "Self-Reliance" seems blandly to reassure American undergraduates with visions of a cultural birthright—a sense of self-worth just the way they are. But for too many, the reading turns out to be perplexing or boring. Teaching the essay as literature is challenging enough. Studies in American Self-Reliance aims both to engage students with Emerson's essay and to forge "an original relation" with some wider aspect of culture that genuinely engages them.

WPI does not regard the Department of Humanities and Arts as a service department or a purveyor of general education. Dozens of students major or double-major, and scores minor, in any of several disciplines based in the department. The humanities and arts requirement, moreover, is one of three substantial projects each WPI student must satisfy: a major qualifying project (the equivalent of three courses, the MQP is typically a team project in the student's major); an interactive qualifying project (also the equivalent of three courses, the IQP is usually a team project, often conducted abroad, examining the interaction of science or technology with an issue having humanistic or social implications [see Mott, "'Monarch'"]); and a humanities and arts requirement (five courses—three of which must be in a single disciplinary area—culminating in an inquiry seminar that meets weekly for two hours). Students choose from approximately seventy-five seminars a year (seven in English or American literature, four of which are also among the present sixteen seminars labeled American studies), each with an enrollment limit of twelve. An inquiry seminar is thus a capstone encouraging students to reflect and synthesize their significant experience in the humanities and arts at WPI.

Studies in American Self-Reliance is designated an American studies seminar and is thus open not only to students with "depth" in literature but also to those with backgrounds in history and philosophy or religion; surprisingly, several international students have also elected the seminar. About one-third of the students already have taken either my American literature (1830–65) survey course, in which we read a half dozen Emerson essays and selected poetry, or my American Dream course, in which we read a brief excerpt from "Self-Reliance" to represent the "idealistic" strain in American life; an occasional student has taken my advanced Concord Writers course, which includes samplings from Emerson's poetry and journals, a sermon, and four essays. Typically, several students have humanities "depth" in literature but have not previously taken my courses. Nearly half have "depth" in history, writing, rhetoric, or another humanities discipline. Most of my seminar students have not previously studied or even read "Self-Reliance," though they are pretty sure they know what it is all about.

Starting our first class, for which simply reading "Self-Reliance" is assigned, I ask students to jot down one or two sentences for each of the following prompts: what self-reliance means to them personally; why self-reliance is considered a central national trait, and what the implications of such a self-image might be; and what Emerson means by the term. This is a rather nasty trap, of course, since Emerson himself avers that self-reliance is a living, protean, dynamic force that verbal constructs cannot define or contain but only hint at ("To talk of reliance, is a poor external way of speaking. Speak rather of that which relies, because it works and is" [*Collected Works* 2: 40]).

As expected, the first question—about personal senses of self-reliance—elicits many definitions driven by immediate life issues such as going off to college ("Doing things by yourself"; "Independence"). Others are unreflective and bland ("Not relying [or 'depending'] on others"; "Taking care of [or 'thinking for' or 'depending on' or 'belief in'] yourself"), even hopelessly circular ("Self-reliance is relying on yourself"[!]). Some reveal career and other practical concerns ("Ability to take care of yourself in any situation—physical, mental, financial, such as making and keeping within a budget"; "Support oneself"). A few grasp ethical and psychic dimensions of the concept ("Give more than you take"; "Holding yourself to a standard"; "The act of looking within for joy and satisfaction"). The instructor puffed up with superiority to these groping definitions should try the exercise! More than any Emerson essay, "Self-Reliance" eludes paraphrase. And in this course particularly, it would be a great mistake to pose as the expert holding the keys to the Emerson shrine.

Our ensuing open discussion of the second question—respecting implications of our culture's ready acceptance of self-reliance as a key national characteristic—ignites the seminar. Several students shed their reserve and declare that in a national context, self-reliance in the United States can be ambiguous, contradictory, illusory—that a fine line can separate self-reliance from selfishness; that scoundrels cloak themselves in the mantra of self-reliance to justify predatory business practices and arrogant foreign policy; that family and friends are crucial to individual well-being; that our founding Puritan and revolutionary rhetoric has conditioned us to think that the United States is "special," "the best," leading us to believe that we have no need to cooperate with other nations; that "we think our hard work is what gets us ahead" (our being "set off geographically," one student asserts, fed our national myth of individualism and the conviction that we are "economically in control of our own fates"—an attitude that still fuels "hypocrisy in debates over welfare and other public affairs"); that virtually all children grow up accepting these notions uncritically. The insights of several international students, moreover, illustrate the maxim that foreign travelers are often the most astute observers and critics of the countries they visit; the seminar affords them useful perspectives on their own native cultures as well as on the United States.

As we turn to what Emerson's essay says and does, these mostly non-English majors quickly grasp that Emerson's volatile essay is not to be scoured for static aphorisms, nuggets of stable truth to be glommed on to as little anchors against confusion; rather, the essay proceeds unpredictably, surprising the reader with self-contradiction and shocks of recognition. As each student briefly presents a challenging passage, we experience Emerson's sense that language and truth are volatile. It follows that Emerson does not employ self-reliance as a pretext for any ideology, and Emerson's style is neither sloppy nor pointless. Somehow, vision and expression in "Self-Reliance" are linked. One student cut short my clever professorial explication by stating the matter concisely: if Emerson had written "Self-Reliance" in traditional expository prose, with a crisp thesis statement, telegraphed transitions, and a neat concluding summary, he would have violated his very principle—that self-reliance must be earned by the reader as well as continually rediscovered and asserted by the alert, ethical person.

Having spent our first meeting freshly engaged with Emerson's seemingly self-evident but disturbingly slippery essay, and having exposed their own unrehearsed sense of self-reliance, in the second meeting students come prepared for two tasks. Assigned my essay "'The Age of the First Person Singular': Emerson and Individualism," for the first hour they discuss some of the contexts in which Emerson wrote the essay and the historical and contemporary uses and misuses of it. This exercise is not a road map or prescriptive methodology for term papers; it simply complicates an essay and a concept that by now appears far more complex than when the term began. We consider the jingoism and boosterism, the economic exploitation and international mischief, that are often sanctioned by perverse readings of "Self-Reliance." We explore too the moral and creative courage and the sense of empowerment that countless readers, common and renowned, have found in Emerson's essay. Several students have been surprised to discover that Emerson, like most transcendentalists, spent a lifetime keeping in creative tension the demands of self and society. One later wrote, "I really liked how this course got me to think about life/community in ways I never had before."

In the second hour, each student presents a tentative abstract for the research paper—on any broadly cultural implication of Emerson's essay—that will occupy the rest of the term. To spark exploration of unlimited topics and contexts, the syllabus provides a bibliography of classic cultural observations (Tocqueville), historical and literary criticism (Bercovitch; Howe, *Making*), sociological surveys (Bellah et al.), journalistic analyses (Callero; Lipset), and critiques of foreign and military policy (Bacevich).

In the third session, students return explicitly, if briefly, to Emerson, submitting the first substantial piece of writing for their seminar portfolios: an analysis of a "literary" aspect of "Self-Reliance" or, drawing on reading from their previous courses, of a work by any other American writer who in some way responds to Emersonian idealism (Hawthorne has been a popular choice).

The seminar, however, is not substantially *about* Emerson. We turn quickly to revised abstracts for the research paper that is the core of the term. Students must freshly explore underpinnings and assumptions of any issue or field in the context of the nation's cherished, but often unexamined, sense of self-reliance. Some take a global stance. Research can be based on any humanistic discipline. The only stipulation: each thesis must be framed by the student's understanding of what Emerson means by self-reliance or of how others have used or misused the term. Students by now are aware that self-reliance is malleable, paradoxical, and sometimes employed not, as Emerson intended, to provoke but to smooth away hard realities and unpleasant truths. As one student, Thomas Danko, wrote at the end of the term, society plays a complex "role in shaping the individual"; it is therefore delusional to think the "self" can cut itself "off from the world (I believe advocating isolation is one of the biggest misuses of Emerson's work)." The seminar's main value, Danko concludes, is the promotion of "critical thinking."

The richly diverse topics have been limited only by the experience and imagination of the students: Andrew Carnegie as case study of paradoxes of self-reliance; advertising and the psychology of conformity; Hawthorne's critique of Emerson; civil rights and women's education in Pakistan; survey of WPI student opinions of self-reliance; the Electoral College as deterrent to voting; Ayn Rand and Emerson; cultural effects of the evolving Disney princess mystique; "vulnerability" and sexism in the United States; violence in mass media; erosion of the founding principles of Greek life; G. E. M. Anscombe and consequentialism; self-reliance and global environmental policy.

Students also discover the truth of Emerson's insight that self-reliance is hard ("If any one imagines that this law is lax, let him keep its commandment one day" [*Collected Works* 2: 42]). Indeed, the independence the seminar promotes is tempered by rigor and accountability. With Coleridgean polarity, Emerson habitually privileged life itself over analysis and calculation—"Genius" over "Talent" (*Collected Works* 1: 134), "Intuition" over "tuitions" (*Collected Works* 2: 37). Yet even lower orders of intellect, he knew, had their indispensable uses ("[T]he oracle comes, because we had previously laid siege to the shrine" [2: 197]). In education, he averred, "Genius" must be complemented by "Drill," because "[a]ccuracy is essential to beauty" (*Complete Works* 10: 147). Though WPI juniors and seniors will produce massive research reports for the IQP and MQP, a few seminar students report that, until taking Studies in American Self-Reliance, they had never written an abstract, had to paraphrase a source, or known how to incorporate quotations fluently into their own prose. Each of the next four weeks, moreover, involves peer reading of drafts, in-class progress reports, and discussion of aspects of writing and research: rhetorical and stylistic matters, as well as principles of research that concern everyone. Students spend most out-of-class time doing solo research and writing, but the in-class collaboration lends a welcome Emersonian self/society rhythm to the seminar.

In week six each student prepares a peer-reading critique of a randomly drawn classmate's penultimate draft. Almost invariably, the class is surprised that a carefully done student critique resembles my own in most essentials. Many students make suggestions not only about thesis, structure, and argument but also style, grammar, and word choice. The peer reader's critique is included in his or her own portfolio and not that of the person *being* critiqued; though I do not grade these critiques, I consider the care and effort of the peer reader when I determine final grades.

In the seventh and final session, students give formal final reports and complete anonymous course evaluations. Contrary to transcendentalist education theory, today, of course, teaching at every level is judged using industrial-model metrics and outcomes assessment. In more humanistic terms, seminar students also are asked to judge a seminar's success in meeting objectives stated on the syllabus and to offer additional comments and suggestions for improving future course offerings. Students repeatedly express satisfaction with the "independence," "open-endedness," "choice," and "freedom in search of options" encouraged by the seminar: "I thought it was great that we had the freedom to do our own research and go in any direction after reading 'Self-Reliance'"; "I enjoyed how the course required independent work and began with Emerson." What and *how* they learned were equally important: "encouraged to explore our own choice of a multidisciplinary topic . . . was a great way to learn"; "I learned a lot about American culture that I never thought about before." Several like the collaborative aspects of the seminar as much as the freedom: "I enjoyed listening to other people's topics for their papers and getting feedback on my ideas." One was delighted that "my writing, research, and speaking skills improved." Christine Carbone later wrote that the seminar promoted more than good academic habits: "it also provided an opportunity for students to undergo a self-reliant introspection. . . . I find myself questioning whether or not I am self-reliant . . . and constantly examining my actions." Noting that the research paper was clearly "defined" but "different for everyone," Dylan Baranik was impressed that the topics "covered nearly every facet of American culture, and even some other cultures too." He found "the humanities and arts fulfilling and satisfying. . . . It is nice to work with people, literature, and history rather than working with numbers and science all the time."

It's equally gratifying for the seminar instructor to see the enthusiasm and achievement of students working independently on topics that matter to them. The students genuinely teach one another—and me—with perennially fresh topics and ideas. Making it work takes accepting a difficult Emersonian principle: that successful teaching requires abandoning complete control and conscious desire for effect and influence. "Truly speaking," Emerson famously declared in "The Divinity School Address," "it is not instruction, but provocation, that I can receive from another soul" (*Collected Works* 1: 80). Lawrence Buell terms Emerson's pedagogical ideal "the sage as anti-mentor" (*Emerson* 292). As Emerson reflected in his journal in 1859, "This is my boast that I have no school & no follower. I should account it a measure of the impurity of insight, if it did not create independence" (*Journals* 14: 258).

The seminar certainly fostered independence for the chemical engineering major Caitlin Swalec. Having done her IQP on natural resource management in rural Thailand, she found in Emerson support for the emerging global concept of "community self-sufficiency." Learning "how to use research from multiple disciplines (environmental policy and literature, in this case) to create and support a cohesive argument," she now feels "uninhibited by the boundaries of 'science' and 'literature' and 'environment' and 'history.'" In fact, while taking the seminar, she declared a minor in English and attended public lectures on Abraham Lincoln—marking the sesquicentennial of the end of the Civil War—at the nearby American Antiquarian Society. She went on to be selected for the competitive fall 2015 AAS undergraduate seminar on American culture exploring the historical meanings of *union* and *emancipation*.

"Our reading," Emerson complained in "Self-Reliance," "is mendicant and sycophantic" (*Collected Works* 2: 36). Too often classrooms are thwarted as students settle, on exams and term papers, for crude paraphrases of the unparaphrasable "Self-Reliance" and for mimicking the instructor's futile attempts to explicate the essay. Students in this seminar report a sense of mastery and accomplishment. As Rachel Cody concluded, "[T]his was one of the hardest English courses I have ever taken, but it was certainly one of the most rewarding." She added modestly, "While I am not sure I can say I fully understand the concept of self-reliance—if that is possible! —I do feel as though I have a better understanding and awareness of self-reliance."

The seminar reveals the protean nature of "Self-Reliance," an endlessly provocative essay, the uses and misuses of which illuminate contests at the heart of American identity. Challenging and trusting students to pursue the implications of Emerson's vision can be the basis of a significant and sometimes moving experience in humanistic learning—for the student and the instructor.

The Ideals of "Friendship"

Jennifer Gurley

Ralph Waldo Emerson's "Friendship" might be both the easiest and the trickiest of his essays to teach. Read midway through a course (if it is read at all), the title comes as a relief to students daunted by "The American Scholar" or "The Divinity School Address": here, at last, is a topic they think they recognize. So they are thrown by Emerson's unrecognizable demands to know why they "insist on rash personal relations" with their friends, why they "go to his house, or know his mother and brother and sisters," why they must be "visited by him" at their own homes. And they are irritated when he instructs them to "[leave] this touching and clawing" and let their friends be "spirits" (*Collected Works* 2: 123). Students have asked me, rather pleadingly, "What is *wrong* with this guy?"

It's a fair question. The answer is that Emerson doesn't serve up familiar notions of friendship but pursues instead an unusual form of that relation that leads to "truth" (*Collected Works* 2: 119) rather than companionship, trading physical closeness for spiritual intimacy. For him, the latter is achieved by transcending the former. This disembodied way of being a friend—one that shuns actual contact—seems weird and cold and in some ways is. Because I've found that students are very invested in grappling with Emerson on this personal topic, "Friendship" might be better suited than any other text in his corpus for introducing his idealism more generally, in all its severity and beauty. In what follows, I flesh out the features and implications of Emersonian friendship as I present them in the classroom.

The students I imagine addressing here are my own. They are diverse in age, class, and experience (like the members of Emerson's own audiences); few of them are English majors; most of them are new to Emerson. They will read him for a full semester to fulfill my college's core curriculum "major authors" requirement. In other words, most of my students are conscripted. But I like the challenge of trying to turn them on to Emerson and help them come to their own conclusions about why he might be worth reading. The material I present below could also be taught as is in a number of general education courses or a survey or period course in American literature or philosophy for English majors. Whatever the level, I walk the class slowly through sections of "Friendship" as I lead a discussion of its key claims, which derive in part from Plato's *Phaedrus*,[1] one of Emerson's favorite texts by one of his most beloved thinkers. We then work through two poems from Henry David Thoreau (1817–62) and Ellen Sturgis Hooper (1812–48), Emerson's actual friends who take up his conception of friendship in different and, in at least one sense, gendered ways. Emerson and Plato are covered in one 1.5-hour session, Emerson and his poet friends in a second.

For the first of these two classes, students will have read all of "Friendship," plus a short myth from Plato's *Phaedrus* (lines 244a–250c) comparing the human soul to a charioteer leading his two horses, a white horse of moderation and a black one of intemperance (254a), through the heavens in search of a vision of divine truth (247a–b), figured as a merry-go-round of the gods in which that human soul, now fallen, formerly had a place. The purpose of this class is to grasp Emerson's conception of friendship, not to evaluate it (that comes later). We begin with a discussion of what Emerson *doesn't* want: a friend sought "not sacredly, but with adulterate passion" (*Collected Works* 2: 117), or a merely "modish and worldly alliance." He will have no "prostitution of the name of friendship" (2: 121). Here students discuss the key distinctions that drive Emerson's idealism in this essay: the sacred is opposed to the merely worldly and to low lust. The latter gratifies immediate desires (like those of Plato's black horse); students know what that means and can provide many examples.

The former—the sacred—is otherworldly and hence more difficult to imagine. But that is what Emerson *does* want: a friendship of spirits that he defines as a "covenant," a "sacred relation which is a kind of absolute, and which even leaves the language of love suspect and common" (*Collected Works* 2: 119, 123). This "purer" friendship is an "alliance of two large, formidable natures, mutually beheld, mutually feared, before yet they recognize the deep identity which, beneath these disparities, unites them." Because my students are usually lost here (rightfully, I think), I lecture on this abstruse stuff. I begin by explaining that two friends working together in the right way will get past superficial differences and come to see the deeper "likeness" between themselves (2: 122). Eventually, they will grasp the "deep[est] identity": that they are united, each having a unique place within a universal order.

I ask students: what is this correct way of working together, of mutually beholding and fearing? Here we return to Plato's myth of the charioteer (which makes sense to them) to examine therein a "lover" and "beloved" relation that shaped much of Emerson's thinking about friends in conversation. It begins when the charioteer, that human soul trying to find its way back to that divine merry-go-round, catches sight of a beautiful boy, a prospective beloved. This soul of a man recalls a faraway vision of real beauty, of the gods above, into which he was once "initiated" (250b–c). Until this moment, he had forgotten (248c), but now he remembers a pure, divine form of beauty he once knew (254b). In this visual exchange, the lover does not despise his beloved for being an embodied form of the real one. Indeed the boy is an object of "desire" precisely because his material beauty recalls the divine. Only now will the charioteer consummate his desire. What began as a desire to be close to physical beauty results in an admixture of physical and spiritual love. Hence Plato is sensuous about the friend who brings him to truth, believing that it can be recalled and hence experienced when with that other person. Others need not be left behind.

For Emerson, however, they must be. The embodied person is transcended. Emersonian friendship therefore requires that persons be drawn to one another in the interest of truth rather than each other as such: friends are "useful" when they bring us into the "eternal" and worthless when they merely occupy our time. "I do then with friends as I do with my books," he claims. "I would have them where I can find them, but I would seldom use them. . . . I cannot afford to speak much with my friend. If he is great he makes me so great that I cannot descend to converse" (*Collected Works* 2: 126).[2] That mutual beholding and fearing in Emersonian friendship is agonistic because it is also caring, it can be "truthful" (2: 119) because it is "tender" (2: 120)—not in a hand-holding way, but as an austere act of holy "affection" (2: 114) that "may deify both" (2: 126). The true friend is drawn to the other in the interest of a "divine affinity of virtue" that resists the physical and emotional contact normally associated with friendship and yearns only for spiritual growth. Hence true friends do not lean on but work with and against each other, in contact only and exactly as long as it takes to find truth before departing to stand alone once more. With time, friends no longer require actual contact at all. This is how the truest friend becomes a "spirit" (2: 115). This is how Plato's human soul, now cited by Emerson, rejoins its divine cohort of parading gods. "[E]very soul," he writes, "which has acquired any truth, should be safe from harm until another period."[3]

In our second class session, I ask students to consider the ethical consequences of Emerson's conception of friendship. What does it mean, practically speaking, to regard friends primarily as stepping blocks to truth? How are we to deal with our friends' imperfections or embodied needs? How Emerson's ideal played out in his actual friendships varied and cannot be discussed in any useful sense here,[4] but two of Emerson's notable friends picked up on his themes in their poetry in ways that have stunned my students. I ask the class to come prepared to compare these poems' conceptions of care for others with Emerson's. Thoreau's 1841 poem opens:

> Let such pure hate still underprop
> Our love, that we may be
> Each other's conscience,
> And have our sympathy
> Mainly from thence.   ("Let" 71)

Students find, rightly, that Thoreau takes Emerson's claims about friendship to their logical extreme in ways that seem histrionic and hence unpersuasive. Love is a means to truth that is neither erotic nor sensual at any point. Lovers and beloved friends express sympathy not as empathy (or as any kind of feeling at all) but as the work of constant mutual judgment. That requires objectivity, which requires distance, imagined as a fountain of "pure hate" that keeps us true to truth rather than to the vulnerability and fallibility of other persons.

For Thoreau, love is more shared discipline than shared fuzzy feeling. Some students find this severity cartoonish, and others worry about a world in which friendship is based on "pure hate," however defined. They want friends who are more than remote judges.

In contrast, Hooper, a friend and poet whom Emerson mentored, rejects his strictly spiritual manner of relation and would have been appalled by Thoreau's cold excesses. Hooper's spiritual sense enlivens but does not at all supplant the material: actual persons. We consider the following untitled poem:[5]

> Too holy for me, Lord! this temple wrought
> By thine own hands, where I have stopped awhile,
> As some poor peasant, called to daily toil
> At noon-tide hour the way-side church has sought,
> There laid aside his earthly ware, and knelt—
> And in the dim of cathedral air has felt
> Thy sacred presence—from the world unmeshed,
> And with an almost painful awe refreshed.
> He lingers still with lowly reverence paid
> To saint and martyr niched in shadowy Time,
> And though he feels this hour his mortal prime,
> Almost his being here is over-weighed.
> He passes forth to sunlight and to men
> And mingles him with daily life again—
>
> So I, within thy outer natural world—
> Have felt thy presence and my soul bowed low—
> The noble ones it has been mine to know,
> Like saints indwell here—angels with wings furled—
> Life's care invite me forth—since to my ear
> The voice speaks not which stayed the prophet here,
> And bade him give up all—I must return,
> Pilgrim just crossed at nature's holy urn—

A "sacred presence" grounds each stanza and nourishes each speaker before he (the peasant of stanza one) and then she (presumably Hooper in stanza two) "must return" to the duties of "daily life." Unable to suffer the "Too holy" cathedral in which the peasant momentarily has "felt" the Lord's presence "from the world unmeshed," Hooper has "felt" it in "[his] outer natural world." The divine is not an *end* but a *means*: a source of replenishment for caring ("Life's care invite me forth") for that natural realm—the "NOT ME" of daily life, of sunlight and men—over the featureless realm of the "ME,"[6] the world of spirit. Hence the "voice speaks not which stayed the prophet here, / And bade him give up all": she "must return" to her actual friends in all of their embodied bits.

Some students usually want to suggest that Hooper's call for attention to embodied experience is a gender-specific response to Emerson's presumably masculine conception of friendship. Others find such generalizations frustratingly simplistic. Here I lead students through a speculative discussion of Emerson and gender, emphasizing that these textual moments offer places to begin thinking, not to end it. Because Emerson uses masculine pronouns in "Friendship," some students assume that his conception is necessarily masculine; others counter that Emerson always defaults to such pronouns when describing concepts he applies to all and that readers are free to engage ideas as they see fit. I enjoy telling the class that an early line in the essay, "A new person is a great event, and hinders me from sleep," in fact originated in a journal entry Emerson composed after meeting Anna Barker, the young follower and friend of Margaret Fuller, who also sought spiritualized friendship, especially with and for women. Some students claim that Emerson is only being true to his claims when he refuses to wallow in emotions or personal trivia, citing his own rejection of that "vulgar" realm (*Collected Works* 2: 193). Others respond that he is unduly cold and unrealistic in handling human relationships and is perhaps especially prone to find fault with women who merely seek basic expressions of love. A short letter (24 Oct. 1840) in which Emerson rejects Fuller's demand for a confidant can be used to provide additional evidence for the conflicting interpretations (*Letters* 2: 352–53).[7]

Though for a variety of reasons students generally find Hooper more appealing than Thoreau, the point is not to make them choose but to return them to Emerson with these poems in mind as they write their own essays about how his ideal speaks (or does not) to their own friendships. These are text-based arguments in which students first define Emerson's terms and then evaluate them as they assess one of their own friendships by his standards. The results don't divide along gender lines but vary and are often quite interesting, in part perhaps because I welcome rigorous disagreement with Emerson. Students who do poorly are impatient with the text and impose their own understandings or generalize about their love of or loathing for the man; their analyses of their own friendships are equally vague. Those who do well rise to the challenge of attending closely to his words and to the concrete dynamics of their own relationships.

I leave the class with my own conviction that Emerson insists on a friend's spirit over his or her appearance and circumstances in order to make all of us better friends and human beings. A true friend is "magnanimous" in spirit, "emanating" like the sun and never troubling where "his rays fall" (*Collected Works* 2: 126). We receive from such gracious persons not what they "give" but what they "are": we receive simply by being in their presence. This is a vision of grace. My friend does not "hold me" in low, gift-giving exchanges of emotions or services or things but cares enough about me to insist that I stand on my own. And for that my friend is proudly able to say that the "only joy I have in [her] being mine, is that the *not mine* is *mine*" (2: 122).

NOTES

For Hunter Igoe and all my Emerson students.

[1] Because any translation of Plato will do for our purposes, I use the Oxford Classical Texts standard line citation (*Opera: Volume II: Parmenides, Philebus, Symposium, Phaedrus, Alcibiades I and II, Hipparchus, Amatores*). Emerson read various translations but happily welcomed the now widely used *The Dialogues of Plato* (1871), edited by Benjamin Jowett. Translations throughout this essay are my own.

[2] See Emerson's similar claim about the fading usefulness of friends in the "Discipline" section of *Nature*.

[3] Emerson first uses the line from *Phaedrus* (248c) in "Experience" (1844) and finally quotes (but still does not cite) it in his 1858 lecture "The Natural Method of Mental Philosophy" (*Later Lectures* 2: 85).

[4] Emerson's relationship with Thoreau is a focus of *Emerson and Thoreau: Figures of Friendship* (Lysaker and Rossi). Though little has been written on Hooper, Megan Marshall's *Margaret Fuller: A New American Life* describes Fuller's sometimes chilling interactions with Emerson in ways that resonate with the Hooper poem I share with students.

[5] This is one of various untitled poems later privately printed as *Poems*, probably assembled in 1872 by Hooper's son, Edward William Hooper.

[6] Emerson's famous description appears in the opening pages of *Nature*: "Philosophically considered, the universe is composed of Nature and the Soul. Strictly speaking, therefore, all that is separate from us, all which Philosophy distinguishes as the NOT ME, that is, both nature and art, all other men and my own body, must be ranked under this name, NATURE" (*Collected Works* 1: 8).

[7] See Marshall (163–83) for a very precise account of Emerson's interactions with the young women surrounding Margaret Fuller and of Fuller's own ambivalent taking up of Emerson's notion of friendship. See also Gurley, "Reading," in *Ralph Waldo Emerson in Context*.

In Praise of Affirmation:
On Emerson's "Experience"

Branka Arsić

It would be difficult to identify a relevant interpretation of Emerson that doesn't engage in reading "Experience," an essay that appeared in 1844 as a part of *Essays: Second Series*. And yet the reading of this important essay, in the classroom as well as among the critics, has tended to settle upon some questionable commonplaces, namely that this essay reflects a disruption in Emerson's philosophy, a turn from idealism to skepticism. Readers generally agree that it marks a breakthrough in Emerson's thinking, triggered, at least partially, by the death of his son Waldo in January 1842. In fact, Emerson's grieving for his son—commented on in a single paragraph—is what has most preoccupied readers of the essay. Some readers see in his three quick confessions regarding his grief ("the only thing grief has taught me, is to know how shallow it is"; "I grieve that grief can teach me nothing"; "In the death of my son . . . I seem to have lost a beautiful estate,—no more") an opportunity to discover the man himself, to get a sense of what kind of person he was, whether he was really mourning his son or rather signaling, when reporting the shallowness of grief, his incapacity for grieving, thus obliquely confirming that he has the cold heart that he was accused of having so many times (*Collected Works* 3: 29). Others are preoccupied less with the private aspect of Emerson's grieving than with detecting how mourning was enacted through his practice of writing. Still others think that in the wake of Waldo's death the lugubrious tone of the essay reflects a transformation of Emerson's alleged optimism into a more sober pessimism, if not downright skepticism.

But it is difficult to see why "Experience" should pave a privileged road to Emerson the man, since the essay is in fact no more personal than his other essays. In accord with the autobiographical logic of the genre as established by Montaigne, who famously explained that in his essays he "paints [himself] diversely" (St. John 2: 100), Emerson talks about his experiences all the time. Here are some of the most famous examples: in *Nature* he reports an exaltation overtaking him on the occasion of crossing the commons; there also he talks about his fear of losing his sight and obliquely mentions the death of his brother (*Collected Works* 1: 10); in "The Divinity School Address" he relates his disappointment with his preacher, Barzillai Frost, who appeared to Emerson more spectral than the snow surrounding the church, making him think that "[he] would go to church no more" (1: 85); in "Circles" he confesses that taking risks exhilarates him and that nothing is sacred to him (*Collected Works* 2: 188); in "Friendship" he reveals that "a new person is to [him] a great event" that keeps him awake at night (2: 115); in "Illusions" he talks at some length about his visit to the Mammoth Cave in Kentucky and engages in a detailed self-reflection about his confused ways of perceiving the world (*Collected Works* 6: 165–66). Together, the essays outline an image of a man sick to death with New England genteelness; traversed with fears and dissatisfaction; desiring the acute feel of life, intense encounters, and a way to be quicker when it comes to change.

Students should recognize that just as "Experience" is not Emerson's only or even most personal essay, it is also not a site that registers the weakening of his optimism. Emerson's allegedly naive belief, formulated at the end of *Nature*, that a "revolution in things" will come so powerful that "prisons [and] enemies" will vanish "until evil is no more seen" (*Collected Works* 1: 45) and his theory of compensation are sometimes understood as tokens of an optimism that overlooks the injustices and inflictions of the world. But Emerson never meant "compensation" straightforwardly, as if to say that what is lost will be restored in the form in which it was lost and that sorrow will be no more. Surely he knew that a "dead friend, wife, brother, lover" would not be reincarnated (*Collected Works* 2: 73). By "compensation" he meant what he referred to as the "low prudence" of ordinary men (*Collected Works* 1: 115). "Low prudence" is a complex Emersonian concept that, among other things, signifies his affirmative attitude toward life: the conviction that a calamity must not be used as an excuse to hate life and that the endless singing of a lugubrious song must not be taken as the only convincing sign of mental maturity and social responsibility. The theory of compensation thus doesn't advocate overlooking the suffering, for how would it be possible not to register at least one's own pain? Instead, it proposes that saying yes to life, even when life seems nothing but a long "natural history of calamity," will help us to "slowly form" new relations after every disaster, relations that, in reconnecting us to the world, will afford us a "happier mind" (*Collected Works* 2: 72). The ethical effort of compensation is then not in denying suffering and sadness but in recognizing that sadness can't take us out of sadness—sorrow blocks our capacity to fight it, thus engendering its own prolongation. Compensation theory desires to work out the ways of bringing us closer to joyful passions, which alone have the power to move us to action and to fight sadness and suffering. In what follows I will argue that in "Experience" Emerson only intensifies his effort to celebrate the powers of affirmation, thus reinforcing the continuity of his thinking.

That said, instructors and students would do well to reconsider the essay as a significant breakthrough in Emerson's philosophy—the nature of which is explained in the essay itself. Atypically, given Emerson's style, readers will note that the essay is divided into two parts: the first part tells the story of how an ideated, merely mental experience of grief pointed to the failure of his philosophical and practical efforts to bring his mind closer to his body to introduce it to an intense, almost physical feel of life, which would count as experience. At first he is consumed by hopelessness that one will ever be able to really feel anything. But the second part of the essay, in complete accord with the compensation theory, argues itself out of that mournful paralysis. Realizing that demurral generated by defeat is only an excuse for postponing action and hence joy, he proceeds to affirmatively formulate a novel idea of what counts as experience and how to access it.

The philosophical efforts that the first part of "Experience" depicts as wrecked by grief were formulated already in Emerson's first book, *Nature* (1836), the introduction to which famously distinguished between ordinary and philosophical meanings of the word. It was then determined that in common parlance *nature* means everything that exists without being generated by men, such as "space, the air, the river, the leaf," whereas in philosophical vernacular, which interests Emerson most, *nature* means everything that is "NOT ME," that is "both nature and art, all other men and my own body" (*Collected Works* 1: 8). Emerson's definition of the philosophical meaning of the word accurately summarized most of the Western philosophical tradition that, insisting on ontological dualism, claimed the irreducibility of the mind to matter. For a variety of such idealisms, from Plato via Christianity to Descartes, nothing embodied and material, including the "I's" own body, is "I." For Plato, the matter of our bodies is a dense opaqueness blocking the journey of the mind to the light of pure ideas; for Christianity it is dust that will return to dust, whereas our real essence, a living spirit, will be resurrected. For Descartes our bodies, as well as the bodies of animals, are mere automata, our "I" residing in the pure cogito. For the tradition as a whole, my body is not me in the same way in which a tree, a bird, or a painting is not me.

Readers need to see more clearly that what Emerson will find shocking in the idealist taxonomy of the world is not the fact that art is designated as nature (on the premise that both are equally not me), or that the body is nature, or even that, according to those classifications, the "I" is the only unnatural phenomenon, hence more stylized and artificial than any artifact, the most fashioned phenomenon there is. Rather, the most candidly unacceptable consequence of idealism's version of the world's morphology will be for Emerson its insistence that we craft our "I" against the body, lead it in the opposite direction and so ever increase the distance between the two. If such a consequence is intolerable for him it is because to sever an "I" from the body, or mind from matter, is to divorce it from the sensations and affects that make us alive. It is to institute a fissure, in this life, between us and life. Thus, against all those who hurriedly presume that Emerson is an idealist, a commonplace pedagogical narrative, I would argue that from *Nature* to "Experience" Emerson will work against idealism's understanding of the mind as pure spirit in tension with everything that lives, our own body included. His fundamental claim, which can be traced in all his essays from *Nature* on, is that severing the self from what is external to it generates the most flagrantly fallacious existential condition of man being "disunited with himself" (*Collected Works* 1: 43). It "empties" man of all the world, since all the world is in fact not him, not in him. In such a condition we all "stand waiting, empty" (*Collected Works* 2: 184), like all those ideated abstractions emblematized in "The Divinity School Address" by Emerson's formalist preacher, whose cool disembodiedness rendered him spectral and unreal, positioning him in sharp contrast with the snow that concretely instantiated its coldness into reality ("the preacher [was] merely spectral . . . the snow storm was real" [*Collected Works* 1: 85]).

Everything Emerson thinks about is centered around his effort to make the "I" coincide with life, to feel itself living in and as its body, and through this "spirited" body to then gain access to everything else embodied in the world: other men, animals, trees, landscapes. It is such access to embodied reality that he will call "experience." To gain it he experiments with a series of behaviors that he narrates in the essays preceding "Experience." To name just a few: in "Circles" conversation, it is hoped, will enable us to circulate in and out of our minds, to transcend the barrier of the self that separates us from the "nature" constituted by other people. Emerson hopes that the gesture of abandoning ourselves to the minds of others, which is enacted by conversation, will fill our emptiness with what "surrounds" us but that, thanks to our spectrality, seems "trivial" to us in common hours (*Collected Works* 2: 184). In "Over-Soul" patient listening to our surroundings is promoted as a means of finally enacting the contact of the ghostly self with reality (Emerson imagines it as the "influx" of the "sea of life" into us, alternatively calling it ecstasy [2: 173]). In "Love" it is the rare experience of the initial moment of falling in love—when the "force" of passion assumes the lover's nature—that is identified as bringing us closer to reality (2: 104). And because affect—the encounter of the mind with something embodied—offers the intense feeling of being alive that constitutes experience, Emerson will require that it invest even the meaning of the most common words ("the simplest words,—we do not know what they mean, except when we love and aspire" [2: 189]).

"Experience" is of extraordinary relevance for understanding and teaching Emerson, because its first part announces the failure of his efforts to overcome the ghostliness of our abstracted selves, suggesting that if anything, his philosophy experienced only its own impossibility. It opens with the declaration of defeat in the face of idealism's victory. It laments how we are ontologically stuck in idealism's glass prison, since everything seems to be covered by a film of our thoughts; everything—perceptions, others, our bodies—seems to be mediated by ideas that slightly distort it to conform to our perspective, cushioning us in a safer, even if unreal, merely mental existence. The sensuous, the embodied, the affective, seems forever barred from us, and we are fastened to spectrality: "ghostlike we glide through nature, and should not know our place again" (*Collected Works* 3: 27). The world is around us, but without a body whose weight would land us somewhere, we remain unattached to the world, not of it. We glide through life, but life dodges us. And a languor overwhelms us, as if our "self" were always too slow to follow the speed of life, easily tiring and sleepy. Hence the generalized claim of the essay's opening: "sleep lingers all our lifetime about our eyes, as night hovers all day in the boughs of the fir-tree."

Even the self that is eager to live rather than expiate, as Emerson declared in "Self-Reliance" that his was, ends up expiating. To cancel its separateness as a self-sufficient ego that disembodies him into a ghostlike existence, that self was ready to pay more than the price of conversing, loving, and writing, none of which introduced him to the reality of what it is not. As he famously puts it in "Experience," "[F]or contact with [reality], we would even pay the costly price of sons and lovers" (*Collected Works* 3: 29). And pay he did, for when he says the first-person plural "we," he in fact means himself. He is the champion of losses, having won them all: first he loses his father when only eight years old; then in 1831 his first wife, Ellen Tucker, dies when he is twenty-eight years old; three years later, in 1834, his brother Edward dies all alone in Puerto Rico; two years after Edward, Charles, his other brother to whom he always felt closest, dies in New York City. And if he survives all of those losses thanks to being "compensated" by marrying again to the pious Lidian Jackson, with whom he had little Waldo, now, at the opening of "Experience," Waldo is dead too. Waldo's death announces an irreparable calamity—a cancellation of all compensation—since the death of a child is the death of the future, and thus the extinction of time. With all his prospects gone and his world shattered, Emerson feels that cessation is all he is left with: "Nothing is left us now but death. We look to that with a grim satisfaction, saying, there at least is reality that will not dodge us" (3: 29). The feeling described here is paradoxical, for in "nothing," Emerson finds something. In the midst of death there appears some sort of satisfaction triggered by the hope that a devastation so radical can't be grasped only mentally but totally, consuming both mind and body. And even if being consumed in that way would be "unhandsome," it would finally make Emerson feel alive, really experiencing. If the joy that comes from conversing with friends and lovers, or from writing poetry, doesn't make us shiver with life, suffering the loss of a child surely must, even if the tremor is that of horror. Emerson was far from expecting the perversion that meant that the quickening of his being would come through the death of all he loved. But there it is now, promising the "grim satisfaction" that it might afford an encounter with the real.

In fact, the prospect of finally managing to experience reality by living intense grief drugs Emerson into a bizarre mood where he wishes for more suffering ("What opium is instilled into all disaster"; "There are moods in which we court suffering, in the hope that there, at least, we shall find reality, sharp peaks and edges of truth" [*Collected Works* 3: 29]). Students would do well to understand that his primary interest in talking about grief is neither biographical nor invested in something like a more generalized, phenomenological description of the nature of mourning. Rather, it is ontological. For what he wants to know, as he explains, is whether an experience can be so intense as to make "souls . . . touch their objects" (3: 29). Might the death of a child bring about grief so intense that it will not only be felt bodily, like a real pain, but even more radically, taking us out of our minds all the way to their objects, enacting thus an ontological wizardry, the unity of mind and matter, soul and body, me and another, what is living and what is not? For grief, as he imagines it, will remake us by thoroughly unmaking us, so that as the self gets undone, in it the thin veil of thought that divests us from the real will be rent and we will fall hard on the real, smashed on "sharp peaks and edges of truth." This is how he reasons: if "some thing which . . . was a part of me, which could not be torn away without tearing me, nor enlarged without enriching me" dies, and so "falls off from me," then I must be torn away, I must be "falling off from me," no "me" remaining; that would be real (3: 29). For what was "me"—a cluster of mental representations, "colored . . . lenses" that "distort" reality and separate me from everything else—would be shattered (3: 43). What used to be "me" would then coincide with the real; at that point the soul would be introduced to its objects.

But that is not happening. Not because he is not grieving—to the contrary, he reports so much grief—but because while grieving he continues to live isolated in his self. And he interprets that continuation as a sign that nothing has really touched him: his body goes on, his grieving mind goes on, he writes and reads and converses, and, following the loss, he even doesn't find his life after loss meaningless. On that basis he learns that grief is merely mental and ideal. That is what he means when he calls it "shallow." Grief is for him purely psychic and incapable of bringing the mind into the vicinity of the body. As he writes, it doesn't "carry me one step into real nature," into what is not me; instead it reveals itself as something belonging to the domain of "me" and, therefore, like "me," is ghostly. It functions as a spectral protective screen that cushions us against reality. In grieving "we fall soft on [the] thought" that grieving is. That is why "grief too will make us idealists" (*Collected Works* 3: 29).

Emerson's insight sounds like a definitive acceptance that idealism can't be defeated and that we will forever remain grounded in the images given us by the "colored lenses" of our mind, "which paint the world their own hue, and each shows only what lies in its focus" (*Collected Works* 3: 30). We live in a world of nothing other than "the scene-painting and counterfeit" (3: 29), which for Emerson means that instead of giving us reality, unbeatable subjectivism always deals only illusion. "Illusion" and "subjectiveness" become the "lords of life" (3: 47), because we remain clapped in the fetters of our consciousness from which there is no exit; we will never know what the world looks like outside of our head, how things and beings are when we are not looking. Hence the famous verdict of the essay: "An innavigable sea washes with silent waves between us and the things we aim at" (3: 29). We are irrevocably isolated in our own minds, as though crazed in soundproof rooms.

Yet, if this ontological doom is indelible, why doesn't the essay end there or drift even deeper into the sadness caused by the metaphysical illness of idealism? For, as we know, it instead interrupts itself to start afresh.

The second part of "Experience" begins with a claim that the insights formulated in its first part must be rejected for ethical reasons: "But what help from these fineries. . . . We, I think, in these times, have had lessons enough of the futility of criticism" (*Collected Works* 3: 34). Thus, far from being acknowledged as inviolably correct, the work of the essay's first part is identified as mere "finery" and dismissed on the basis of being "critical," a concept that Emerson uses in a twofold sense. First, in the Kantian sense of a critique that seeks to determine the limitations of a faculty (hence, the critique of reason, judgment, or reflection). Emerson signals that he is using the word *criticism* in that sense when he immediately asserts "skepticisms" to be "not gratuitous" but "limitations" (3: 43). And second, *criticism* is used in the more colloquial sense of being negative about something—objecting, judging, and grumbling—an attitude that to his thinking dominates the minds of the times: "Objections and criticism we have had our fill of" (3: 34).

The problem with "objections" and negative "criticism" is that they enhance neither our thinking nor our actions but instead merely disorient both by trying to limit, question, or block them. And since there is nothing perfect—nothing that could avoid criticism and stand in the calm, righteous zone of what is perfectly pleasing—everything is exposed to it. Criticism thus becomes a universal ("omnipresent") attitude that, in devaluing everything, generates only the indifference of melancholia: "There are objections to every course of life and action, and the practical wisdom infers an indifferency, from the omnipresence of objection" (*Collected Works* 3: 35). For if—as the first part of the essay together with the spirit of the times proposed—it is in vain that we hope we will reach others, that we will relate to the world, that we will overcome our illusions and prejudices, and even that we will ever feel alive, what is the point in trying anything? Because this pessimism makes everything equally illusory, everything becomes a point of indifference. Far from being a vestige of ethical maturity and political realism, pessimism—as well as the negative and the judgmental on which it rides—is thus only a vehicle of indifference, which, because it demobilizes investment and interest in others, is unethical. Pessimism is merely an attitude of the beautiful soul that claims our engagements with the world are not really consequential in order to make them really impossible. That is why such an attitude must be resisted—just as Emerson resists it when he interrupts his essay—to enable the force of the affirmative that it negates. "Skepticisms are . . . limitations of the affirmative statement" (3: 43), but demystifying their spell will weaken the isolation to which it consigns us (thereby also weakening our "subjectiveness"), thus helping the force of affirmation.

What exactly the new affirmative theory will look like we don't yet know, trapped as we are in idealism and subjectivism. But in what Emerson calls our "liberated moments"—rare instants when we feel, without knowing how or why, that the yoke of limiting subjectivism is loosening—we realize that the most essential, most affirmative attitude available to us now is to *believe* in the possibility of affirmation even if we can't philosophically formulate it or empirically know it. Emerson is asking us to believe in the possibility of everything the first part of the essay declared impossible, for "*the universal impulse to believe* . . . is the material circumstance, and is the principal fact in the history of the globe" (*Collected Works* 3: 42). It is the force of belief against everything we know that will make us begin to live as if things and beings outside our minds were perhaps palpable and not the mere pictures we paint of them; it will make us begin to behave as if souls can touch their objects, as if men and women "were real" ("treat the men and women well: treat them as if they were real; perhaps they are" [3: 35]). And this new way of behaving will slowly reveal to us that the continuity of what is supposed to be substantially different (mind and body, souls and objects) is indeed possible. Out of this humble and uncertain beginning— out of a breeze of joy that traverses us thanks to the fragile belief in the unity of mind and object—and despite all pessimism and negativity, the new affirmative theory will be glimpsed. First we live, then we think: "In liberated moments, we know that a new picture of life . . . is already possible; the elements already exist in many minds around you, of a doctrine of life which shall transcend any written record we have" (3: 43).

Even if only obliquely, Emerson must have included himself in the cluster of minds he references here, since the second part of the essay actually formulates some elements of the new theory of life that can at the moment, he claims, only be prognosticated. Its basic premise derives from the claim that the doubling of life—the image of it in which we live and the reality of it that remains inaccessible to us—must be fallacious, for "life will be imaged, but cannot be divided nor doubled. Any invasion of its unity would be chaos." If dualism were real, then either souls or feelings would be acknowledged as "twin-born" material and living reality, some sort of "co-life" running parallel with real life, in which case souls would be reduced to some "spectral" accompaniment of the real, less valued than the real (*Collected Works* 3: 45). Or, alternatively, the embodied would be acknowledged as lifeless and inert matter, an irrelevant appendage to the spirited. Dualism generates an uneven status of minds and bodies, and the consequences, in both variants, would be ethically disastrous.

To avoid this ethical crisis, an affirmative philosophy must be premised—this is the essence of the belief that will bring it about—on the substantial unity of the embodied and the mental. The one and the same substance of which everything is made sometimes expresses itself as consciousness, other times as bodies, but the two are versions of the same. In a similar way, Emerson says, signaling that he understands Christianity as a monistic theology, in Christian vocabulary, it is sometimes called the spirit or God, other times the "flesh of his body" (*Collected Works* 3: 42). Spirit and matter are manners of the same substance.

As "Experience" makes explicit, the new affirmative philosophy to come will have to be formulated according to the model of the "vast affirmative being." Just as that being "swallows" all negations, so the "new philosophy must take them [skepticisms, limitations] in, and make affirmations outside of them" (*Collected Works* 3: 43). *Yes* to *no* undoes the power of the *no*. That is the final lesson of "Experience." Subjectiveness can't be overcome and for that reason is our "lord of life," but that conclusion of the first part of the essay is, by the affirmative twist of its second part, shown to be an erroneous consequence of subjectiveness itself. For affirmative philosophy will show us how to overcome the "subjectiveness" that "I find . . . in my way," revealing to us that even if it is true that "I am a fragment" of the totality of the world, "subjectiveness" is only "a fragment of me" (3: 47). Subjectiveness is therefore already transcended by the forces of life that are in us, if not accessible to us—forces that will "swallow" it in the same way that vast affirmative being swallows all such negations. When that happens—when the intense life in us transcends the limitations imposed on it—we will come closer to reality, to the "sharp peaks and edges of truth." We will finally come to know what experience is.

Teaching Emerson in
the Nineteenth-Century Poetry Course

Christoph Irmscher

In *Nature* (1836) and even more assertively in "The Poet" (1844), Emerson expressed his vision of a poet who would "integrate all the parts" of the world (*Collected Works* 1: 9). This was a vision both somewhat aristocratic (in that the poet can do what we currently can't) and democratic (since ideally, if we pay attention to Emerson, we are all going to be such poets). Emerson himself felt that he "was a poet born," as he wrote in a letter to his future wife Lydia ("Lidian") Jackson, though he added that his voice was a "husky" one (*Selected Letters* 142–43). This assessment was echoed in a recent review, by the poet Dan Chiasson, of a volume of Emerson's poems. It says something about Emerson's poetry that, more than 150 years after the publication of his first collection, it still packs enough of a punch to get a bad review in *The New Yorker*.[1]

I regularly teach a selection of Emerson's poems in my survey of nineteenth-century American poetry. We use only one textbook in this class, the college edition of John Hollander's anthology *American Poetry: The Nineteenth Century*, so as not to distract ourselves with a mass of supplementary material from the poetry itself. My challenge in this class is how to treat the works of the poets we discuss not only historically (i.e., in relation to the poets who came before and after them) but also as literary works in their own right. In order to give Emerson the poet a fair hearing, I discuss his poems mostly without any reference to his essays. Instead, I encourage my students to immerse themselves in the poems themselves, to take at face value what they ask us to do.

I often begin with "Merlin I," and although I dutifully explain—supported by Hollander's explanatory note (983)—that Emerson's Merlin has more in common with the Welsh bard Myrddin Wyllt than with Geoffrey of Monmouth's much better-known reinvention of that figure as the wizard at King Arthur's court, I don't mind when my students confuse the two. I usually ask a student to read out loud the poem's first section. For many, the poem's assertive, life-affirming tone—its take-no-prisoners attitude to what it identifies as the right kind of writing—comes as a surprise, especially after the tentative mode of Lydia Sigourney ("Think ye"?) and the safe backward glances in William Cullen Bryant's work. "Thy trivial harp will never please / Or fill my craving ear," exclaims Emerson's speaker. "Its chords should ring as blows the breeze, / Free, peremptory, clear" (*Collected Works* 9: 223). As one student observed, "This is a glimpse of the wildness Bryant only remembers." Students like the distinction Emerson makes between the dainty sounds of the "serenader" and the thunderous noises made by the poet, who bangs on the piano with a hammer or a mace and thus tells us of a world beyond our understanding, where we travel among "Secrets of the solar track, / Sparks of the supersolar blaze" (9: 224). These sibilant lines prepare us for the fantasy of sounds that follow, in which the speaker, in rapid succession, imagines forest trees rocked by the wind, rivers breaking through their wintry prison of ice, the beating of human hearts, cannons booming on battlefields, and so on.

Students comment that it's less important what any of this means than what it *does*, which quickly opens up for them, and their instructor too, a new view of Emerson's work as a poet. For *work* it is, and the traces of the poet's labors have attached themselves permanently to his texts. Emerson didn't want his poems to be exercises in shallow versification. What he was after was poetry as *lived* experience, poems that would have as much of an effect on us as they did on him when he was writing them. That is why he makes us watch the poet "climb / For his rhyme," moving up the "stairway of surprise" (*Collected Works* 9: 224). A miniversion of Dante's ascent toward paradise, perhaps. But the revelation at the end of Emerson's "Merlin I" comes "sudden, at unawares," and it's over before the poet-pilgrim knows what it really was. In Emerson's poetry, perfection remains a goal, not a secure possession (9: 225).

In my experience, it's not at all difficult to plead for the relevance of Emerson's poetry in classrooms filled with students who grew up reading Harry Potter novels. They already know about worlds to which "a greater spirit bids thee forth / Than the grey dreams which thee detain" ("Monadnoc," *Collected Works* 9: 121). Once they get hooked on Emerson the poet, they find a universe more animated with the powers of nonhuman presences than that of Walt Whitman or Emily Dickinson, a world in which things constantly change shapes and the speaking self surrenders its authority to the voices of trees, animals, mountains, rivers. Emerson once wonderfully describes nature as the "infinite paroquet" ("Xenophanes," 9: 269), as repeating one and the same sound but in so many different manifestations. Finding the one in the many and many in the one, experiencing the world as constant metamorphosis, is the source of never-ending pleasure: "It makes us dance and sing. It delights all. All men are poets" ("Poetry and English Poetry," *Later Lectures* 1: 303).

Emerson's poetry, while not as carefully crafted and self-consciously hermetic as that of Dickinson and not as sensuously raucous as that of Whitman, is more spell than cadence, more magical than resonant. It has an incantatory quality, with nouns piling on nouns, as if the sheer act of uttering words could make something happen. We don't usually think of Emerson as pagan,[2] but in poems such as "Woodnotes" a sensibility announces itself that I have found readily speaks to readers of Rick Riordan's bestselling Percy Jackson series.[3] Consider the description of the "eternal Pan" in "Woodnotes II," also included in Hollander's anthology, in words spoken by a pine tree:

> He is the essence that inquires.
> He is the axis of the star;
> He is the sparkle of the spar;
> He is the heart of every creature;
> He is the meaning of each feature;
> And his mind is the sky,
> Than all it holds more deep, more high.   (*Collected Works* 9: 113)

When I teach Emerson in the graduate version of this course, I occasionally find it helpful to make connections with Jane Bennett's theory of vital materialism, which in many ways is merely an update of the kind of thinking Emerson would have encountered in the works of, for example, the German philosopher Johann Gottfried Herder. Of particular relevance here is Herder's critique of Spinoza, notably Herder's refusal to find the world of things enlivened by anything other than God's will. Matter, stipulates Herder, is not "dead but lives, for in it . . . manifold living forces are at work" (Bennett 92–93; Herder 64).

Emerson's friend, the poet Caroline Sturgis, once said about his "Bacchus" (also included in Hollander's anthology) that it "made the day wider" (*Collected Works* 9: lxviii). The liberating, life-affirming impact of Emerson's poetry on a generation of readers who had barely survived Puritanism is perhaps lost on college students today. However, a poem such as "Blight" allows us to situate his reverence for nature—a nature that we should never think of as separate from us—in the context of a critique of the scientific method. An ecocritical reading of the poem would separate the "scholars" invading the hills, pillaging nature for what it might yield to them (classificatory data, profit), from those who choose to tread lightly on the earth, wanting to imagine themselves as, in Emerson words, "part of the round day, related to the sun." In language that will resonate with students who have an interest in ecology, Emerson contrasts the plundering "thieves / And pirates of the universe" to the gentle "unitarians of the united world" of the past, who weren't yet "strangers to the stars" (9: 273–74).

In "Saadi" Emerson more fully develops a poetics grounded in the enjoyment of everything life has to offer in the here and now. (The fact that this poem is a tribute to a Muslim, the medieval Persian poet Saadi Shirazi, adds modern relevance to Emerson's text.) Saadi does not need to leave his cottage to conjure a magical world where "life pulsates in rock or tree" (*Collected Works* 9: 247). His muse tells him that the doors to paradise are the people around him: his neighbors, his servants, those who listen to his poetry. Saadi embodies precisely the commitment to one's immediate environment the contemporary nature writer Scott Russell Sanders urges us to rediscover in his book *Staying Put: Making a Home in a Restless World*.

On the afternoon of 1 January 1863, President Lincoln issued the Emancipation Proclamation, freeing, at least on paper, millions of enslaved human beings in the country. At a special jubilee concert held that evening in Boston's Music Hall, Emerson read his "Boston Hymn" with a steady, beautiful voice, observed Henry James, who had been in the audience. "The slave is owner," thundered Emerson, "And ever was. Pay him" (*Collected Works* 9: 383). Thanks to the debate about reparations for slavery that was recently initiated by Ta-Nehisi Coates, these lines sound more pertinent than ever.

That same evening, Emerson repeated his performance at a private reception at the twenty-six-acre estate of the wealthy merchant George L. Stearns in Medford, Massachusetts. Stearns and his wife, Mary, were staunch abolitionists, proud of having provided money and arms to John Brown. In fact, the party at their house was in honor of Brown, whose life had ended at the gallows three years before. A statue of Brown was unveiled, and Emerson read his poem again, this time before a much smaller audience, which included Bronson Alcott and his daughter Louisa May; Julia Ward Howe, author of "The Battle Hymn of the Republic"; and William Lloyd Garrison (Reynolds, *John Brown* 3–12). To commemorate the evening, Mary Stearns afterward asked Emerson and other attendees to send her written tributes to Brown. She provided them with special paper, thick and adorned with red borders. Emerson, who had already left for a lecture tour, complied but not without apologizing for having wasted her paper: "I send the copy of the Hymn, although the eagerness to write fairly on your sumptuous paper has cost you, by blot and error, two sheets."[4] Mary Stearns had Emerson's poem, along with other entries by Louisa May Alcott, Lydia Maria Child, and the transcendentalist minister Samuel Johnson, bound into an album that she dedicated to her son Henry, an ardent admirer of John Brown. The album and Emerson's letters to Stearns are now among the holdings of the Lilly Library at Indiana University.

A fairly incidental story, some might say, but not to my undergraduates. In my classes, I regularly assign research projects involving original materials from the Lilly Library, to provide a more hands-on experience to undergird our discussions in the classroom. An immediate benefit of these projects is that they allow my students to cast themselves in the role of investigators, rather than the docile recipients of a professor's accumulated wisdom. While I am happy to help when asked, these projects remain the responsibility of the individual researchers. Students will, I tell them, eventually know more about their chosen sources (an autograph poem, a letter, a journal entry) than I do. The student who transcribed the (still unpublished) Emerson letter to Stearns was excited to know more about the mundane side of Emerson it revealed. It showed, she wrote, not "Man Thinking" but "*Emerson* Thinking" (obviously she had by now read "The American Scholar"). She relished the subtle irony Emerson displayed when he reminded Stearns of the "cost" of her "sumptuous" paper, which he had so carelessly wasted when he wrote out a fair copy of his poem for her album. Emerson must have known how odd his poetic challenge to compensate the slave had sounded in Stearns's mansion on the night Lincoln had freed the slaves.

Stories such as this one help to anchor Emerson's poetry in real-life contexts. I am lucky to have the Lilly Library's collections in my backyard, but similar experiences can be provided to students almost anywhere. For example, scans of both the Boston and the London editions of Emerson's first volume of poetry, *Poems* (1847), are freely available on *Google Books, Wikisource,* and *Archive* *.org.* Emerson had rushed his manuscript to his London printer, whose typesetter often had trouble deciphering his handwriting. Students will be amused to find the discrepancies between the two editions—and they will wonder what difference it makes when Saadi (in the British edition) "shines" rather than "smiles," as he does in the Emerson-approved version.

We mostly teach poems by themselves, in splendid isolation from the contexts for which they were intended. Studying the collection in which a poem was first published or the sequence in which it was first written can be an eye-opening experience for undergraduates, and I regularly assign first editions of Emerson's poetry—in digital or physical form—for independent research projects. Is it a coincidence, for example, that in *Poems* Emerson's life-affirming "Saadi" is preceded by "The House," a poem invoking the "cadence of the whirling world / Which dances round the sun" (*Collected Works* 9: 241)? And was Emerson making a point when he decided to have "Saadi" followed by the deceptively titled "Holidays," in which the poet tells himself to grow up and accept that he "has duties" (9: 252)?

For his final paper in a class on transcendentalism I taught a few years ago, one of my students, Robert Smith, took it upon himself to read some of Emerson's sermons, specifically the one on the Lord's Supper, given when he resigned his ministry (Myerson, *Transcendentalism* 68–78). Robert discovered that even when Emerson dealt with biblical texts, he was a "creative reader," a role he would more fully explore in "The American Scholar." Creative reading makes the text come alive for us today. Whatever facet we find significant (and whatever other facets we decide to discard or ignore) always depends, Robert wrote, "on the reality of the era in which we live." Creative reading is proudly selective, unabashedly presentist, perhaps even biased. It focuses on what is good in a poem and not on what is bad—not on the "dust and motes," as Thoreau once wrote, but "on the light and air which float them" ("Best Criticism"). The beauty of this approach, at least in Emerson's case, is that it derives its legitimacy from the author's own practice.

This is the eclectic method of interpretation, then, that shapes my teaching of Emerson's poems—poems that were neglected or shunted aside and won't, and manifestly don't want to, satisfy the critic's desire for a self-sufficient work of art. I will never insist that students clarify every single line in an Emerson poem. Instead, I encourage them to add to our discussions whatever else they are passionate about in their own previous or current reading, whether that be Rick Riordan or Ta-Nehisi Coates. And when my students do their research, I invite them to think about how their projects might spill over into their own lives. Creative reading means listening to Emerson when he imagines how people once listened to Saadi the poet—with rapt attention, sympathetically, "in ecstasy." Above all, it means listening to yourself as you read. As for the literary critic, "spare thy vanity" (*Collected Works* 9: 244).

NOTES

[1] For a reevaluation of Emerson as a poet, see Irmscher.

[2] See Emerson's journal entry from October–November 1845: "Does he [Swedenborg] not know . . . that every poetic mind is a pagan, and to this day prefers Olympian Jove, Apollo, & the Muses & the Fates, to all the barbarous indigestion of Calvin & the Middle Ages?" (*Journals* 9: 313–14).

[3] In *The Battle of the Labyrinth*, demigod Percy Jackson and his friends discover the great god Pan in the underworld, but he is already dying: "The wild . . . is so small now, so shattered, that no god can save it. My realm is gone" (Riordan 314).

[4] Emerson to Mary Stearns, 10 Jan. 1863.

Teaching Emerson's Antislavery Writings

Len Gougeon

Emerson's antislavery writings are an important component of his canon. The relatively recent addition of these texts broadens our understanding of Emerson as a central figure of nineteenth-century American culture, while also aiding in the presentation of his life and thought in the classroom. One of the most challenging aspects of teaching Emerson is establishing his relevance to the issues of life in the modern world. While many scholars see him as America's first public intellectual, to nonexperts his writings often seem abstract and remote. Fortunately, the works produced in his long career in the cause of antislavery can serve as a helpful corrective. They show that Emerson was no aloof scholar. He was an active, engaged, and determined social reformer who addressed head-on many of the challenging issues that still face American society today. I usually teach selections from Emerson's antislavery writings in conjunction with other examples of antebellum reform writing, specifically Frederick Douglass's *Narrative of the Life of Frederick Douglass, an American Slave, Written by Himself* and Margaret Fuller's *Woman in the Nineteenth Century* (both 1845). Both of these works show a strong Emersonian influence. Like Emerson's reform writings, they demonstrate that transcendental values and principles, ridiculed by some contemporaries as intellectual moonshine, could be effectively deployed in the pursuit of social justice. In teaching Emerson's antislavery writings, it is helpful to know something about his active participation in this, the most important reform movement of the antebellum period.[1]

Emerson's first major antislavery address, "The Emancipation of the Negroes in the British West Indies" (1844), celebrated the abolition of slavery throughout the British Empire a decade earlier. It was presented before a large audience in his hometown of Concord, Massachusetts. The town had already gained a reputation as a "transcendental Mecca" (Conway), and it is not surprising that a number of notable transcendentalists were there for the occasion. Among them were Margaret Fuller, Bronson Alcott, and Henry David Thoreau. The crowd was there primarily to hear Emerson speak, but also on the program that day was a young, talented black orator and former slave who worked for William Lloyd Garrison's American Anti-Slavery Society. Frederick Douglass was then on the threshold of a career that would eventually catapult him into national prominence as the nation's best-known and most respected African American orator and reformer.

In his speech, Emerson applauded the efforts of the West Indian slaves themselves in winning their freedom. He emphasized their personal courage in this collective effort. "They won the pity and respect which they have received," he stated, "by their powers and native endowments. I think this is a circumstance of the highest import. Their whole future is in it" (*Emerson's Antislavery*

Writings 30). The reason this circumstance was so important to Emerson was because he believed personal courage was essential in the work of reform. As he declared in "Self-Reliance" (1841), "God will not have his work made manifest by cowards" (*Collected Works* 2: 28). Every individual must live in accordance with personal values that give meaning, purpose, and dignity to life. Thus, for Emerson, "Nothing is at last sacred but the integrity of your own mind" (2: 30). It is this personal sense of integrity and self-worth that informs the individual's relationship with society. It must be maintained at all costs, even in the presence of oppression, since "[n]othing can bring you peace but yourself. Nothing can bring you peace but the triumph of principles" (2: 51). For Emerson, self-reliance was an essential prerequisite for social reform. You must believe in yourself before you can believe in a cause. This is a point often missed by contemporary critics who view Emerson's emphasis on self-reliance as antithetical to collective social action. Emerson saw no such contradiction. In his "Lecture on Slavery" (1855) he made this point explicitly. "But whilst I insist on the doctrine of the independence and inspiration of the individual," he declared, "I do not cripple but exalt the social action. . . . A wise man delights in the power of many people" (*Emerson's Antislavery Writings* 103). This "power" is especially important in a democracy, where "what great masses of men wish done, will be done" (28). It is at work in nature as well as in human society. As Emerson goes on to note in his "Emancipation" address, it is "the grand style of nature," and

> it will save only what is worth saving: and it saves not by compassion, but by power. . . . So now, the arrival in the world of men such as Toussaint, and the Haytian heroes, or of the leaders of their race in Barbadoes and Jamaica, outweighs in good omen all the English and American humanity. . . . [T]he might and the right are here: here is the anti-slave: here is man: and if you have man, black or white is an insignificance.   (30–31)

Douglass must have been thrilled as he heard these words. In less than a year, he would publish a compelling first-person account of his own transformation into the "anti-slave" in *Narrative of the Life of Frederick Douglass*. In this classic work, Douglass demonstrates through his transformational struggle with the slave-breaker Edward Covey that belief in oneself is a necessary antecedent to both resistance and reform. In the same year, Fuller would make a striking declaration of the rights and responsibilities of American women in *Woman in the Nineteenth Century*. In this work she, like Emerson and Douglass, emphasizes the integral relationship between self-reliance and collective social action. "Union is only possible to those who are units," she declared (106).

Emerson spoke again the following year on the anniversary of West Indian emancipation. He used the occasion to excoriate the racism and vile sentiment conveyed by what is referred to today as the infamous n-word. This brief address offers an excellent opportunity to raise the issue of racial "branding" with students. The question to be asked is, "Why was Emerson so obviously outraged by this one particular word?"—a question that resonates loudly today. "What is the defense of Slavery?" he asked. "What is the irresistible argument by which every plea of humanity and reason has hitherto been borne down?" The argument is summed up with one word: "*Niggers!*—a word which . . . is reckoned stronger than heaven." "They who say it and they who hear it," said Emerson, "think it the voice of nature and fate" proclaiming an inescapable "inferiority of race" that renders all the arguments of the reformer moot (*Emerson's Antislavery Writings* 35, 36). This obscene racism struck at the very heart of Emerson's transcendental notion of divine justice and human dignity. "This damnable atheism," he thundered, violated "the sentiment of right," which is the very basis of civilization (37). Emerson was staunchly opposed to the racist theories of his day, on both moral and scientific grounds. He was convinced, before Darwin, that we all evolved from the same source. He declared in "Self-Reliance" that "All men have my blood, and I have all men's" (*Collected Works* 2: 41). Also, the notion of a fixed and determinate reality that denied human freedom to an entire race violated his most fundamental beliefs. In his early essay "Circles" (1841), he insisted that "[t]he universe is fluid and volatile," and he challenged all efforts to stifle this progressive flow. His goal was always to "unsettle all things" (2: 179, 188). He also believed that the universe was moral at its core, and any theory of law or science that attempted to visit upon any group of people a damning determinism was clearly out of sync with moral law. Like slavery itself, theories of deterministic racial inferiority were clearly inconsistent "with the principles on which the world is built" (*Emerson's Antislavery Writings* 86–87). Those principles constitute a divine "Higher Law," hence Emerson's declaration that the deterministic racism expressed in the word *niggers* is a "damnable atheism." He believed that we all share equally in the divine "Over-Soul," and in a later lecture called "Morals," he condemned the Supreme Court's infamous Dred Scott decision (1857), which declared slaves and their descendants to be property, as a "blasphemy [that] . . . does not honor the moral perceptions of the people" (*Later Lectures* 2: 140).

Emerson's resistance to slavery grew more militant throughout the 1840s. He accepted invitations to speak at antislavery gatherings despite growing opposition to the movement. Cheap southern cotton was a source of profit for northern textile mill owners, and these "gentlemen of property and standing" (Richards 3) as well as others who gained indirectly from the institution of slavery were determined to resist any movement that threatened change. The "Lords of the Loom," as Charles Sumner called them, found common ground with the "Lords of the Lash" (Taylor 267). National tension grew following the Mexican-American War (1846–48), which added a vast territory to the nation. Would the new states carved out of this territory be slave or free? Congress attempted to defuse the situation with the Compromise of 1850, which consisted of five separate bills. The Fugitive Slave Law, passed in September 1850, was one of them. It required that free-state citizens cooperate with authorities in the arrest and detention of people accused of being fugitive slaves. It also mandated substantial fines and imprisonment for those who aided in the escape of fugitive slaves. Before the passage of this law, fugitives who made it to a free state like Massachusetts were protected by personal liberty laws that forbade their forcible return. The new federal law, in effect, voided such protections and made all free citizens potential slave catchers. Not surprisingly, the law caused an uproar among northerners, many of whom had been indifferent to the slavery question earlier. Emerson was shocked, appalled, and outraged by the measure. He was especially angry that Massachusetts's own senator Daniel Webster had vigorously supported passage of the law. Such a backward development challenged Emerson's faith in moral progress. At first, most believed that the law simply could not be enforced. But after several attempts were made to do so, even in Boston, it was clear that the federal government had every intention of enforcing the law. Emerson responded. In a letter published in Garrison's *The Liberator*, he called for militant civil disobedience. "At this moment," he wrote, "it seems imperative that every lover of human rights should, in every manner, singly or socially, in private and in public, by voice and by pen—and, first of all, by substantial help and hospitality to the slave, and defending him against his hunters,—enter his protest for humanity against the detestable statute of the last Congress" (*Emerson's Antislavery Writings* 51).

Just weeks after Emerson's letter appeared in *The Liberator*, a young fugitive named Thomas Sims was seized by authorities in Boston and, after a brief hearing before Chief Justice Lemuel Shaw, he was returned to his "owner" in Savannah, Georgia, where he was publicly whipped. The South had its victory. It was this event that prompted Emerson's "Address to the Citizens of Concord on the Fugitive Slave Law," which he delivered on 3 May 1851. It is a dramatic piece. Emerson's anger is palpable. In teaching Emerson's antislavery writings, this address is my favorite. It shows clearly how Emerson deployed his transcendental principles in addressing what was now a social and political crisis. In setting up classroom discussion, I provide students with the following set of questions in advance. The goal is to demonstrate how Emerson's argument is the product of his transcendental beliefs.

> What is the basis for Emerson's opposition to the Fugitive Slave Law? (Answer: Intuitively perceived truth, i.e., "Higher Law.")
>
> Could his argument be used against *any law* that a citizen does not like? (Answer: In a moral universe, only unjust laws elicit widespread opposition, as in the civil rights movement.)
>
> Why is Emerson so especially angry with Daniel Webster? (Answer: Webster, a natural conservative, supports the status quo even though it is corrupt. Because slavery is a historical reality, he believes it should continue. This is a great example of "a foolish consistency" [*Collected Works* 2: 23].)
>
> What gross deficiency of American society does the passage of the Fugitive Slave Law reveal? (Answer: Materialism. Slavery is tolerated in the North and South because it is integral to a robust economy. Morality is subordinate. Each of these points is developed below.)

In "Self-Reliance" Emerson famously declares, "Society is a joint-stock company in which the members agree for the better securing of his bread to each shareholder, to surrender the liberty and culture of the eater. The virtue in most request is conformity" (*Collected Works* 2: 29). The goal of such conformity is to ensure that the material status quo is undisturbed. People who value material comfort more than social justice, in Emerson's view, do so because they lack moral and spiritual substance. Their "reliance on Property" erodes the dignity of life, as they "measure their esteem of each other by what each has, and not by what each is" (2: 49). Slavery is a toxic by-product of this corrosive materialism. It defines people as property and seduces ostensibly moral citizens into tolerating a gross immorality because it is both legal and profitable. In his address, Emerson says, "Boston, spoiled by prosperity, must bow its ancient honor in the dust, and make us irretrievably ashamed." Recent events had clearly demonstrated that individuality and self-reliance, the keys to moral conduct, were subverted, as prominent citizens—representatives of the "establishment"—cooperated in the reenslavement of Thomas Sims: "the whole wealth and power of Boston . . . are thrown into the scale of crime; and the poor black boy, whom the fame of Boston had reached in the recesses of a rice-swamp . . . on arriving here finds all this force employed to catch him" (*Emerson's Antislavery Writings* 56).

At this point, I often remind my students that transcendentalists believed that every individual knows right from wrong through intuition and instinct. Emerson called this the "sentiment of right," as noted earlier. This concept is empowering to any individual who feels compelled to oppose an immoral law that everyone else seems willing to obey. Famous reformers like Mohandas Gandhi and Martin Luther King, Jr., found in Emerson a confirmation of their own beliefs in moral self-reliance. Many transcendentalists saw this principle at work in the Founding Fathers' declaration of "self-evident" truths. In our own time, the United Nations' Universal Declaration of Human Rights reflects this idea when it refers to "the equal and inalienable rights of all members of the human family." The document also notes that "disregard and contempt for human rights have resulted in barbarous acts which have outraged the conscience of mankind." (In discussing this, I usually ask my students if they think that humanity has a "universal conscience" and, if so, what its source is.) Emerson anticipates the modern notion of universal human rights when he asserts that the Fugitive Slave Law is an abomination because "it is contrary to the primal sentiment of duty" and, therefore, all truly moral people are "found to be [its] natural enemies." Indeed, he declares, "If our resistance to this law is not right, there is no right" (*Emerson's Antislavery Writings* 58, 57). Slavery, for Emerson, was a crime against humanity.

Here, I usually ask my students how one can know when a law is immoral. The answer usually gets around to the idea that you just "know it" because you can see and feel the injustice, as in forced segregation. This is, of course, Emerson's point. I sometimes tell my students the story of Rosa Parks, the African American woman who many believe sparked the modern civil rights movement by refusing to give up her seat on a Montgomery, Alabama, bus to a white man because she felt the law requiring her to do so was unjust. Her action from principle was intuitive, self-reliant, and very Emersonian.

In "Address to the Citizens of Concord," Emerson saves his harshest criticism for Daniel Webster, one of the most respected men in America at the time. Because Webster was willing to sacrifice morality to placate the South, Emerson refers to him as "a white slave" (*Emerson's Antislavery Writings* 65). According to Emerson, Webster claims to be a patriot and applauds the Founding Fathers, but he is actually an obedient servant of a corrupt status quo, a conservative defender of what is rather than a crusader for what should be. "In Massachusetts, in 1776," Emerson proclaims, "he would, beyond all question, have been a refugee. He praises Adams and Jefferson; but it is a past Adams and Jefferson that his mind can entertain. A present Adams and Jefferson he would denounce." Webster has failed as a leader because "he has no moral perception, no moral sentiment," which, for a transcendentalist, is an unpardonable sin. Webster's material goal was to preserve the Union at all costs, but Emerson insists that "as soon as the Constitution ordains an immoral law, it ordains disunion" (67). Therefore, "this law must be made inoperative. It must be abrogated and wiped out of the statute book; but whilst it stands there, it must be disobeyed" (71).

In summary, this address, like Emerson's other antislavery writings, offers an excellent view of transcendentalism in action. Resistance to the Fugitive Slave Law is based on an intuitively perceived "Higher Law." In a society that insists on conformity, such resistance requires a courageous commitment to self-reliance. In 1850 a lack of self-reliance and moral courage in national leaders precipitated a national crisis. Enacting immoral laws to support an immoral institution brought social protests and civil unrest, as good people resisted the evil through civil disobedience. The conflict came about because of an immoral compromise in the past that was reinforced by the gross materialism of the present. This "foolish consistency" led to a social and moral crisis. Finally, the primal sin of slavery itself was that it denied the most fundamental principle of transcendentalism, the divine unity and universal dignity of all human beings.

NOTE

[1] *Emerson's Antislavery Writings*, edited by Gougeon and Myerson, is the standard scholarly edition. The collection includes a detailed historical introduction and abundant annotations for all selections.

Teaching the Practical Emerson through the Sermons and the Early Lectures

Carolyn R. Maibor

Like many public institutions of higher learning, Framingham State University's students come predominantly from middle- and working-class backgrounds. For them—and their families—a college education has far more to do with finding a job than finding themselves. The study of literature (or any of the humanities) is already a hard sell, and an author such as Emerson, whom students might well perceive as an abstruse writer unconcerned with helping us negotiate the difficulties of living in the real world, presents a particular challenge. And the anthologies don't help. There are good reasons to anthologize the best and most widely read of Emerson's essays; however, immediately confronting a class with a text like *Nature* or even "The American Scholar" only confirms students' worst fears: his style is contradictory and frustrating and punctuated by obscure allusions. But there is a "practical Emerson" very much concerned with the dilemma of most undergraduates, whatever their backgrounds: finding meaningful work that will bring them not only self-fulfillment but also a purposeful connection to their surroundings and a means of contributing to others. Good results flow from beginning with some of the lesser-known texts, such as the 1832 sermon "Find Your Calling" and the 1837 lectures "Trades and Professions" and "Doctrine of the Hands." These afford students a way into Emerson and show overtly how relevant Emerson's words from the nineteenth century are to today. Building on this foundation, readers become receptive to the effort the more complex and esoteric texts demand.

In a survey course with only a few classes to devote to Emerson, "Find Your Calling" (sermon 143) has the advantage of being short and accessible. First delivered in 1832, the same year Emerson would rebuff his own familial and societal pressures and resign from the ministry, the sermon outlines both the spiritual and practical concerns at stake in choosing a vocation. Cleverly targeted to two different audiences, it aims at inspiring young congregants to take seriously the need to find work that will be meaningful to them and cautioning older congregants against interfering in that process, however well-intentioned—something most students facing a Thanksgiving table full of relatives asking, "And what are you going to do with that major?" can appreciate.

The opening line of the sermon connects the highest spiritual concerns with the most mundane: "The Christian doctrine of the immortality of the soul gives the greatest importance to all the events of this life as they in some degree affect the whole being of the soul" (*Complete Sermons* 4: 65). While students may not share the particular religious perspective presented, it is worth pointing out the underlying emphasis Emerson places on the quotidian. This emphasis will prepare students to appreciate Emerson's experience of the sublime crossing the muddy commons in *Nature* and help illuminate his call at the end of "The American Scholar" for a "philosophy of the street" and insight into today (*Collected Works* 1: 67). It is what you do every day—the general course of your life—that matters.

In stressing the relation between work and self-development—you are what you do—Emerson emphasizes the high stakes involved in choosing and pursuing a profession (the pressure of which most students already feel). But through his emphasis on the education one receives through all kinds of work and the need for a vast diversity of workers, Emerson also gives his young audience members, both then and now, a defense against those who value only certain professions. In a list that sounds more reminiscent of Whitman than a passage from Emerson, the third paragraph of the sermon asks us to "[l]ook at the great throng the city presents. Consider the variety of callings and pursuits," and goes on to name a number of workers, including everything from a laborer to a student, a merchant, a sailor, a healer, a criminal, and a judge. "They do not perceive, who make up this sad and cheerful scene, that they are placed in these circumstances to learn the laws of the universe, and that these various implements and callings serve the same use as the child's slate and spelling book . . ." (*Complete Sermons* 4: 65). It is through work that we learn about our individual powers, which is why Emerson tells his congregants that their true callings may take a while to find, through a process of experimentation with other vocations. However, "all other callings are temporary," whereas the "high calling" of each individual is permanent (4: 68). Through each step taken, workers gradually "unfold" themselves and uncover their talents and powers.[1] They also learn the "laws of the universe," "invigorate" their faculties, and form their virtues. This lays the groundwork for students to better appreciate the meaning of the "old fable" that begins "The American Scholar," in which Emerson discusses the division of labor in both its ideal and degenerate states (*Collected Works* 1: 53). As he writes in "Find Your Calling," through the distribution of work into various professions and the specialization it engenders, the worker's "more efficient action is gained to the common good" (*Complete Sermons* 4: 66). Following one's true calling, and ignoring societal pressure, ultimately results in greater service to society. It is important to note that Emerson values meaningful work, and not all work qualifies, but what makes work meaningful is not intrinsic to the work but rather depends upon the worker, which is why individual choice is crucial. What you can best do—what you feel called to do—is also how you can best serve yourself and make your greatest contribution to others.

When the call of the individual's "temper" is in conflict with that of his friends and family, he must follow his own character. This is the only path to a complete unfolding of one's powers and to a complete spiritual fulfillment, and while it may be difficult and problematic to turn away from the advice of friends and family, in associating the call of the inner voice and tendencies with God, Emerson makes it blasphemous to turn away from the self. He also makes it clear that only by following his own proper vocation can a man best serve the society of which his friends and family form a part: "Let a man have that profession for which God formed him that he may be useful to mankind to the whole extent of his powers" (*Complete Sermons* 4: 341). Through reading Emerson's insistence here on the need to turn away from outside influences and follow the inner voice—but ultimately in the service of others—students can intuit that the self-reliance Emerson outlines is not a call for solipsism but a defense of the necessity of the individual to contribute through his unique gifts. It is useful to remind students of this line when they turn to "Self-Reliance" and read, "Your own gift you can present every moment with the cumulative force of a whole life's cultivation; but of the adopted talent of another, you have only an extemporaneous, half possession. That which each can do best, none but his Maker can teach him" (*Collected Works* 2: 47). Seeing the later essay in conjunction with the sermon helps students view some of the passages that typically garner resistance—including those on charity and "shunning" family members in favor of the inner voice—in a different light. No matter how intrinsically valuable a given vocation may be, if it is not one's individual (and for Emerson divine) purpose, it is not the means through which one can best serve others.

In imploring his congregants to find their callings, Emerson emphasizes the role work has in self-development, knowledge, and finding the meaning and purpose in one's life. It is through our work that we realize the importance of each individual and the value of diversity. In his insistence on the power of the individual mind, Emerson charges each person with the responsibility for his own self-culture and education: "Be content then, humbly and wisely to converse with yourself; to learn what you can do, and what you cannot; to be deterred from attempting nothing out of respect to the judgment of others if it be not confirmed by your own judgment" (*Complete Sermons* 4: 69). The search for one's vocation is a process of self-discovery. It is a process of trial and error as well as reflection, through which, by attempting a variety of roles, one learns what one can and cannot do, and so "unfolds" one's powers. The emphasis is on the process itself as a process of self-discovery. The gradual unfolding of one's powers is an unfolding, or unlocking and enlarging, of the self. We must begin by exerting our powers if we are to realize their extent. This necessitates experimentation and exposure to a multitude of disciplines. It also requires patience, despite increasing pressure on students to specialize earlier and earlier.

If time allows, reading "Trades and Professions" and "Doctrine of the Hands" along with "Find Your Calling" emphasizes Emerson's stress on the spiritual within the practical. "Trades and Professions" prefigures "The American Scholar" with a description of various vocations, including arts, trades, and "learned professions," all leading to "one and the same system of right and prudent action" (*Early Lectures* 2: 126). As the lecture emphasizes, it is the fidelity of one's service and not the particular trade or profession that matters. While "Doctrine of the Hands" is most concerned with celebrating the education of natural laws derived from manual labor, it echoes the ideal of self-development through all work outlined in "Find Your Calling," arguing that "infinitely more important than any outward ends which his work is to answer, abides the permanent and supreme end of the amelioration of the workman himself" (2: 234). And nothing is a better defense against the question "What are you going to do with that major?" than Emerson's insistence in "Doctrine of the Hands": "I must esteem this right and duty of choosing his pursuit one crisis in each man's life. Nothing is more sacred" (2: 237). Also noteworthy in these lectures is the number of references Emerson makes to both male and female workers. He acknowledges that the education of natural laws from work typically allotted to women is equal to the education derived by male workers, and in the conclusion to "Doctrine of the Hands," he explicitly applies the "right and duty" of choosing a profession to both genders: "Let me say to the man and to the woman that would draw out of nature and the soul its highest counsel on this point that if they desire the most costly and enduring ornament of a human being they will find it by applying their faculties in the most earnest manner to what they can best do, without the least regard to highness or lowness of repute" (2: 245).

In all three texts, Emerson shows an acute awareness of the challenges young people face in choosing a profession—challenges that have not vastly changed over the centuries. His understanding that the work we do ultimately gives us our sense of purpose emphasizes how critical this decision is and how only the individual worker can make that choice. This emphasis gives students a sense of power, particularly if they are being pressured in a direction that goes against their own sense of who and what they are, but it also places a tremendous amount of responsibility on them. They have to be willing to expose themselves in a genuine way to a wide variety of disciplines, and they have to spend some time reflecting on their values, in particular what constitutes a meaningful and productive life.

Reading "Find Your Calling" aloud in the classroom re-creates for students the experience of this text as oratory. As young people on the cusp of adulthood, they are the target audience Emerson identifies and addresses throughout most of the sermon, and often they can hear that more easily than they can read it. For some students, this is enough to inspire their own reflections on what has influenced their decisions regarding majors and vocations. For others, specific assignments can get them to connect to the texts through their own experiences,[2] and relating on a personal level to these texts often translates into a willingness to seek those connections in the later essays.

By approaching Emerson in the manner described, our classrooms become points through which intriguing parallels are established. In discovering Emerson heuristically, students are led to self-discovery. They are introduced and reintroduced to the timeless injunction to "know thyself" and to the equally persistent rewards of meaningful work. These thought-provoking writings, occasionally couched in antique language and the quaint notion of vocational calling though they might be, have the power to make their thoughtful student readers alive to an Emerson who is more, not less, relevant and needed in the twenty-first-century academy.

NOTES

[1] Though I have sought to avoid gender bias in my discussion of the sermon, Emerson uses male pronouns and assumes a male worker. Later in the essay I discuss places where Emerson refers specifically to both male and female workers. As I have argued elsewhere (see *Labor Pains: Emerson, Hawthorne, and Alcott on Work and the Woman Question*), Emerson's views on the importance of work for women evolve. While his use of the male pronoun in his early work may be understood in a universal sense, his later works on women—especially "Discours Manqué"—state explicitly that the search for one's vocation is equally fundamental for both genders (*Later Lectures* 2: 16–18). In upper-level seminars, this is an illuminating text to pair with Emerson's earlier works.

[2] For instance, I ask students to find their own connections in text pairings and to explain Emerson's idea of how we "unfold" ourselves through our work. I also often ask them to apply Emerson's theory to fictional characters who exhibit this unfolding and to provide examples of the problems that arise from these characters' failure to develop their own powers. The celebration of difference that comes through a focus on work also opens a discussion on how Emerson's idea of the uniqueness—and therefore necessity—of our work embraces a need for a wide variety of workers not only from different classes but also genders, races, etc.

Emerson, Gender, and the Journals

Jean Ferguson Carr

Emerson's practice of dramatizing himself as a writer (scholar, preacher, bard, poet) in his essays and journals makes visible the workings of power and public pressure, and as such, it offers a valuable frame for understanding gendered issues of nineteenth-century literary culture. Emerson's writing practices opened up a rhetorical space that women and other emerging writers could exploit. He articulated as a shared politics what women often assumed as a personal burden, documenting for himself and for American writers more generally the struggle to emerge from the shadow of British traditions and the past.

Emerson may seem the last writer of his time who should be recast in terms of gender struggles. He rarely addresses women readers directly or differentially and is seldom linked in literary histories with any women except Margaret Fuller, his colleague and coeditor of *The Dial*. Little is made of his influence on contemporary women writers, perhaps because the writers who cite his importance to them do so when they are still schoolgirls. Instead critics have insistently figured Emerson as the "father" of a masculinized American literature, launching a long line of male writers and focusing attention on male-dominated arenas: Harvard, preaching, and oratory. Portraits of Emerson graced the walls of nineteenth-century libraries and schoolrooms. His role as the leader of the "American Procession" (Kazin) or as the guiding spirit for the "American Renaissance" (Matthiessen) seems to isolate him as a godlike figure—bard, American scholar, poet. His reputed disinterest in reading novels, the genre in which American women writers excelled, isolates him from a popular literary culture crowded with socially engaged writers like Harriet Beecher Stowe, or what Nathaniel Hawthorne mocked as "the d——d mob of scribbling women" whose "trash" "occupied" the "public taste" (75).

One of the problems of pairing Emerson with contemporary women writers is the generational gap: he is mature and successful by the time writers like Stowe or Louisa May Alcott begin to write. His career (and his extensive writing about the nature of the American scholar and the poet) sets standards for the writers who come after, whether they follow him directly or not. His career influences theirs simply by its being so successful and public. For younger writers like Alcott, Emerson was a revered family friend as well as an eminent writer whose attention she valued. Alcott referred to him as "the god of my idolatry" (May 1860; 99) and mourned him, at his death, as "our best & greatest American" and "the man who has helped me most by his life, his books, his society" (27 May 1882; 234). She chose an epigraph from his essay "Experience" to usher in her 1864 book, *Moods* (itself an Emersonian topic), and dedicated her first book of poems to his daughter Ellen. Her journals remark on his generosity to younger writers, his willingness to back her up when the Concord elders disapprove of a reference in her poetry to John Brown, and his gift of a volume of Goethe.

Elizabeth Stuart Phelps expresses a more conflicted relationship to the eminent poet and critic. She describes at length a visit "the seer" paid to Andover (44–49), framing it as a contest of wills between the distinguished visitor and the somewhat impolitic schoolgirl. She strikes the first blow, describing him "—not to speak disrespectfully—in a much muddled state of his distinguished mind. . . . His blazing seer's gaze took us all in, politely; it burned straight on, with its own philosophic fire; but it wore, at moments, a puzzled softness." Her story pushes back at the challenge of the seer with the "look of the eagle," whose attention "concentrated like the light of a burning glass" on the schoolgirls. She reports his astonishment at finding the girls have a Chaucer club (and represents him as "taken aback . . . as if he had found a tribe of Cherokees studying onomatopoeia in English verse"). Phelps thus attempts to deflect Emerson's low expectations (of girls) by aligning herself with what might have been, at the time, an even more surprising literary group (Cherokees). Phelps misreads Emerson's prejudices, however, since he had supported Cherokee cultural literacy in a public letter of 1838 he wrote opposing the Cherokee removal ("Letter to President Van Buren," *Emerson's Antislavery Writings*, 1–5); furthermore, Cherokee schoolgirls of the time, like Phelps's Abbott Academy schoolmates, did in fact have literary clubs in which they read Shakespeare if not Chaucer (Mihesuah). At the center of her story is a public disagreement with Emerson over the value of Chaucer, the "Father of English Poetry." Phelps casts herself as a "dissenter," opposed to her peers' "idolatrous enthusiasm" and "too much of a modern" to prefer Chaucer. Although she might expect to win approval from the modern poet in this contemporary battle of the books, she finds herself "demolished by the rebuke of the great man." She might be demolished, but she is not convinced: "I must say that I have never loved the Father of English Poetry any better for this episode." Phelps's story dramatizes the burden Emerson represents to the young female writer. But Phelps does not end her story with the conflict; instead she adds an anecdote about a subsequent pilgrimage to Concord. Touring Emerson's house and study, she wonders if she ought to "rewrite" her "interpretation" to address the writer she might have valued had they met in simpler, more equal circumstances.

Emerson models relationships to nature and art that renegotiate the terms of literary success. He claims as his own, and indeed as an "American" value, what may have initially seemed to emerging writers liabilities for literary success. In his introduction to *Nature* (1836), Emerson advocates seeking an "original relationship to the universe" (*Collected Works* 1: 7), and he urges his American scholar to prefer the primary influences of nature to the secondhand experience of books or travel. In "The Poet," he argues against the privileged value of elegance—the quality so prized by "those who are esteemed umpires of taste"—and calls instead for a poet who will "chaunt our own times and social circumstances" (*Collected Works* 3: 3, 21). Women writers of the time evoke these dichotomies, although usually as apology instead of bold assertion. They claimed for themselves the value of attention to the everyday and the local, to "crudeness" (signaling authenticity and insistence on the real) over "elegance" (signaling artificiality, the blindness of wealth and privilege). Emerson encourages experimentation and empathizes with the difficulties faced by emerging American writers, stuck between the challenge of Britain's literary traditions and the disdain of an American public with little time or interest in letters. "Doubt not, O poet, but persist," he counsels at the end of his essay "The Poet." "Say, 'It is in me, and shall out.' Stand there, baulked and dumb, stuttering and stammering, hissed and hooted. . . . The world is full of renunciations and apprenticeships, and this is thine" (3: 23, 24). His imagined dialogue invites lesser writers to see their outsider status as momentary, to withstand criticism until the world learns how to read their work: "Insist on yourself," advises Emerson in "Self-Reliance"; "[n]ever imitate" (*Collected Works* 2: 47).

To explore these competing understandings about the nature of literary value, I ask students to read women writers in a kind of attenuated dialogue (or, at times, debate) with Emerson. This is unfamiliar work: it asks them often to compare radically different genres (domestic fiction and philosophic essay) and styles. It asks them to compare writers working in different times and contexts as if they were peers, and at the same time, it asks them to take seriously the shaping forces of gender, class, and race, of educational opportunity and worldly experience. In many important ways, Emerson and the women writers are not alike. But I encourage students to see that they are similarly invested in arguments about the nature of art, of originality, style, and authority.

I frame classwork on Emerson and women writers by asking students to examine a set of short "literary credos" (in multiple genres) written by male and female writers. The handout includes the opening paragraph of Emerson's *Nature*, a brief section from Melville's "Hawthorne and His Mosses," opening stanzas of Whitman's "Starting from Paumanok," and three prefatory passages by women writers (I vary this but have used Anne Bradstreet, Susanna Rowson, Fanny Fern, Caroline Kirkland, Harriet Wilson, and Stowe; the passages come from novels, short stories, memoirs, and poetry). I ask students to work with passages by male and female writers as if they were in dialogue with each other. Students are initially struck by the confidence of the male writers and by the women writers' tone of apology. But they also come to see that the confidence is often like whistling in the wind—a matter more of assertion than full surety. Each set of writers argues against prevailing assumptions and values; each attempts to transform failings into potential value. Writers contest the expectations of art, as Kirkland does in the preface to *A New Home—Who'll Follow?* (1839), by arguing for the value of "an unimpeachable transcript of reality; a rough picture, in detached parts, but pentagraphed from the life" (iii). The passage from Wilson's preface to *Our Nig* confesses "her inability to minister to the refined and cultivated, the pleasure supplied by abler pens." But it turns out the problem is not with Wilson's inability but with the readers' demand for *pleasure*. "It is not for such," Wilson insists, "these crude narrations appear" (iv). In her preface to *Rose Clark* (1856), Fern goes further, expelling the harsh *"dictionary on legs"* who finds fault with her domestic production, sending him away "to the groaning shelves of some musty library, where 'literature' lies embalmed, with its stony eyes, fleshless joints, and ossified heart, in faultless preservation." Having banished both critic and "literature," Fern can settle down with her carefully constituted domestic audience to share her "unpretending story" (iii–iv).

Reading women's credos in tandem with Emerson's opening passage to *Nature* helps students to see women's writing as something more than defensive apology. They can see that Emerson has as much stake as do the women writers in challenging traditional standards of writing. Emerson frames his book by "apologizing" for the failings of his age, which doubts itself in comparison to the past. He then turns apology into challenge, critiquing traditional values and inviting American writers to step forward from the "sepulchres of the fathers" and the "dry bones of the past" to "demand" their own "works and laws and worship." Women writers might well have heard Emerson's call to action—which pitted the older British traditions against emerging American attempts—as an invitation that could include them as well: "Why should not we have a poetry and philosophy of insight and not of tradition, and a religion by revelation to us, and not the history of theirs?" (*Collected Works* 1: 7).

The credo exercise works partially because the texts are "equal"—relatively short, excerpted, of a scope that allows students to study them as rhetorical and intertextual documents. When students begin to read Emerson's journals, I make a similar pedagogic decision, asking them to read a small sampling of his college journals, slowly, closely, and in tandem with those of the African American writer Charlotte Forten Grimké. Grimké is a generation younger than Emerson, she is African American, and she is female—there are significant differences between them. Yet in many other ways, they are similarly positioned: they both come of age in Boston, they have literary aspirations but also chafe at the conventions of literary and educational culture of their time, they write extensive journals both as literary training and as an exercise in self-monitoring. They use their journals to report on their reading, but also to observe their time and place. The comparison allows students to consider literary careers in the context of literacy, schooling, and material considerations—to see that excellence is not simply a matter of talent or will, or even of hard work and diligence, but also a matter of access and visibility, an effect of gendered education and modeling. Emerson has opportunities that are not open to most women writers of the time—and especially not open to a young African American woman like Grimké: education, economic support, international connections, the ability to travel, a sizable library, educated peers. He is expected to read philosophy and poetry, to spend time in reflection, to engage in serious conversations and correspondences. He is not, as Grimké is, expected to spend time sewing or learning to paint; he is not restricted from reading newspapers or going to public events.

And yet Grimké is not completely shut out from those kinds of cultural and material concerns. She leads a relatively privileged life, given her race and gender—the child of middle-class, educated African Americans, living in

Philadelphia, able to send their daughter to the integrated schools of Boston. Of course, integration at the time meant that Grimké is allowed to go to school as the single African American in a school full of white students, with white teachers. She is allowed to "pass" and to sample white culture, even though she is also painfully aware of the turbulence around race during the pre–Civil War years in which she wrote. Her Boston is a place of oratory and newspaper accounts about escaped slaves, about the trouble brewing in the South, about freedom and imprisonment. When she reads the approved books of poetry and travel, she focuses on the contrasts between freedom and enslavement, between rich and poor. When her teacher recommends a book about the "homes of the authors," she is struck by their privileged difference from the tents of Indians (71). When she read about Europe, the banks of the Rhine and the pastoral beauty of England, she instead thinks of travel in terms of escape from the conditions of slavery and racism in the United States.

I ask students to pay attention to what styles or topics are available to each writer and what helps them fill those blank pages. What allows them to write with confidence? Reading Emerson's college journals as a body of material—rather than reading the famous quotations that often represent his journal writing—makes the comparison with Grimké a more equal one. Both Emerson and Grimké struggle with what they have been taught to value, with learned styles and appropriate topics. Both develop strategies to extend themselves beyond the limits of their training, to explore competing notions of what writing can and should accomplish. Reading them side by side allows students to see both of them as shaped by their reading, by educational practices, and by their political and personal situations. The pairing helps students to notice Grimké's silences; it helps them make sense of Emerson's extravagances. Most of all, it helps students become interested in them both as emerging writers, in shared but differing contexts—not as master and apprentice. They see that Grimké often "queers" the lessons she is offered, the culture she is invited to tour. She is encouraged to write about the weather; she instead writes about the misery of the enslaved (66). She is obligated to appreciate a book of engravings given to her by her teacher ("we gazed admiringly at the beautiful homes") but writes about the experience as a form of antithesis (the homes of the American authors are contrasted with the miserable condition of American Indians encamped in the pastures [72]).

Students expect Grimké to feel at odds with her culture, but reading Grimké with Emerson allows students to see that he also "queers" the values he is offered. As a young man, he faces particular forms of privileged culture: the classics, the wealth and traditions of Europe, the conventions of religion, the ability to compose elegant prose and harmonious poetry. He cannot live up to those values, partially because of his own position as an American, with little classical training or ability, with relatively meager libraries, and without the larger educated audience or supporting culture of Europe, but also because he seeks a radically different way of being an "American" scholar-poet.

Reading Emerson in terms of gender thus challenges many of the existing depictions of Emerson himself and helps students to face him with less awe (and trembling). It reminds students to read Emerson as part of his times, not removed at the head of a literary procession, not rendered transcendent. It also usefully challenges discourses about gender, seeing it as a more complicated exchange of concerns and values, not the responsibility or property of women writers in isolation or in defensive posture.

A Natural History of Intellect? Emerson's Scientific Methods in the Later Lectures

Meredith Farmer

Undergraduates are almost always frustrated by Emerson's "famous inconsistencies" (Dimock, "Scarcity" 84) or the ways that his content "slip[s] through our fingers then when we clutch hardest" (*Collected Works* 3: 29). In fact, asking students to describe the experience of reading Emerson yields answers like "confusing," "baffling," and "impossible," alongside acknowledgment that his work can be "deep," "profound," and even "uplifting" at the level of individual sentences. The struggle in reading Emerson that students eventually identify is in moving from individual insights or aphorisms to comprehension that extends to an entire essay. And the solution I've settled on in my course on the connections between nineteenth-century "literary" and "scientific" methods is to respond to students' frustration by shifting our focus from Emerson's content to his form. Students and teachers alike might benefit from thinking more seriously about the method—or the systematic procedure—that Emerson proposes in his frequently overlooked project to produce a natural history of intellect. This interest in method or process is visible in Emerson's first secular lecture, but it is especially evident in later work like "The Powers and Laws of Thought." Those late lectures become our focus, alongside a number of supplementary materials, including Lee Rust Brown's essay "The Emerson Museum," images of nineteenth-century natural history museums, and entries from Emerson's journals.

In 1833 Emerson visited the Jardin des Plantes and the Cabinet d'Histoire in Paris. There he had what Robert D. Richardson describes as a "moment of vocational epiphany," viewing both objects in glass cases and living plants in the ground, classified according to different naturalists' taxonomies (*Emerson* 139). Those "compositions" demonstrated a particular kind of order. Or as Brown frames it in "The Emerson Museum," spectators had the opportunity to actually see classifications. The medium of display made conceptual "depth" or "higher" orders visible (59, 66) and offered Emerson "a version of precisely the kind of writing to which he had long aspired" (59). He responded by declaring, in his journal, "I will be a naturalist" (*Journals* 4: 200). Then Emerson began to index his journals, treating words and sentences as "elemental units" and "vehicles" that would ferry him toward some higher order (Brown, "Emerson Museum" 72, 62). Brown refers to this as Emerson's "writing 'up' from journals and notebooks," and Emerson referred to it as his "'new pattern of order'" (59, 71). But Brown's insight is that we might consider Emerson's essays as classifications, culled from a collection of "statements and thoughts that could not be completed" but that collectively built up toward some productive whole (71).

More concretely, the conceptual shift we might derive from Emerson's turn to natural history is that Emerson presents not "Experience" or "Circles" but anecdotes or aphorisms that build back towards those concepts. The essays simply serve as a container for collection and display. And this is certainly the reading we encounter in *Natural History of Intellect*, where Emerson's literary executor, James Elliot Cabot, frames him as offering a surprisingly atypical declaration of his methodology: "My contribution will be simply historical. I write anecdotes of the intellect; a sort of Farmer's Almanac of mental moods." Here we find a powerful account of Emerson's supposed practice: "he who contents himself with dotting a fragmentary curve, recording only what facts he has observed, without attempting to arrange them within one outline, follows a system also" (*Complete Works* 12: [10–11]). Students quickly identify this passage, and the idea that we eventually unpack is that Emerson's coherence may be in his work's form. Instead of offering final or fossilized answers—"forcing" his observations "into a circle or ellipse"—Emerson "only draws that arc which he clearly sees" (12: 11–12). Each unit of Emerson's writing becomes a record of a fragment of his lived experience. And his essays, in turn, chart these "anecdotes" without resolving them. Even so, Emerson's process of indexing—this process of induction, or the drawing of an arc—enables these anecdotes to be arranged and then "seen through," much like the museum's objects in glass cases.[1]

This "natural history of intellect" project was central for Emerson for almost forty years. Cabot described the work as "the chief task of his life" (2: 633). And Richardson opens his biography by explaining, "Emerson's main project, never realized to his satisfaction, was to write a natural history of intellect" (*Emerson* xi). Even so, this work has been "largely overlooked" thanks to its "long and tangled history," which I'll briefly rehearse here (Robinson, *Emerson* 182). Less than a month after returning from England in 1833, Emerson launched his secular career with the lecture "The Uses of Natural History." By 1837 Emerson's "I will be a naturalist" gave way to a new goal: to "write the Natural History of Reason" (Cabot 2: 633). In 1841 Emerson published an essay on "Intellect," explaining that he would "gladly" unfold "a natural history of the intellect" if he could somehow find a way to "mark" its "transparent essence" (*Collected Works* 2: 193). And Emerson's second trip to England in 1847 exposed him to scientific discoveries that gave new life to this project (Robinson, *Emerson* 112, 182–83). By 1848 Emerson delivered the lecture series titled Mind and Manners of the Nineteenth Century, including "The Powers and Laws of Thought." This developed into the series Natural Method of Mental Philosophy ten years later (Bosco, *"His"* 15; Arsić, *"Brain"* 77). And, finally, in the 1870s this project culminated with Emerson's final lecture series at Harvard, which was tellingly titled Natural History of Intellect.[2] Emerson never had the opportunity to complete this long-term project, but Cabot published a reconstructed version of it as *Natural History of Intellect* in 1893. Lawrence Buell describes Cabot's edition as "bowdlerized" (*Emerson* 229). Maurice York and Rick Spaulding call it a "strange patchwork" (xii). And Ronald A. Bosco offers a more detailed critique.[3] But the absence of a definitive text should not prevent teachers from discussing Emerson's "chief task" and his "main project" in the classroom. In fact, its consistent importance and continued development seem to suggest that it deserves a place next to more popular texts.

With three days to focus on Emerson, we begin with "The Poet" and excerpts from *Nature*. I ask students to describe their reading experiences, which consistently leads to a sense of collective frustration—along with at least a few passages that inspired admiration. Next we shift to important background information about Emerson before moving through the first pages of *Nature* very slowly. Finally I pose a deceptively complex question: how would you describe Emerson's Poet? As class ends students almost always conclude that Emerson's descriptions of "the Poet" work together in ways that cannot be compressed into one clear account. This frustration with attempts to synthesize Emerson's various accounts of "the Poet" leaves students ready to seriously consider what I frame as Emerson's method, or the procedural steps that he followed as he developed his essays and lectures from the records in his journals.[4] To do this I have traditionally assigned the first chapter of Cabot's *Natural History of Intellect*, alongside Brown's "The Emerson Museum." But because of the complex reception of Cabot's edition, in the future I plan to use his most important source: Emerson's 1848 lecture "The Powers and Laws of Thought" (found in Bosco and Myerson's *The Later Lectures of Ralph Waldo Emerson*, 1: 134–51).

We open our first class on Emerson's later lectures with images of natural history museums. These help students develop a stronger sense of Brown's suggestion that placing "specimens" in glass armoires or cabinets "clarified their classification to the viewer" ("Emerson Museum" 66). We consider this technology at a number of scales, looking at cases with bones, bugs, and butterflies—and then turning to entire arrangements of collections at the Wagner Free Institute of Science in Philadelphia, which has preserved its design since the nineteenth century (Montgomery and Largent 441). Our discussion of classification leads to questions about Brown's essay. Then students work in groups to identify Brown's argument. Groups also identify especially important passages from the text, which they add to a class summary in *Google Docs*. (Each group is responsible for three or four key pages of Brown's essay.) After ten to fifteen minutes we talk through the material together, focusing on explication and comprehension.

Next we turn to Emerson's own discussion of method, beginning with the problematic idea of "true reporting." Here we look back at *Nature*'s "transparent eyeball," along with discussions of the historical rise of "objectivity," which we examined at the start of the semester. (We read excerpts from Lorraine Daston and Peter Galison's *Objectivity*.) But we also learn that Emerson's reporting reaches across the variety of his experiences—or across his "mental moods."[5] This opens a series of questions about perspective. And eventually students sort out that Emerson doesn't only consider his own shifting affect. He also foregrounds the location of a viewing subject, asking, for example, "What is life but the angle of vision?" (*Later Lectures* 1: 147). Ultimately we unpack the idea that Emerson records his thoughts at a time when his moods change, his perspective changes, and the world around him changes.

Depending on the direction of our class discussion, here several new topics become possible. We consider, for example, the ways Emerson's work seems to anticipate developments in the social sciences, psychoanalysis, and pragmatism. The expansion of the sciences, in general, is clearly called for when Emerson asks, "Could we have, that is, the exhaustive accuracy of distribution which chemists use in their nomenclature and anatomists in their descriptions, applied to a higher class of facts; to those laws, namely, which are common to chemistry, anatomy, astronomy, intellect, morals and social life;—laws of the world?" Here Emerson tellingly continues, "Why not? It is high time it should be done" (*Later Lectures* 1: 137). If students have any working knowledge of psychoanalysis, we also discuss Emerson's claim that "the laws and powers of the Intellect" are complex "objects of Science" that "may be numbered and recorded like stamens and vertebrae" exactly because they are "at once observers and observed" (1: 137). Here Emerson proposes the unfiltered recording of ideas that can be analyzed only after they've become external records. (In classes with students who are interested in psychology, comparing this process to a description of free association can be useful.) Student comments and questions might also lead us to Emerson's connections to American pragmatism. For example, Cabot offers the intriguing reconstruction, "My metaphysics are to the end of use" (*Complete Works* 12: 16). Here I might tell students about Emerson's role as William James's godfather. Or I might outline debates about whether Emerson is a "literary" figure or a "philosopher," an artist or a pragmatist.[6] Finally, if my literature and science students are more interested in biology, we discuss the fact that Emerson's way of thinking about classification is inextricable from pre-Darwinian cosmology. To do this I draw on Lauren Klein's extension of Lee Rust Brown's work, which compares Emerson and Darwin.

After we simplify, we complicate. We might discuss the natural history project's vexed publication history, thinking about the development of Emerson's ideas or the questions about authorship that arise with Cabot's allegedly "bowdlerized" edition. Or students might push on the idea that "data points" could ever represent observations and ideas. (The logic of "dotting a fragmentary curve" may not hold when plot points include generalizations and oracular claims.) As class ends we turn to a few pages from Emerson's journal, including Emerson's now-familiar "I will be a naturalist." Here I ask whether Brown is exaggerating when he calls it a "vow" ("Emerson Museum" 59). I also share Kerry Larson's related concern that Brown affirms "a symbiosis of metaphysics and method" that "oversimplifies a complex situation" (395). Ultimately I invite students to think about published work as material that they can simultaneously appreciate and challenge.

For our third and final meeting, each student selects an additional canonical essay—"History," "The Over-Soul," "Circles," "Experience," or "Self-Reliance"—and prepares a brief written response that speaks to the question, Does the essay that you've selected seem compatible with Emerson's purported method? Or does it open new ways to question or challenge ideas from either "The Emerson Museum" or "The Powers and Laws of Thought"? The idea is for students to explicate and then evaluate the descriptions about method that we find in both Emerson and Brown. Students bring six copies of their essays to class and work in groups to develop informal collective responses, which we discuss together. Answers differ widely. Students engaging with "Circles," for example, tend to focus on the ways it resonates with our readings about method. But students focused on "Self-Reliance" often push back, suggesting that Emerson seems to be doing far more than just observing, recording, and rearranging his ideas.

This assignment is grounded in the broader context of my lower-division course called Literary and Scientific Methods, which challenges students' assumptions about the distinctions between literature and science by moving through a series of nineteenth-century "literary" authors who changed the forms of their writing in response to specific developments in science. But this short paper also helps students develop their higher-order writing skills. (This is often the first time students have been asked to evaluate secondary texts.) Engagement with Emerson's natural history project would also work well in a much wider range of settings and conversations, from the transnational (this method was inspired by Emerson's European tours) to the psychological (decades before Freud, Emerson used writing as a tool to externalize and analyze his "intellect"). It is deeply interdisciplinary, centrally about the writing process, and a clear invitation to consider genre. Last but not least, this shift to considerations of Emerson's form helps students draw on their initial frustrations to produce productive readings.

NOTES

[1] Cabot's edition of *Natural History of the Intellect* is contested, as I will discuss. But even that edition's strongest critic, Ronald A. Bosco, draws on this passage in the introduction to *Emerson in His Own Time*. And both sets of notes from Emerson's final Natural History of Intellect lectures at Harvard discuss this "farmer's almanac of mental moods" (Bosco, *"His"* 27, 55): a phrase that appears in Emerson's journals (*Journals* 11: 438) and in "The Powers and Laws of Thought" (*Complete Works* 12: 11). One student described Emerson's course as being about "mere observation," reporting that he described himself as "jotting down observed facts" in a way that was "historical." Her account also refers to a "curve of personal observation," along with Emerson's suggestion, "It is much to record your results in sentences. 'Tis more to add method, and report the

spirit of your life symmetrically . . . to arrange many general reflections in their natural order, so that I shall have one homogenous web" (Bosco, *"His"* 55; Emerson, *Complete Works* 12: 12–13). In short, this image is clearly part of Emerson's thinking, even if I am citing Cabot's synthetic reconstruction.

[2] See Bosco (*"His"*) for a thorough discussion of the notes from Emerson's university lectures at Harvard. They have been framed as Emerson's "best effort towards condensing, summarizing, and putting forward what he considered to be his best thoughts" (Richardson, *Emerson* 449; see also York and Spaulding i, ix). But this may not be accurate. Emerson was allegedly "composing lectures only hours before giving them," struggling to keep up with a teaching, writing, and travel schedule that would have exhausted almost anyone (Bosco, *"His"* 21–23). Emerson drew heavily from older material, which was his standard compositional method. And he told his classes at the end of both semesters that his goal was to "give a greater completeness" to the "sketches" he had shared (Bosco, *"His"* 25, 12; see also Walls 203). So we can't discount these lectures, but we also can't frame them as definitive.

[3] Bosco suggests that the praise modern editors have offered Cabot's work has not and should not be extended to *Natural History of the Intellect*, because "these essays are simply not reflective of the comprehensive treatment of intellect Emerson developed across those sixteen lectures at Harvard," and he is skeptical of work with editors' "treatment of how Emerson might have transformed those lectures into essays had he enjoyed the health and reserve of energy necessary to see the work through himself" (*"His"* 17). Laura Dassow Walls frames this differently, claiming instead that Emerson's major project was "much closer to completion than he realized" (204). And York and Spaulding compellingly frame Cabot as "trying to re-create Emerson's method" of reassembling pieces of lectures and essays into a logical order (xii).

[4] For an especially helpful discussion of Emerson's method, see Robinson's *Emerson and the Conduct of Life* (185).

[5] Arsić offers an especially helpful account of "moods" in "Brain Walks: Emerson on Thinking" (59–62, 67, 69, 72–73).

[6] For a discussion of Emerson's connections to pragmatism, see Cavell ("What's the Use"); Grimstad; Levin; and J. Richardson, along with William James's references to "The Powers and Laws of Thought" in "Address at the Centenary of Ralph Waldo Emerson" (307–13).

"These Flames and Generosities of the Heart": Emerson in the Poetry Workshop

Dan Beachy-Quick

In Conference

Among the many circles to which we find ourselves apprenticed, perhaps none so affects the teacher of poetry writing as the overriding sense that the conversation between professor and student in the private confines of the office is the very same conversation in the more public space of the classroom—the circumference has only grown wider. When students come asking for advice, mostly they want to make their poem "better." Perhaps that is an easy thing to do, to teach. But each time I hear in the back of my mind Thoreau's distrust of those who would do good on behalf of another, fearing that my help would come as does the "parching wind of the African deserts called the simoom, which fills the mouth and nose and ears and eyes with dust" (*Walden* 74). Maybe my fear is basic, shared by most teachers of creative writing, extending its reach as the circle of my influence expands. I fear that there is an error inherent in teaching another person how to write a poem, that in offering to others those peculiar sparks that drive for myself the green fuse through the flower, I fill their vision with my own sight, fill their mouth with my voice, and what to me is seeing and song, though students might not know it, is but dust to them. But maybe I'm wrong—I want to be wrong—and it is in Emerson that I find a way not only to counter my pedagogical fears but to move forward through them.

Emerson suggests, early on in "The Poet," that we must find a way to restore "perception of the instant dependence of form upon soul" (*Collected Works* 3: 3). This plaiting together of perception, form, and soul is a subtle braid, one whose threefold strength relies on the very sensibility under threat in Thoreau's dismissal of do-gooders. It is the fact of the sensuous life, that wounded condition of self, in which—through eyes, ears, nose, mouth, hands—the world keeps insisting that it is as real as we who live in it. The instant of perception reveals a numinous world. This poetic equation, this strange economy, wherein perception weaves into soul weaves into form, eases the opposition of Emerson's double claim: that poetry should be *vascular* and that it should be *ensouled*. Body and breath, but breath is *pneuma* and so tied to the spirit. Sometimes the form the soul depends on is just a word; sometimes it is the word *soul*. Perception here is a kind of precipice, and the good teacher of poetry ushers students to the cusp. There the mind finds itself disturbed from the ease of its reason. Emerson has stood there: "Here we find ourselves, suddenly, not in a critical speculation, but in a holy place, and should go very warily and reverently. We stand before the secret of the world, there where Being passes into Appearance, and Unity into Variety" (3: 3). The ideal and the actual reveal their interdependence, and so of soul and form . . . but this all goes unspoken, or mostly so, between student and teacher, with just a desk in between.

What I can offer is the advice Emerson gave a woman who asked him how to write. Take two notebooks. In one, on the left-hand page, write down any image that grabs your mind as beautiful, startling, apprehensive; on the opposite page, write down every thought the image gives you. In the other notebook, reverse the pattern. On the left-hand page, write down any thought that comes to you that seems worthy of the attention; opposite it, note the images that come to mind when considering the thought (R. Richardson, *First* 20). Far more than an exercise, these notebooks—faithfully kept for even a short while, even a day, even an hour—insist reality begins in the beauty of the world we perceive, and the mind must learn to think by finding a sympathetic idea born out of that immediate perception. These notebooks insist that what is real begins in that idea of old, in εἶδος, in Form, and our perceptual life is there to recollect from memory those images that might best allow us to imagine the world in such a way that our thinking about it is as real as a tree, as iron, or as a stone.

This Emersonian advice to young writers might do its best ministry in secret. It encourages without giving certainty; it undermines talent and asks us to think and to see. More profound, underneath the vague and striving ego, down in the roots and grammar of experience, it unsettles our most basic assumptions about cause and effect. The world creates the mind; then the mind makes the world. Emerson writes, "People wish to be settled; only as far as they are unsettled is there any hope for them" (*Collected Works* 2: 189). Suddenly, our ideas about Idea are both humbled and vaulted, cast in the dirt and lofted to the stars. The roots of εἶδος bear it out: *that which is seen, beauty of person, habit of body, form, kind, nature, specific notion, meaning, idea,* all the way to *written statement* and *poem.* "Cause and effect are two sides of one fact," Emerson says (2: 186). The true student realizes that both notebooks are more truly understood as one. What results from the work is what the poet most dearly wants: the poem.

In Classroom

But this advice is of the office, of the private conversation, and workshop is public, a community that once or twice a week arranges the rows of desks into a circle and day by day tries to find a way to talk about the art all there want to practice: poetry. The question these years that has most filled my mind veers away from any use of Emerson, whose first result is a prompt or an hour's lesson, or even anything that feels immediately of use. I don't want to give my students a tool, a techne, an artifice, for their art. I've wondered instead what a long approach, what an unspoken ethic, derived from Emerson, might mean, might do, within the circular confines of the poetry workshop.

The circle itself is where to begin.

As the workshop of old, maybe it's best to consider those of us sitting in its circle apprentices of a sort. Truer to say, though, not that we "sit in a circle," but we are ourselves the circle. "The eye is the first circle; the horizon which it forms is the second; and throughout nature this primary figure is repeated without end," Emerson says (*Collected Works* 2: 179). The very shape the workshop takes, the geometry it forms out of itself, creates within the four walls of the classroom a cosmic space, not where many are in the gravitational orbit of one, but where each is forming the horizon of our utmost reach. The goal isn't simply to fill the circular space with meaningful conversation about one another's poems but, by speaking fully into and through those poems, to break apart the horizon into its greater diameter. It's not a commensurable expansion but a spiritual one: "Our life is an apprenticeship to the truth that around every circle another can be drawn; that there is no end in nature, but every end is a beginning; that there is always another dawn risen on mid-noon, and under every deep a lower deep opens" (2: 179). One way to imagine the workshop: each poem a student writes and brings to the discussion is but a pebble dropped in the center of the circle, a stone in a pond, and equally important as the comments to come is the strange measure the poem makes of the circumference of the whole. It ripples out and marks our limit; it ripples down and marks our depth; and though inches and feet over the course of a semester will mark no appreciable difference, no workshop counts as a success that hasn't, week by week, drawn a wider circle around the shattered arcs of the orb that in the last class we abandoned.

That notion of "success" is as central as it is debased. Abandon the assumption that the work workshop does on a poem is done to improve it, to make it good, to make it publishable, and without a sound one of the prisons in which we place our hearts has been undone and opened. It is disorienting to be set free; mostly, it doesn't feel like freedom. It removes us from the lesser demands of our own expectations for ourselves and puts us under the command of genius. Talent is the circle we draw around ourselves, lodging like a dim sun in the center. Genius makes center and circumference one, excuses us from our own centrality. Emerson knows this as deeply as any writer in the language: "Talent can frolic and juggle; Genius realizes and adds" (*Collected Works* 3: 7). Strange as it is to say, the hardest thing one can convince a young poet of is that he or she is a genius; it's hard because it has so little to do with him or her. "The one thing which we seek with insatiable desire," says Emerson, "is to forget ourselves . . ." (*Collected Works* 2: 190). To accept the workshop as working toward genuine desire—the only kind that can "realize and add"—shatters the economy we've been handed and so alters the laws of the house, so that "what is of value?" again becomes the question of dearest commodity. To ask it means that the self-same authority of each poet—the *I*—has gone missing, has gotten lost; it's grown expansive where it used to be conclusive, and rather than being the arbiter of actuality, it becomes instead this site of genius in which the experiment of the world takes place. One might say genius is what we hold in common; if so, the workshop is the circle that with genius must fill, belonging to no one, because it isn't ours. Genius lays its claim on us, not us on it. Success comes to the poets who vault over their talent, who put it down as does a child a toy, or who, as the tern, leave the nest to migrate north, and so discover only in flight are they at home.

Lofty goals, I know—and none seems to come to any proof. It is a pedagogy that points at the facts as they return to the ether, all discoveries to be made but never to call one's own. A student may write a wonderful poem, but as of the poem, so of life: "The way of life is wonderful; it is by abandonment" (*Collected Works* 2: 190). The poem too is a shape that fills itself with itself, seeks the nature of its own limits, and then asks to be broken apart. What talent clings to as rescue, genius lets go as the thresher does the thrown seeds. Emerson knows "that which builds is better than that which is built" (2: 180). So it is in the deep etymology of the word *poet*. ποιητής means both maker and poet, and the verb that accompanies the noun, ποιέω, means "to make," "to do," but in the middle voice—not present in English; in ancient Greek that form is both active and passive at once—means "to consider."

We should think about what our work is. It is a high demand, though it sounds so humble; Emerson demands it of us, as he demanded it of himself. One could say his greatest essays, those informing most deeply this one—"Circles," "The Poet," "Experience"—all are written in the middle voice, all are made so as to consider themselves, for only the made thing can consider itself . . . but we have no such voice in our language to claim it. What seems true, at least for those of us in Emerson's workshop, is that the made thing considers itself, and we are makers of that thing, which does not mean we have the answer but that we are allowed—sacred permission—to eavesdrop on the poem as it whispers to itself.

And what do we hear?

Sometimes nothing. For Emerson's workshop has taught us also to "suspect our instruments" (*Collected Works* 3: 43). Poetry is an art in which we are our own instruments, for the soul depends instantly on form, and that form so often is a word as doubtful of its existence as we are of our own.

Or we hear silence: "An innavigable sea washes with silent waves between us and the things we aim at and converse with" (*Collected Works* 3: 29). Then we might ask ourselves, How did I build this bridge only to create more distance? And how do I cross it? For it is here, in what I might call the "ideal crisis," that workshop does its work, not by excusing us from the fear that words never touch what they love and aspire toward but by letting us dwell there in something other than desperation. Maybe it is only there, in the workshop expanding to its next orbit, that Emerson's sense that "every word was once a poem" and "every new relation is a new word" come to bear their curious fruit (3: 11). Poems that unsettle the world they name, and by the world are themselves unsettled. Such writing as poets in Emerson's workshop write must be found in the "focal distance within the actual horizon of human life" (3: 30). Which is to say, they are with us, even as they break us apart.

Between the Disciplines and beyond the Institution: Emerson's Environmental Relevance

T. S. McMillin

Sundry arts and crafts bear Emerson's adages, proving his words can still inspire (and still sell), that his star still shimmers as a hitching post for our wagons. And every now and again a novel or film character or other such object of art will be perfumed with Concord sage. But just how relevant is Emerson's thought? This problem of relevance arose recently during a faculty review and planning retreat for environmental studies at my institution. We had learned from surveys of senior majors that a number of them doubted the relevance of certain courses to their major, including an offering in the natural sciences. What factors, I began to wonder, determine the relevance—as perceived by students—of a particular course or a particular body of works (Emerson's essays, say) to a discipline or area of inquiry? What does it mean to teach Emerson under the circumstances, in the present?

In general, relevance involves meaning or value, especially in relation to someone. Herein lies one of its important aspects: relevance does not refer to a special meaning inherent in a particular thing but rather regards meaning that arises from someone's relation to the thing. F. C. S. Schiller, in an essay on relevance in the context of philosophy, enumerated the concept's many advantages, chief among them being "subjectivity": relevance, Schiller wrote, "is not conceived as a quality residing in the thing thought of *per se*, but *lies in its value for us and in our attitude towards it.*" Something is relevant less because of the qualities of the particular object than because of what the object does for a subject. Working with the word's etymology, Schiller asserted that "'relevant' is that which is *helpful* and affords us *relief*" (155). In other words, the value inherent to "relevance" is that its value is not inherent; it means something to someone and avails that person.

As in the environmental studies example, I suspect that a course deemed by some as irrelevant to the major is not inherently valueless to the major; rather a subject (the student) has not been able to find help, relief, or meaning in the object (course). Assuming the assessments are correct, there are various actions we might take in pursuit of making the course more relevant: we could revise the object to make its meaning more broadly and more readily recognizable; we could teach the subject how to connect with the object more effectively; and we could do a little of both as we more generally rework the set of relations between subject and object. That last, most encompassing action entails making "relevance" itself—with its meanings and values, its objects and subjects—our topic. And that, more or less, is how I have come to approach teaching Emerson at a liberal arts college. The advanced course, titled Nature and Transcendentalism, counts toward both the English and environmental studies majors and, as such, raises many questions regarding value, the humanities, and interdisciplinarity. The course takes relevance as an opening question and as an open question—one that leads to related questions, not the last or the least of which is "relation" itself.

What is and will be relevant as global conditions change? What changes can we make in higher education to meet the new challenges? How relevant is literary study and how might it be rendered more so? My approach to interdisciplinarity supposes that not only might one set of questions be relevant to the other, but they actually *refer* to one another. Interdisciplinarity is not a magic cloak that you put on or a state that you obtain; it is a reflective and referential process, a series of thinking events that can produce different ways of understanding the world from those that are available through any one disciplinary perspective. Its relevance is that it treats relevance as arising between disciplines, not just within one. The philosopher Ted Toadvine writes about various "myths of interdisciplinarity": that it requires little special effort and minimal additional resources; that the humanities are inutile for problem-solving; that humanistic input is most valuable for prettying up communication skills. To my mind, the main myth of interdisciplinarity regards relevance, a quality mistaken to be static and obvious. Interdisciplinary studies require thinking between disciplines about the nature, value, limits, and potential of each to each, trying disciplines in relation to one another and connecting them into something new.

This "trying" of disciplines relates to reflective movement between disciplines, and that movement is part of how I define transcendentalism. In four consecutive paragraphs near the beginning of "The Method of Nature," for example, Emerson addresses the titular phrase directly, urging his readers to explore "the *method of nature*. Let us see *that*, as nearly as we can, and try how far it is transferable to the literary life" (*Collected Works* 1: 123). Seeing nature "nearly" and transferring that to literary understanding lead to Emerson's thoughts on our inability to fully analyze the system of nature, which lead to his thoughts on incessant "emanation," which lead him to endless interreferentiality: "This refers to that, and that to the next, and the next to the third, and everything refers" (1: 125). Potential relevance, then, in the case of Nature and Transcendentalism, might be said to arise from transference between disciplines as well as the study of inter- or trans-*reference*—learning to pursue meaning in the varying relations among multireferential systems.

For environmental studies students in the course, but also biology, geology, and neuroscience majors, the transfer involves learning and applying the methods of humanistic inquiry (attention to texts and contexts, cultural history, interpretation, imagination) to questions of nature and ecosystem. For literary students, but also religion, philosophy, and art history majors, it involves in part revising the principles of study: taking the complexity of nature and the fact that we dwell within it as a starting point for interpretive investigations. I try to use the combination of such principles and methods to cultivate what might be deemed a version of scholarly "reverence." Reverence, according to the philosopher Paul Woodruff, "begins in a deep understanding of human limitations . . ." (3). Defining it as a capacity for awe, he links the quality of reverence to a deep sense of belonging to nature, community, ecosystem, cosmos.

In no other course that I teach, including those that also count for environmental studies credit, do I experiment with the kind of textual belonging implied here by "reverence." Students who take Nature and Transcendentalism learn early on in the course that we will be questioning the subject-object split: a recent iteration of the syllabus warns, "In order to discern the nature of transcendentalism, we will attempt to know that nature as 'transcendentally' as we can—that is, we will try to understand transcendentalism from the inside, as it were, rather than viewing it exclusively from some sort of (questionably) detached position." Two significant consequences follow from this premise, one involving interpretation and the other communication.

Weeks before we come to Emerson's "Circles," we consider the figure of circular worldviews that the essay articulates. Rather than approach a given Emerson essay as if we were dissecting it in a laboratory under perfectly controlled conditions, we consider the circle of conditions from which we attempt to make sense of the text. Our goal then is not to sit in judgment of the text but to engage with it in such a way as to take the measure of our reading, as the philosopher Stanley Cavell might say, including the where and when in which we are implicated, the circle within which we read. A stable, discrete, independent subject is not empirically analyzing a stable, discrete, disconnected object. In this way, students come to understand reading as the movement between subject and object, between present and past—a movement that describes a sort of circle of interpretation.

When practiced reflectively, and with care, the circle's limit becomes fluid, permeable, allowing for revision and a flow of ideas. At the heart of any literary study is a theory of interpretation, and students in my course are encouraged to reflect on the nature of interpretation while advancing their skills in its practice. To assist the process, we break interpretation down into phases that don't necessarily occur sequentially. One phase involves examination: paying close attention to the text and contexts, to its elements and structure, and to its historical moment and rhetorical situation, as well as identifying key (that is, most relevant) parts. Another phase involves explicating those parts, connecting them to one another and making them meaningful by investigating their role in the text as a whole. A third phase revolves around extrapolation, drawing out larger meanings from the text, imagining its potential relevance to related situations. A fourth phase requires self-reflectively retracing one's steps in making meaning with a text, trying to interpret one's interpretation—its method(s), values, goals—in relation to the text being interpreted. For example, one of the first Emerson essays we interpret is "The Transcendentalist."[1] Examining the essay, we pay attention to the rhetorical situation implied by its subtitle: "A Lecture

Read at the Masonic Temple, Boston, January, 1842." We think about the historical moment: what's going on in the United States, where the moment falls on the timeline of transcendentalism, when in Emerson's career it occurs. And we outline the essay's structure, discussing key parts and the general movement from beginning to end, connecting this with its rhetorical situations—specifically the lecture's delivery in Boston and its publication.

We concern ourselves with not only what the essay means in terms of Emerson and transcendentalism; we wonder too about what it might mean for us, for nature, for our thinking about nature. How might Emerson's propositions inform our course? What does the essay suggest for literary study? Or for environmental studies? We build off the conclusion of "The Transcendentalist" by asking what it would mean to "reorganize [our]selves in nature, to invest [our]selves anew in other, perhaps higher endowed and happier mixed clay than ours, in fuller union with surrounding system" (*Collected Works* 1: 216). And as we respond to such questions, we circle back through examination, explication, and extrapolation, reflecting on the process of interpretation as a whole and observing the conditions under which we have produced meaning with the text.

The other consequence that follows from studying the literature of transcendentalism "transcendentally" revolves around student participation in developing and communicating relevant ideas. I organize student assignments using some of the forms of communication in which Emerson and company engaged: journal, essay (at midterm and semester's end), conversation (occasional small-group discussions following Margaret Fuller's model), lyceum (a weekly forum in which students give a minilecture on nature, transcendentalism, etc., to the class), and letter (more on this below). Conversation, the lyceum, and letters are all forms of "inside" communication. In these modes, students understand the rhetorical situation to occur within the class, directed toward people who are invested in understanding the course's topics of inquiry and the materials being studied. "Inside" forms of thought and communication, in other words, carry a presupposition of relevance: they are pertinent to the matter at hand. Conversations occur around an assigned problem based on readings for a given week, issues that refer to particular texts and that relate to the class's general interests. A student can craft and deliver a lecture to the lyceum expecting an informed and interested audience, one gathered together for the shared pursuit of understanding nature and transcendentalism.

The lyceum, while involving a lecture delivered to a semicaptive (and, when accomplished particularly well, captivated) audience, foregrounds the issues orators face: a rather severe time limit and the necessary efficacy of particular styles and gambits within the time limit, the ephemeral nature of oral communication, the challenges of communicating in regard to sometimes abstruse material and thought, the expectations and proclivities of the audience, the purpose of the assignment, etc. Even though the nineteenth-century lyceum was, as Kent P. Ljungquist has described it, "A 'performance-based medium' that 'often defied traditional literary conventions,'" and thus in its contemporary manifestation allows for experimentation with ideas as well as styles of presentation, the course's version clearly operates within a relatively definite circle (340–41). It occurs in class, in the context of the course, within the larger context of an undergraduate institution. A lecture is given by a student of the course, for students of the course; it does not have to be relevant for anyone outside of this particular circle, at least not immediately. The same may be said for conversations, in which a designated facilitator works to ensure the discussion's relevance to the assigned task and a designated secretary records and reproduces, for the benefit of the rest of the class, the conversation's most salient aspects.

How "inside" assignments might differ from "outside" assignments can be seen in some of the rhetorical conventions employed to distinguish the letter from the essay. Letters are bipartite, biweekly assignments. The first week, each student writes a one-page, single-spaced letter to another student in the class on an assigned topic; the following week, each recipient of a letter writes a one-page response to the originating writer. (Playing transcendental postman, I have experimented with different ways of establishing the corresponding parties but invariably vary them so that no two students form a lasting epistolary bond.) The assignment has two main functions: to help students develop their interpretation of transcendentalist writings and ideas and to help them take their ideas a step beyond the journal in an attempt to communicate meaningfully and effectively with another student. Regarding the latter, I emphasize that a letter is written to someone else; the writer must envision his or her audience, try to make contact with that person, and attempt to communicate meaningfully within a rhetorical situation of recognizable limits. Because the writing takes place within a particular circle, writers know more about the potential readership and can make some assumptions regarding shared background of reference materials; they can traffic in at least some set of values or meanings held in common.

While an essay might be directed toward a broad audience consisting of people well beyond an author's personal circle, in some ways the writing's goal is to expand the original circle by inviting readers into it. An essay reaches out in order to bring in. Something similar occurs in letter writing: the personal perspective on relevance (as developed in the journal) is converted into a private interaction with another (the letter), potentially extending its circle of relevance further into the public. Much of the correspondence among historical transcendentalists was "done with the knowledge that others would see it" (Myerson, *Transcendentalism* xxx). A value of "inside" assignments is that they help students think more expressly about audience, purpose, method, and relevance. What is learned from practicing "inside" writing can then be applied to "outside," to expanding the circle(s) of relevance.

Teaching Emerson's essays in Nature and Transcendentalism is an expression of the belief that the study of literature matters, that it is pertinent to the study of Earth (to which we belong) and the cosmos (to which it belongs). Associating

Emerson with questions of relevance, I hope students learn not that literature has the answer to our ecological problems or that Emerson is the answer to everything (or to anything). What I want them to learn from Emerson is the necessity of asking questions and the responsibility of pursuing questions, of being pursued by questions. In the end, I'm less interested in establishing that Emerson is relevant than in using his texts (as well as those of Thoreau and others) in pursuit of relevance: in looking for it, determining it, and expressing it. What matters and why? What next? Transcendentalism, I hope, will help students examine our circles and experiment with drawing new, better circles. Perhaps, within the institution, the study of transcendentalism will lead to something like transdisciplinarity: "the cross-fertilisation of knowledge and experiences from diverse groups of people that can promote an enlarged vision of a subject, as well as new explanatory theories" (Lawrence 126). Perhaps, in an even more optative mood, it will lead beyond the institution. Abandoning the customary, asking questions, promoting experiment, and fostering connections, we look to the world beyond the classroom, beyond the disciplines, glimpsing the nature and challenges of the present in illuminative flashes, pursuing relevance even in the ensuing shadows.

NOTE

[1] Emerson's essays form the centerpiece of roughly the first half of the course, along with selected poems, writings of other transcendentalists, works providing some historical context, and pertinent critical responses. "The Transcendentalist" is followed by *Nature*, "The American Scholar," "The Divinity School Address," "The Poet," "Self-Reliance," "The Over-Soul," "The Method of Nature," "Circles," and "Experience."

Emerson in Media Studies
and Journalism

David O. Dowling

Ralph Waldo Emerson commented extensively on the media, especially the periodical press, and its capacity to generate what we now call mass culture. Approaching Emerson from a media and communication studies perspective immerses students in his vast sea of media commentary—ranging from vitriolic to celebratory—on the power of mass communication technology in shaping intellectual life. Students encountering Emerson as media critic can typically see immediate connections between contemporary digital culture and his antebellum print revolution. As a celebrated figure in mass media, Emerson endorsed and supported the use of the commercial press as an amplifier of transcendentalist thought. Instructors can benefit from framing Emerson as a media critic and a celebrity through his writings, in addition to presenting him in the socially embedded roles of his relationships with Henry David Thoreau, Margaret Fuller, and Horace Greeley, which reflect directly on his actions within the publishing industry itself. By considering Emerson first as media critic and then as media star, students can come to a greater understanding of his commentary in the light of his active engagement with figures like Fuller and Greeley, who dedicated their careers and lives to the popular press as a means of serving what Greeley called "The Practical Education of Man" (*Hints* 88) and as "the only efficient instrument for the general education of the people," according to Fuller (*Papers* 138).

As an extension of broader Romantic reactions against industrialization, Emerson's media criticism pairs well with today's Luddite reactions against the Internet and digital technology led by Nicholas Carr (*The Shallows*) and Thomas Cooper (*Fast Media / Media Fast*). Useful for framing the teaching of these critiques are two histories of affective responses to media technology, Lisa Gitelman's *Always Already New: Media, History, and the Data of Culture* and Brenton Malin's *Feeling Mediated: A History of Media Technology and Emotion in America*. Instructors can emphasize from the outset Gitelman's foundational claim that "[m]edia aren't the instruments of scholarship in the humanities, they are the instruments of humanism at large, dynamically engaged within, and as part of the socially realized protocols that define sites of communication and sources of meaning" (153). In this sense, journalism and mass communication approaches to teaching Emerson illuminate how the study of such protocols "offers nothing less—if not a great deal more—than the material cultures of knowledge and information" (153).

Gitelman and Malin help students situate Carr's and Cooper's appropriation of Emerson among the array of cautionary arguments about the commercialized environment of the Internet. The loss of deep reading, what Carr calls "the literary mind," to the Internet's distracting and increasingly superficial headline-driven content seems to have produced a nation of superficial readers (111). Such claims resonate with Emerson's concern for the intellectually and morally corrosive effects of his era's unprecedented mass consumption of popular literature and sensationalistic news. But was Emerson a Luddite? Debate activities on this question encourage students to examine his media commentary as evidence. Other assignments might showcase the contemporary relevance of Emerson's assault on media's role in fueling materialism and consumer culture; one such activity is the media fast Cooper prescribes. The media fast requires that students abstain from selected electronic media to assess their impact on their lives and reevaluate from a critical distance their own media consumption and communication patterns. The objective is to empower students with a more mindful understanding of the media products they use and to historicize the critical perspective on media Carr and others call for.

The current movement in slow journalism is consonant with Cooper's media fast assignment. Slow journalism platforms such as *De Correspondent* and *Delayed Gratification* illustrate how the movement has leveraged digital technology to immerse audience attention rather than scatter it throughout the Internet via a multitude of advertisers' links. Such meaningful, deep reading presents itself to readers willing to "turn off the 'speed up' world long enough to slow down and take personal inventory" of consumption patterns, Cooper observes (5). This awareness of "how and if each medium should be ingested or could be creatively employed" calls into question the low standard of journalism within the Internet's attention economy. The key to the process, especially "[i]n a world of fast media where new technologies, programs, software and publications come faster than one can digest the old," is "to *slow down* . . . to the speed of comprehension and overview," a deep understanding "where Emerson and Thoreau, among others, found transcendence" (16) over what Thoreau called "this nervous, bustling . . . nineteenth century" in which "we are in great haste to construct a telegraph from Maine to Texas; but Maine and Texas, it may be, have nothing important to communicate" (*Walden* 323, 24).

To draw attention to Emerson's own historical moment, instructors can situate his most slashing criticism of the liabilities of the antebellum popular press in the light of his own publishing activities. "I think [nature] more grateful and health giving than any news I am likely to find of man in the journals," he wrote, blaming print media for plaguing mass culture with the trivialization of American intellectual life and the stultifying effects of vocational specialization, allegations at the core of his Romantic reaction against modern industrialization (*Collected Works* 8: 153). He famously defined in "The American Scholar" this commodification of humanity's "fountain of power" into industrial roles to be "distributed to multitudes, and has been so minutely subdivided and peddled out, that it is spilled into drops." In the process, he was enjoying free publicity through the profusion of glowing reviews, excerpts, and reprints of his work that filled the pages of Greeley's weekly *New-Yorker* and, later, the mighty *Tribune* (*Collected Works* 1: 53).

Emerson's activities in the publishing industry on behalf of his many followers alert students to the complexity of his media commentary. Ellery Channing, who had Emerson to thank for landing his position as a staff writer for the *Tribune*, chafed against what he unfairly deemed "certain hateful elements in the Tribune office in N.Y. and seems to have resisted a crisis of spleen." Emerson felt the *Tribune*, especially the structures and routines of news gathering and reporting, might have a curative effect on Channing's wayward romantic impulses. "[T]he Tribune office might be good treatment for some of his local distempers," Emerson allowed, but in Channing's case it "seems a very poor use to put a wise man & a genius to" (*Letters* 7: 618).

Beginning with the "Commodity" section of *Nature* (1836), in which Emerson lauds technological development, telling passages from his journals—particularly those that extol the virtues of the press as a democratic force providing a moral check on its citizens—challenge students to reconcile the tension in his stance toward media proliferation. Ample evidence of this other side of Emerson, the media star and publishing industry insider, reflects his paradoxical advocacy of commercial media expansion, which he wished to refine into a "keener avarice" geared toward individual and cultural liberal reform (*Collected Works* 6: 126). To achieve this objective, students can be introduced to Emerson's own vigorous and often mercenary use of communication networks and technologies to advance his career and those of his followers, as exhibited by his relationship with Greeley and his tutelage of his protégée, the journalist Fuller. Of use are portions of Fuller's *The Memoirs of Margaret Fuller Ossoli* (which Emerson edited) and Greeley's *Recollections of a Busy Life*, particularly the chapters "The Vocation of Authorship," "Socialistic Efforts," and "Literature as a Vocation." These complicate and contextualize Emerson's more idealistic strains on authorship in "The Poet," which are brought into sharp focus concerning their compensatory reaction to the less than ideal economic condition for literary enterprise at the time. "Authorship," by Evert Duyckinck, his first article published in *Arctus* in 1840, provides context for what Greeley called "the grand chorus of complaint" in which authors protested their economic exploitation at the hands of publishers and editors (Everton 34).

When framing Emerson as media celebrity, it is important to highlight that the keener avarice he advocated should not be confused with unfettered capitalism for its own sake. This relation to capital is crucial in forwarding an accurate understanding of Emerson's eagerness to harness the latest technologies of mass communication to advance his career. He emphasized not material extravagance but sustenance enough "that [individuals] may spend in spiritual creation and not in augmenting animal existence." Any remuneration for his efforts he gladly accepted, noting in his journal in 1836, "The philosopher, the priest, hesitates to receive money for his instructions—the author for his works.

Instead of this scruple let them make filthy lucre beautiful by its just expenditure" (*Journals* 5: 120).

Emerson's unique approach toward capital here—its elevation from filthy lucre to the stuff of beauty through just expenditure—is readily applicable to his attitude toward the periodical press. When he was not disparaging the press for generating mass culture that minimized the influence of the intellect, he was exhorting his readers and protégés to elevate its moral status, particularly as a vehicle for popular reform. Emerson enjoyed "a triple visibility: as a publishing author, as a lecturer, and as a subject for newspaper columnists." The last category functioned as an especially potent means by which to reach the widest audience possible, since he "gained huge popularity when [his lectures] were reported or reprinted in newspapers" (Reynolds, "'Chaos-Deep Soil'" 294). In this manner, Emerson's lectures became "an antidote to depraved popular newspapers," a means of ridding them of their diseased sensationalism and gore (295). "There goes the diseased newspaper," Emerson observed with disgust, nonetheless harboring hope in his influence through "the corrective pustule— the 'report of last night's lecture'—inserted by the reporter's quill," a tonic made more potent "by the very circulation of the disease itself, the healing principle is carried to the extremities of the land" (qtd. in Cameron, *Transcendental Log* 69–70). Anticipating today's digital ecosystem, Emerson's metaphor of viral media suggests that it contains toxic fare to be sure, but it also accommodates for edifying and restorative content such as his own lectures, powerful enough to counteract its decadent influence.

Exposing students to Emerson's commentary on Fuller's influential newspaper career in *The Memoirs of Margaret Fuller Ossoli* alerts them to the reform agenda at the heart of his role as a celebrity author who otherwise might appear to have manipulated the media only to advance his own career and those of his followers. In describing Fuller, Emerson asserts, "such a truth speaker is worth more than the best police and worth more than the laws of governors; for these do not always know their own side, but will back the crime for want of this very truth speaker to expose them. That is the theory of the newspaper," he concluded, "to supersede official by intellectual influence" (Emerson et al. 1: 30). The press could be at least partially cured of its predilection toward distorted partisan bias, he argued, with truth speakers such as Fuller. To cleanse the press through such transcendental reformist influence also meant countering its rhetorical one-way subjugation of readers with journalism designed instead to empower and enliven them. In this manner, Fuller's affinity toward her post at the *Tribune* as a socially efficacious platform derived from her belief that "newspaper-writing is next door to conversation," which she actively cultivated at gatherings hosted at the educator Elizabeth Peabody's Boston bookstore (140).

In framing Emerson's own quarrel with mass culture and his views toward the periodical press, implications emerge for "the individual circumstances of authoring technologies like word processing and beyond, as well as the bookseller's marketplace, networks for electronic dissemination, and readerly histories that spill across the whole of the Web 2.0 landscape" (Kirschenbaum and Werner 426). Exposure of students to Emerson's active use of media circuits and knowledge networks to build his fame and that of his followers adds significance to his views and animates the antebellum media ecosystem. Such historical data invites students to resolve for themselves Emerson's ambivalence toward the commercial industrialization of publishing.

Emerson and the Digital Humanities

Amy Earhart

When teaching Emerson we are faced with the challenge of giving students skills with which to engage with Emerson's seemingly dense and difficult writing. Through careful use of digital humanities tools, we might guide students through exercises that provide access points to Emerson's work, aid in interpretation and evaluation of Emerson's ideas, and spur classroom discussion. To illuminate how digital pedagogy might enhance the study of Emerson in the classroom, what follows are sample exercises for classroom use that will help students 1) develop an understanding of textual accuracy and transmission, and 2) use digital methods to analyze Emerson's work. Though focused on specific tools and techniques, these examples highlight the way by which digital pedagogies deepen student engagement with and understanding of literary texts.

One of the concerns of scholars is that students do not understand the importance of textual accuracy and transmission. To address this concern, I have used the *Juxta Commons* digital collation tool to help students understand why reliable texts are crucial to scholarly inquiry. Jerome McGann's brainchild, *Juxta* was developed under the auspices of Nineteenth-Century Scholarship Online (NINES) and allows the user to compare versions of texts (collation, a classic technique in editing) and to complete various tasks related to digital edition building. A free, Web-based tool, *Juxta* is designed to create "interpretive comparisons" that the user might then examine to fulfill "the basic humanities interpretive act: critical comparison" (McGann). The use of *Juxta* in the classroom teaches students to see the impact of textual reliability on the way that we understand and interpret Emerson. More simply put, a flawed literary text will produce a problematic, even inaccurate scholarly analysis. A comparison of various editions or versions of an Emerson essay allows the instructor to emphasize the importance of textual variability and to create points of engagement for student analysis of the text, what Amanda Gailey calls "attentive reading."

The first challenge instructors face is to identify reliable electronic versions of Emerson's writings. Emerson's works have been digitized at a rapid pace, though the quality of texts is varied. Much of our current digital textual data is limited because of such transcription issues. Large-scale projects such as Google Books or Eighteenth Century Collections Online (ECCO) use optical character recognition (OCR), the translation of images to machine-readable files, of variable quality. This impacts not only the readability of materials but also the searchability, as most full-text searches of large literary data sets are based on OCR'd documents—an issue well documented by critics including Geoffrey Nunberg, who has been outspoken in his critique of misnaming, misdating, and other metadata errors in *Google Books*. Since Harvard's *The Collected Works of Ralph Waldo Emerson*, the most trusted edition of Emerson's work, is not available in manipulable digital format, I have turned to the Ralph Waldo Emerson Society's Web site, which includes links to higher-quality digital transcriptions of Emerson texts on its "Related Sites" page. When teaching Emerson's "New England Reformers," for example, the instructor could have students compare two different versions of the essay: an 1844 essay, such as the version from Jone Johnson Lewis's *Emerson Central*, to a Centenary Edition essay, such as in the University of Michigan's digitized *The Complete Works of Ralph Waldo Emerson*. Given critical concerns regarding Edward Waldo Emerson's editing of his father's texts, the comparison of the two versions makes for interesting class discussion and reflection regarding the way that editing choices impact the texts we study.

Once the primary texts are located, using *Juxta* is relatively simple. Students create a free account through the Juxta Commons Web site and then upload a digital file of the Emerson text or texts. *Juxta* accepts a wide variety of file formats (html, doc, and pdf), making it a versatile program as the instructor doesn't have to spend a great deal of time producing documents for analysis. When the digital versions are uploaded into *Juxta* they must be converted into "witnesses" and grouped into comparison sets, simple tasks to complete with the easy-to-use tool. Once the texts are converted and grouped, students may begin to use the visualizations created by *Juxta* to compare the 1844 and Centenary versions of Emerson's "New England Reformers." *Juxta* creates a heat map (textual differences suggested by gradations of color), a side-by-side visualization, a two-text comparison with lines linking differences in texts, and a histogram (a visualization of the overall rate of change). The first two visualizations prove most helpful for pedagogical purposes. The heat map of the two witnesses of "New England Reformers" displays several textual differences (see "Heat Map," dx.doi.org/10.17613/M68D7D).[1]

In this particular paragraph the differences expressed are primarily punctuation and capitalization. For a closer look at the differences, students may use the side-by-side comparison (see "Side-by-Side Comparison," dx.doi.org/10.17613/M64M43). As they look through the text, students will notice that the witnesses include word choice differences. For example, Emerson writes that the university is either "ludicrously styled" or "ludicrously called." Such substantive differences will surprise and engage students and allow the instructor to emphasize that even small editorial changes might impact the way we understand a text. Such "interactivity and visuals" in digital pedagogy approaches, argues W. Michele Simmons, "increase opportunities for learning but also simultaneously introduce complexities."

Students will also be interested in the discrepancies in document structures, including the paragraph breaks, spacing, and punctuation. For some scholars, such as Peter Shillingsburg, the issue of digital accuracy is central but also revealing: "Error can be just noise. We correct it or ignore it just as we talk and listen over the noise of a passing train or when surrounded by cocktail chatter. Error can also be serendipitous discovery, leading us to new insights and allowing for repurposing of old texts" (161). Student manipulation of texts, then, helps them to engage in the important conversations about literature, texts, and the creation of information in the digital age.

While these exercises hint at the importance of a reliable text, assignments explicitly designed to require students to examine textual editing are also productive. Some critics, such as Gailey, situate such concerns in the digital humanities, noting "the continuation into the digital age of the disciplines concerned with the materiality and representation of texts, such as textual studies and editorial theory" (192). A *Juxta* assignment that allows students to locate corruptions in an Emerson text not only emphasizes the materials and representations of texts, but it reminds students of the importance of textual accuracy. With a digital collation project students learn "to be attentive to small details, discovering that changes in small details—even when not authorized by the author—can alter dramatically interpretation" (Hawkins 138). For this assignment, I choose two different versions of the same text: Lewis's carefully edited 1844 text of "New England Reformers" and the same essay from the 1909 Harvard Classics series, found on the *Internet Archive* that has been machine transcribed from the *Google Books* digitization (English Traits). I ask students to think about what they might find when they collate the two versions. After the first exercise, students recognize that the two versions will have differences, but they are unaware of the differences introduced by the machine transcription. When collated, students learn that there are numerous substantive differences beyond the two differing versions of the essay (see "Collation Heat Map," dx.doi .org/10.17613/M60X1T).

In the exercise students realize that the file title is incorrectly translated ("Ralph W,|UX) Emer5on") and individual words are incorrectly rendered. Such inaccuracies cause great difficulties with text mining and with full-text searches. The distortion of *hospital*, for example, would mean that a search looking at the word choices Emerson uses in his entire corpus that reference disease would miss this important reference. Important when teaching with digital techniques is to reveal the limitations of the analysis that might be made with technological innovation. Side-by-side comparisons reveal that the primary differences in the text are errors introduced by the machine transcription (see "Collation Side-by-Side Comparison," hcommons.org/deposits/item/hc:13665).

While collation tools are useful to engaging students in understandings of textual accuracy and transmission, the use of topic-modeling software provides additional teaching possibilities. Topic modeling is described by Miriam Posner as "a method for finding and tracing clusters of words (called 'topics' in shorthand) in large bodies of texts." Topic modeling is central to digital humanities work, and student familiarity with such an approach to textual analysis is increasingly a centerpiece of digital pedagogy. Though there are numerous tools that might be of use, Stefan Sinclair and Geoffrey Rockwell's.Web-based plug-and-play set of tools, *Voyant*, has long been my go-to for undergraduate students. *Voyant* is fairly easy to use and produces high-quality visualizations for analysis. In addition, the tools are currently being revised, a fairly unique occurrence among start-up digital humanities tools, which often run out of funding and are often unmaintained, unstable, and unacceptable for classroom applications. *Voyant's* new updates should reassure instructors that assignments developed for the *Voyant* tools will be possible in the future.

Topic modeling allows students to visualize large-scale patterns across multiple texts. Paul Fyfe describes this as a sort of "'hybrid' critical work" that "allows for specificities within close contexts as students read, and for connections within and across texts." In a course where students are reading multiple Emerson essays, for example, topic modeling might aid students in understanding his shifting ideas over time. In a class focused on Emerson and slavery, for instance, the instructor might have students upload three related Emerson texts to *Voyant* for comparison: "Address on Emancipation in the British West Indies" (1844), "The Fugitive Slave Law" (1854), and "The Emancipation Proclamation" (1862) (see "Cirrus Word Cloud," dx.doi.org/10.17613/M6RD6C).[2]

Once the texts are uploaded, *Voyant* performs multiple visualizations using a suite of tools. The Cirrus tool produces a word cloud that represents the number of times a word appears in the text, which allows the instructor to ask the students to interpret Emerson's repetition of certain words. Because Cirrus highlights Emerson's use of *man* and *men* as the most used words in these three Emerson essays, the instructor might prompt students to place Emerson's essays in the context of other literature of the nineteenth century, such as contemporaneous slave narratives, including *Narrative of the Life of Frederick Douglass*, that reclaim *man* for African Americans. Discussion of the repetitive words used by Emerson, such as *man, power, good,* and *slavery,* might also prove illuminating, revealing to students "that they are creating knowledge and creating it through acts of interpretation" (Hawkins 139).

Voyant's Corpus Text tool provides additional information for such discussions. When multiple documents are added to *Voyant,* the Corpus Text tool shows the trend of individual words between documents (see "Corpus Terms," dx.doi.org/10.17613/M6MM5T). Since the three essays have been uploaded in progressive order, trends across time and essay are revealed. When students examine the visualizations they might posit that Emerson's use of *slave* might have dropped between 1844 and 1862 because of the Emancipation Proclamation (1863). Or that the use of *man,* which peaks in usage in Emerson's "The Fugitive Slave Law," reveals how Emerson understands slavery in relationship to the individual. The tool's ability to reveal such patterns, then, allows the instructor to encourage the humanistic interpretations that are the basis of literary analysis.

In addition to tracking individual word repetition throughout multiple texts, *Voyant's* Links tool encourages students to think about what concepts of the texts are interrelated. Links reveals that Emerson uses the term *men* in relationship to a host of words, including *colleges, England, accomplished, law, class,* etc. (see "Links," dx.doi.org/10.17613/M6GX0S). What is Emerson saying about men in college? Why the connection to England or to law? Students might begin by hypothesizing what Emerson might be suggesting by the relationship and, after initial discussion, return to the essay. If students thought that Emerson was interested in sorting out men according to class status, then we might locate the passage from "The Fugitive Slave Law": "For every man speaks mainly to a class whom he works with and more or less fully represents. It is to these I am beforehand related and engaged, in this audience or out of it—to them and not to others" (*Complete Works* 11: 218 [U of Michigan]). Reflecting on the association of *class* and *man* might lead a student to revise his or her opinion of Emerson's ideas about class. While the movement between tool (a distant reading of the text) and text (a close reading) may not provide a brilliant aha moment, using visualizations does ask the student to engage in the text in a deeper and more interactive method than would be easily accomplished in a traditional lecture class. Students feel far more invested in their interpretation of the text in such an approach, leading to a more engaged discussion of Emerson.

The use of digital pedagogical techniques within the classroom allows the instructor to provide a window into what students perceive as the dense and difficult language of Emerson. Through the use of carefully designed assignments, students might find Emerson's texts challenging puzzles for interpretation. The digital tools that I have discussed are open access, easy to use, and applicable to varying pedagogical approaches and classrooms. The tools allow us to emphasize the best practices in our field: interpretation through distant and close reading, contextual interpretation, and attention to the transmission of a document.

NOTES

[1] All figures are stored at the MLA commons CORE repository (mla.hcommons.org/core).

[2] For this assignment, I use texts from Lewis's "Ralph Waldo Emerson Texts" Web page.

Emerson's Transatlantic Networks

Leslie Elizabeth Eckel

In my advanced undergraduate course Global American Literature, Ralph Waldo Emerson's "The American Scholar" (1837) serves as both an answer to a historically specific question about the origins of literary culture in the United States and a provocation to interrogate this national way of thinking. Ever an accessible and appealing text for students, who understand that it was written for "young men [and women] in libraries" and appreciate what looks like a very clear structure in contrast to other essays by Emerson, the address invites readers to share in familiar formulations of national pride even as it deeply questions them and demands that they be considered in the contexts of individual development and wider revolutions (*Collected Works* 1: 56). The deceptive simplicity of Emerson's wake-up call to "the sluggard intellect of this continent" is the ideal entry point into a course that values American literature for its connections to larger networks of transatlantic, transnational, and global cultures (1: 52).

After hearing on the first day about the English critic Sydney Smith's 1820 challenge, "In the four quarters of the globe, who reads an American book?" students normally rush to defend the status and imaginative possibilities of American literature, just as Emerson's contemporaries did in the early decades of the nineteenth century (79). Who would dare accuse a country that nurtures such writers as Walt Whitman, F. Scott Fitzgerald, and Toni Morrison of failing to contribute to world literature? At first my course encourages this response, gathering in the second week a group of readings that seem to assert a distinct American national identity, including Emerson's "The American Scholar," John Louis O'Sullivan's blustering "The Great Nation of Futurity" (1839), and selections from Washington Irving's *The Sketch Book of Geoffrey Crayon, Gent.*

(1819–20), such as the essay "English Writers on America" and the short stories "Rip Van Winkle" and "The Legend of Sleepy Hollow." Margaret Fuller's 1844 review of Emerson's essays in the *New-York Tribune* is the odd one out in this group, but it offers a key that turns "The American Scholar" in an entirely different direction from the rest (*Margaret Fuller*).

Students prepare for these discussions by completing a reading response on "Sources of American Creativity," which prods them to identify the ways in which each writer meets Smith's challenge by evoking desirable national elements such as "American patterns of thought," "American inspiration," and "American style." As they build up this evidence, students are asked to consider each text as an "argument for nationality" and to determine which of these claims they find the most persuasive and why. The response assignment suggests that these roots branch out into different models of American literature that animate the nineteenth century and grow into the twentieth century—the time frame the course itself aims to cover. Already invested in the narrative of American literary nationality, students arrive in class well prepared to discuss the "Americanness" of these writings in relation to one another.

"The American Scholar" is first on the agenda. Discussion begins with questions: At the beginning of this address, where is Emerson's "America" in time? What problems does he believe the country must confront? Students recognize the tone of defensive belatedness that appears to be a natural response to an insult like Smith's. Emerson seems to demand that the United States respond to the "postponed expectation of the world" with an original, autochthonous literature that represents "[e]vents, actions . . . that must be sung, that will sing themselves" (*Collected Works* 1: 52). An invitation such as Emerson's could be taken as a starting point for a self-consciously American literary tradition that readers might trace from Emerson to Whitman to, in turn, his twentieth-century respondents such as Langston Hughes and Allen Ginsberg. Indeed, Emerson's concerns about a condition of "dependence" and a "long apprenticeship to the learning of other lands" align this address with ideas about an American postcolonial literary culture explored by Robert Weisbuch and Lawrence Buell ("Postcolonial Anxiety") that could provoke further reading and discussion in a graduate seminar on American literature (*Collected Works* 1: 52).[1]

After considering the opening pages of "The American Scholar," students reach a consensus on Emerson's effort to identify a pressing agenda for the promotion of national culture. Yet the address almost immediately takes a different course, as Emerson sketches the abstract figure of "Man Thinking" and prescribes healthy doses of nature, books, and action to cure his currently "degenerate state" (*Collected Works* 1: 53). Although these sections provide fascinating material for discussion in themselves, I ask students how Emerson's claims relate to the state of American literature with which he seems so vitally concerned at the start of the address. Silence normally ensues as they struggle to reconcile these two modes of thought. After all, the authors Emerson mentions in his section on books are either classical or English: Cicero, Locke, and Bacon;

Chaucer, Marvell, and Dryden; Plato and Shakespeare. I push them further by asking if Emerson is using American language at all in the rest of this address. This is usually a difficult yet productive moment, as it asks the students to turn away from their assumptions about the text's central concerns and to loosen their grip on the "American" imperative of "The American Scholar."

On the one hand, Emerson's argument is an American one, but on the other, it concentrates its energies on the cultivation of global awareness and the growth of individuals who inhabit that globe. If students are familiar with "Self-Reliance" (1841), they might see the roots of that essay in such statements as "In self-trust, all the virtues are comprehended" (*Collected Works* 1: 63). At the same time, Emerson seeks to situate the scholar and his country within a larger world that can nurture his understanding and provide a sense of purpose for his endeavors. Unlike in "Self-Reliance," where Emerson warns against travel as a "fool's paradise," in this explicitly "American" address, he embraces global ways of thinking and knowing (*Collected Works* 2: 46). "I will not shut myself out of this globe of action," he writes, urging his audience to venture abroad, to "sail for Greece or Palestine, follow the trapper into the prairie, or ramble round Algiers to replenish their merchantable stock" (*Collected Works* 1: 60). Emerson becomes in this moment an advocate not only of action but also of international education, exhorting his listeners to take their studies abroad in order to "replenish" their minds and the home country they serve.

Within the context of my Global American Literature course, this adventurous outlook points students toward writings such as Margaret Fuller's dispatches from Europe (1846–50) and Ernest Hemingway's *A Moveable Feast* (1964), which, when encountered later in the semester, suggest that the wisest American travelers are those who practice a form of transplantation, seeding American soil with ideas from other countries. Here, Emerson also resembles Henry Wadsworth Longfellow, whose efforts to modernize the Harvard curriculum in the 1830s and 1840s included offering lectures on European literatures, which he hoped would draw students as well as members of the general public into dialogue with other contemporary world cultures.[2] In fact, students in my course have already been exposed to this broader perspective, as during the first class meeting they read a passage from Longfellow's little-known novel *Kavanagh* (1849), which contains a debate between two characters who advocate for national literature and international openness. While Longfellow's characters repeatedly clash, leaving these matters unresolved, Emerson manages to reconcile multiple interests in "The American Scholar," which considers American nationality in tandem with a familiar transcendentalist message of self-culture and an unexpectedly global point of view.

The multiplicity of Emerson's address stands in stark contrast to the single-mindedness of O'Sullivan's "The Great Nation of Futurity" and the transatlantic anxieties of Irving's "English Writers on America." Voicing the naive optimism of the Young America movement, O'Sullivan envisions the United States in a "disconnected position as regards any other nation," with "little connection with the past history of any of them"; instead America is at "the beginning of a new history" (426). O'Sullivan's answer to Smith insists that a global network of readers has little relevance to a "disconnected" United States, which stands not in belated relation to other world cultures—the position that Emerson acknowledges yet desires to surpass—but rather at the "beginning" of the only national history that matters. In contrast to O'Sullivan's willful isolation of the United States, Irving sees the nation as far too connected to its European counterparts. Overrun by English writers ready to judge its "national character . . . yet in a state of fermentation," Irving's "infant giant" of a country produces a literature that is perpetually on the defensive, for he imagines that "every day we live a whole volume of refutation" (44–45). O'Sullivan's and Irving's essays help students see the extremes of this debate about national literary identity: the one insisting on complete independence and the other on intellectual dependence.

Despite the threat to a nascent national culture represented by "the courtly muses of Europe," Emerson does not hesitate to embrace his contemporaries across the Atlantic. Indeed, he asserts that such writers as Goethe, Wordsworth, and Carlyle (along with their predecessors Goldsmith, Burns, and Cowper) embody the "genius" of the age (*Collected Works* 1: 68). Emerson perceives this "age of Revolution; when the old and new stand side by side, and admit of being compared," as a definitively Atlantic era, not an entirely American creation (1: 67). In class, this is the ideal moment to discuss Emerson's involvement with British Romantic writers both in his detailed reading of their work and in the visits he made to Wordsworth, Carlyle, Coleridge, and others during his travels abroad in 1833 and 1847–48, first as a tourist and later as an invited lecturer. Emerson's lasting friendship with Carlyle in particular served as a conduit for knowledge of European Romanticism, and Carlyle was Fuller's point of entry into Europe in 1846, when Emerson introduced her to him as "our citizen of the world by quite special diploma" (*Correspondence* 407).

A more advanced course might include examples of scholarship by Leon Chai, Joel Pace, David Greenham, and Samantha Harvey that illuminate the extent to which Emerson's thought developed in conscious and unconscious dialogue with his transatlantic Romantic colleagues. In this Anglo-American vein, Christopher Hanlon identifies Emerson's line of "nearly continuous connection to England" as he examines *English Traits* (1856; xii). Whereas a more deliberately nationalist writer might have written a book about the United States, Emerson turns away from these local concerns, firmly situating both *English Traits* and *Representative Men* (1850) on European ground. Emerson's thinking was so thoroughly transatlantic, in fact, that he identified the core of *Nature* (1836), what he called the "first philosophy," just as he made his crossing home to the United States in 1833 (*Journals* 4: 79). This statement of purpose, drawn from Emerson's journals, helps illustrate two points of significant value for students: the degree to which Emerson needed non-American figures like Wordsworth and Coleridge to push against even as he articulated his own vision, which often seems so authentically American, and the extent to which American literature's concept of itself is born from a transatlantic genealogy.[3]

It was Fuller, Emerson's collaborator in the transnational intellectual project of *The Dial*, who was among the first to recognize the contradictory nature of Emerson's Americanism. Although her *New-York Tribune* review of "Emerson's Essays" does not respond directly to "The American Scholar," but rather evaluates *Essays: Second Series* upon its publication in 1844, Fuller perceives an ongoing pattern in Emerson's thought. She comments, "If only as a representative of the claims of individual culture in a nation which tends to lay such stress on artificial organization and external results, Mr. Emerson would be invaluable here. History will inscribe his name as a father of the country, for he is one who pleads her cause against herself" (*Margaret Fuller* 2). Fuller imagines a way of thinking like an American, even as a founding father of sorts, by going against the grain. Emerson does so, she argues, by focusing on "individual culture" rather than collective "results." As entangled as "The American Scholar" might be in questions of geography, students are surprised to see that Emerson subordinates nations to individuals, as he asserts, "The main enterprise of the world for splendor, for extent, is the upbuilding of a man" (*Collected Works* 1: 65). As this man gains power, he himself incarnates the nation, and Emerson envisions a world in which "man shall treat with man as a sovereign state with a sovereign state," leading "to true union as well as greatness" (1: 68).

Instead of pursuing Americanism as an end in itself, as O'Sullivan does, Emerson seeks to align the culture as a whole with the goals of the individual thinker: a model Henry David Thoreau follows in "Resistance to Civil Government" (1849), in which he holds the state to account for its failure to meet his own moral standards. Within the next few weeks of my course, Thoreau's essay follows Emerson's lead (as interpreted by Fuller), networking the transcendentalists into the theory and practice of civil disobedience developed in the twentieth century by Mohandas Gandhi and Martin Luther King, Jr. Fuller's reading of Emerson as at once for and "against" the United States in its quest for national identity not only aligns him with Thoreau, Gandhi, and King but lays the groundwork for our subsequent encounters with Frederick Douglass's *My Bondage and My Freedom* (1855), Herman Melville's *Benito Cereno* (1855), and Charles Johnson's *Middle Passage* (1990)—texts that leverage their Atlantic and oceanic frameworks to critique, to ironize, and to empty out assumptions about maintaining a cohesive American national narrative.

In "The American Scholar," Emerson's simultaneous engagement with and disengagement from the demands of American literary nationalism that occupied his peers place him in an unusual position, tied to the United States yet inspired by the larger world. Never quite leaping into the heart of European revolutions, as Fuller would in 1848, but also never declaring earnest allegiance to patriotic concerns, Emerson left the doors of his mind open to ideas from within the nation as well as from without. Emerson's writing encourages students to understand the potentially productive multiplicity of thinking like a scholar who is both personally connected and deeply committed, as he was, to a wider world of thought and action.

NOTES

[1] Weisbuch discusses Emerson's rejection of such "dependence," arguing that it had to be either one or the other: "it could never be Emerson and Europe but can only be Emerson or Europe" (193).

[2] For further information about this phase of Longfellow's career, see Eckel (28–29).

[3] In *Atlantic Republic*, Paul Giles makes a similar argument from an English perspective, as he notes that documenting the development of the United States helped English literature define itself. Joseph Rezek has also addressed this phenomenon of Americanization as a transatlantic process.

Teaching the Latin American Emerson

Anne Fountain

Emerson is an early and important hemispheric "border crosser"; his poetry and ideas about nature headed south to Spanish-speaking countries before the end of the nineteenth century. Although the impact of Emerson in Latin America is profound, it is not widely known. Emerson's ideas traveled most successfully through the influence he had on the Cuban poet and patriot José Martí, who translated portions of Emerson's prose and poetry in the 1880s and 1890s and who considered him a kindred spirit. The American transcendentalist probably never imagined that a Cuban living in exile in the United States could give his thoughts an extraordinary contemporary reach, yet that is what has happened. This essay shows how José Martí, Domingo Faustino Sarmiento, and Rafael Pombo introduced Emerson to the Spanish-speaking world and how their interpretations of Emerson's work can be taught in courses in Latin American studies, Spanish American literature, and translation. Reading and understanding Emerson in a broad hemispheric framework contributes to a significant literary and cultural dialogue.

I am a professor of Latin American literature and a specialist on Cuban literature and José Martí, and I have included a focus on Emerson in courses taught in both English and Spanish. The approaches described below are suitable for undergraduate as well as graduate classes. For me, the starting point for introducing Emerson is José Martí, whose outsize role lends itself to connections and comparisons with other Spanish American writers.

José Martí is famous as the national hero of Cuba, as a prolific New York–based correspondent for Spanish American newspapers in the 1880s, and as the author of the seminal essay "Nuestra América" ("Our America"). He is also the person who most fully and faithfully introduced Emerson to Latin Americans. The Cuban exile "discovered" Emerson by reading newspaper obituaries and tributes published in New York after Emerson's death, and with trembling hand, he began to share his newfound knowledge. The essay "Emerson," published in the Caracas newspaper *La opinión nacional* ("The National Opinion") on 19 May 1882, was the start of a sustained association and affinity with the poet of Concord and his ideas, and it is the starting point for any study of the Martí-Emerson ties. Emerson's "Fable," translated by Martí as "Cada uno a su oficio" ("To Each His Own") and published in Martí's magazine for children, *La edad de oro* ("The Golden Age"), in 1888, continues the Cuban's focus on Emerson and provides a case study in translation, literary adaptation, and poetic aesthetics. In addition to the published essay, a shorter follow-up article, and the translated poem, Martí produced fragmentary versions in Spanish of "The World-Soul," "Good-bye," "The Test," and "Blight." He made generous reference to Emerson in his notebooks and clearly considered the American author a source of inspiration. Emerson's impact is clearly evident in Martí's most famous book of poems, *Versos sencillos*.[1]

Another admirer of Emerson's was Domingo Faustino Sarmiento, the president of Argentina from 1868 to 1874, a prodigious writer, and the author of the landmark work in Latin American letters, *Civilización y barbarie* ("Civilization and Barbarism"; 1845).[2] Sarmiento met Emerson in 1865 while serving as Argentina's ambassador to the United States, and following Emerson's death he published, in June 1882, a two-page tribute in Buenos Aires.

The Colombian poet Rafael Pombo, a third contributor to the Latin American Emerson, resided in the United States from 1855 to 1872, working as a diplomat, writer, and translator. Pombo's years in North America (except for a brief return to Colombia in 1856–57) and his sustained engagement with American letters, especially correspondence with Longfellow and Bryant, are thoroughly treated in Kirsten Silva Gruesz's *Ambassadors of Culture*. Pombo's handwritten Spanish version of Emerson's "Fable," dated 1871, was found in Longfellow's home and published posthumously in *Fabulas y verdades* ("Fables and Truths") in 1916 (Englekirk 28).[3]

Teaching Approaches

My primary pedagogical goal is for my students to see Emerson's literary influence as a matter of cross-cultural translation. But I take a variety of approaches as appropriate for the different courses. In a class where students are reading Martí in English, whether an American literature course, a Latino studies course, or a Latin American studies course, the accuracy and effectiveness of the translation is important. My classes use Martí's *Selected Writings*, translated and edited by Esther Allen.

The Emersonian imprint on Martí is evident throughout the article sent to Venezuela in 1882 and published in *La opinión nacional*. Here is what we know about the work. This article conforms to a pattern that Martí established during his years in the United States (1880–95), which was to peruse American newspapers and journals, synthesize what he read, and convey the information in Spanish through letters sent to the South American and Mexican press. His trademark was the creation of the *crónica* ("chronicle"), a piece of writing that rested between journalism and literary portraiture and through which he offered a detailed picture of America in its Gilded Age. Martí's chronicle about Emerson is an excellent example. It expresses the writer's emotions and enthusiasm for the subject, gives statements of fact, and explains why Emerson should be known. It also conveys many of Emerson's basic concepts, including twenty-three allusions to *Nature*, many of them translations or paraphrases, and references to "The Over-Soul," "Montaigne; or, The Skeptic," "Self-Reliance," and the poem "Wealth" (Fountain 46). Martí's empathy for his subject was so intense that many times it is difficult to discern where their thoughts diverge.

In fact, the Cuban and the American had much in common as writers. Both excelled in essays and poetry; both translated; both composed discourses and letters of literary value; both recorded thoughts, points of inspiration, and explanations in their notebooks; both relied upon repetition and illustration; both had the tendency to jump from one thought to another; and both are famous for creating widely quoted maxims. Finally, both became pioneering figures in their respective cultural worlds; José Martí is one of Latin America's greatest writers.

A useful exercise for students reading the essay in English is to ask them to consider key statements from the essay and discuss whether they refer to Emerson, Martí, or both. I typically give ten or eleven examples (two sample statements are given below). To do this exercise responsibly, respondents need to be knowledgeable about both Martí and Emerson. It makes students think and discuss but also prompts them to look back at the reading itself.

> When a person has lived well, the hearse is a triumphal chariot.
>
> (Martí, *Selected Writings* 116)

> Some of his poems are like a grove of oak trees in bloom. . . . And other poems of his are like trickles of precious stones, or shreds of cloud, or shards of lightning.   (129)

This assignment prompts lively discussion, but the nearly unanimous class response is that the statements describe both writers and underscore Martí's identification with his subject. For students well versed in Emerson but not Martí, a challenge might be to critique Martí's essay: How effective is it as an introduction? What points are missing? How does it reflect the time in which it was composed? And would it be suitable for readers in the United States today? To emphasize historical sources, students can consult newspaper and other print accounts at the time of Emerson's death.

In classes taught in Spanish, we study Martí's translation of Emerson's poetry and the discernible Emersonian imprint in *Versos sencillos*. For an undergraduate translation class, students compare Emerson's "Fable" and the translation published in *La edad de oro*. Students in a graduate seminar also study "Fable" but in a comparative context, where they analyze specific examples that link Emerson to the poetry of *Versos sencillos* and apply translation studies precepts, such as those given by Lawrence Venuti.

A doctor-ordered period of rest in 1890 sent Martí to the town of Haines Falls near the Catskill Mountains, a locale not unlike the natural world of Concord. As Martí tells us in the prologue to *Versos sencillos*, this was the setting where the poems were composed. Gonzalo de Quesada y Miranda, whose father knew Martí in New York, was one of the first to detect an Emerson air in *Versos sencillos*. He connected the lines "Arte soy entre las artes; / En los montes, monte soy" ("I am art among the arts / In the woodlands I am at home"), in the second stanza of the first poem, with Emerson's philosophy and profound communion with nature (19). These lines, in fact, suggest a direct link to the introduction to *Nature*, where Emerson states, "*Nature* in the common sense, refers to essences unchanged by man; space, the air, the river, the leaf. *Art* is applied to the mixture of his will with the same things as in a house, a canal, a statue, a picture" (*Collected Works* 1: 8). Effective translation of the word *monte* is vital to understanding the connection. While many translators (including myself initially) have misconstrued *monte* in this context as *mountain*, for Cubans it implies woodlands or forested land and readily prompts the concept of nature. Art and nature. *Arte y monte*. Martí is likely incorporating key concepts from *Nature* in this stanza.

Fast-forward to Pete Seeger and his popularization of Martí's verses in the song he called "Guantanamera," and we have a subtle but real echo of Emerson in music that is literally sung around the globe (for a complete account see the introduction to my translation of *Versos sencillos* [12–13]). In the twenty-first century a new version of the poetry, sung by the Spanish pop group Laredo, emphasizes the "arte y monte" refrain in the song "Mi verso" ("My Verse"). I use these musical versions of Martí's poetry—both "Guantanamera" and the Laredo selections—to emphasize the surprising cross-cultural transfer of Emerson's thoughts through song.

When students in an undergraduate translation class compare "Fable" with the Martí translation that appears in *La edad de oro*, they focus first on vocabulary choices such as Emerson's use of the expression "little prig" (*Collected Works* 9: 141), which Martí conveys as "presumidilla" ("full of one's self," "vain") (*Obras* 18: 325). There is usually lively discussion as to whether the version in Spanish is faithful to the original and about the challenges of translating verse while taking into account message, meaning (of individual words), and rhyme and maintaining poetry. They note that "Fable" has nineteen lines and the translation has twenty-two, and that the translation very nearly duplicates Emerson's rhyme.

In courses where students contrast Martí's version of "Fable" with the rendition by Rafael Pombo, they note that the titles signal two very different approaches to translation. Martí's title is message focused—"Cada uno a su oficio" ("To Each His Own")—and Pombo's is more literal—"El monte y la ardilla" ("The Mountain and the Squirrel"). Although in general Pombo hewed closely to literal interpretations, he introduced God, which neither Martí nor Emerson did, as the creator of nature's differences. Pombo arranged the verses in eight stanzas of four lines each, with *abab* rhyme in each stanza, conforming to a desire for structure that Martí had noted in his overall critique of the Colombian's poetry. Like Emerson's, Martí's version is much freer, with lines of differing length and a variable but consistent rhyme. Although the two translations are quite distinct, they both convey the poem's meaning effectively. Because "Fable" is part of *La edad de oro*, a classic collection of children's literature that has reached generations of Latin Americans and is especially dear to Cubans, and because Pombo is a very popular Colombian writer whose verses continue to be published, this single poem is no doubt the most widely disseminated Emerson work in the Spanish-speaking world.

To understand the principal way in which Emerson reached nineteenth-century Spanish America, students in a graduate course in Spanish read the 1882 essay that Martí sent to *La opinión nacional*. This is a classic Martí *crónica* that takes liberally from press sources in the United States, translates spontaneously, and adds critical comment throughout. My close reading of both Emerson and the *crónica* documented more than twenty-five examples of Martí translations and paraphrases of the American author's thoughts, principally from *Nature* but from other works as well, and that sleuthing allows me to demonstrate for students the value of close reading in more than one language (Fountain 46). The discovery became the primary basis for understanding Martí's intense identification with Emerson and informs work by José Ballón as well as Oscar Montero's description of a "Bilingual Emerson" in his book *José Martí: An Introduction* (105). In the seminar we highlight the translations in the Spanish text to show how they are interwoven in the essay.

Contrasting the thirteen-and-a-half-page essay Martí sent to Venezuela and the two-page necrology published by Sarmiento in Buenos Aires shows students the great disparity in what and how much Spanish American readers learned about Emerson from the two pieces. Although Sarmiento personally met Emerson, considered him a great man, and was familiar with his writings, the brief piece published in Buenos Aires rests lightly with its readers. It is reminiscent in nature. Sarmiento made reference to Emerson's associates, mentioned *Representative Men* and *Nature*, and declared that the American had inspired an "Emerson School of ideas" (375). By contrast, the Cuban writer's tribute leaves a reader swept up by Martí's enthusiasm for his subject and with a representative sampling of the American writer's work to absorb. The essay mentions key titles and offers a physical description of Emerson the man. It presents him through symbols of energy and greatness, such as a mountain, an eagle, a pine. His character is likened to a star, and his verses are wings of gold. No brief comment can do justice to the layers of praise and the tapestry of ideas in the Emerson introduced to Latin Americans by the article Martí sent to Venezuela in 1882. It remains the most comprehensive way that those in the Southern Hemisphere learned of America's transcendentalist.

Understanding Emerson through dialogue with Latin American writers shows the extraordinary global reach of the man from New England. And for many students in Spanish classes, especially heritage speakers, it is a first and surprising connection between their cultural world and literature from the United States. Examples in this essay show how Emerson's work can be introduced in courses in Spanish, Latin American studies, and translation and with a variety of approaches that include close reading, comparative analysis, and a focus on translation strategies. Reading Emerson in a broad hemispheric literary and cultural context crosses language borders, connects the nineteenth century to twenty-first-century music, and confirms the universal and contemporary appeal of an icon in American letters.

NOTES

¹ *Versos sencillos* is a book of forty-six rhymed poems. The title belies an easy translation into English, although conventionally scholars and translators have used "Simple Verses." The problem with this rendition is that the verses are complex, not simple, and the facile translation conveys a false message. In my *Versos sencillos* I explain the title by saying that the verses are the "sincere songs of an honest heart" (3). In this chapter I maintain the original Spanish title.

² *Civilización y barbarie*, a work that describes the life of a savage but savvy gaucho, Juan Facundo Quiroga, is commonly called *Facundo*. Sarmiento's sustained contacts with prominent Americans included Mary Mann, the widow of Horace Mann, who translated *Facundo*.

³ Martí (1853–95), Sarmiento (1811–88), and Pombo (1833–1912) are linked to Emerson and to one another. Sarmiento and Pombo served in diplomatic missions to the United States. Both wrote extensively, Sarmiento on a wide range of subjects and Pombo mainly poetry and children's literature. Pombo's and Martí's translations of "Fable" appeared in collections of children's literature, and Sarmiento's and Martí's tributes to Emerson were published in newspapers. Martí knew of Sarmiento as an author and reporter for the Argentine press, and Sarmiento knew the Cuban through his vigorous chronicles about the United States. Nothing indicates Martí's acquaintance with Pombo or an awareness of the Colombian's translation of "Fable"; however, the Cuban penned a tepid three-page critique of Pombo's poetry (*Obras completas* 7: 406–08).

Emerson and Nietzsche

Herwig Friedl

Ideally, advanced undergraduate and graduate students in American studies with some background in the history of philosophy and preferably with some competence in German will prepare for their course on Emerson and Nietzsche by reading an anthology of parallel texts of the two thinkers put together by their teacher, who may draw freely from the examples provided by Eduard Baumgarten, Stanley Hubbard, George Stack, Herwig Friedl ("Emerson"; "Fate"), and others. This anthology would be a starting point for an adventure of ideas on which the students will embark once they immerse themselves in major works by Emerson and Nietzsche, which should at least include "The American Scholar," "The Divinity School Address," "History," "Self-Reliance," "Circles," "Fate," and "Power," as well as Nietzsche's second and third *Untimely Meditations*; maybe selections from *The Gay Science, Thus Spoke Zarathustra, On the Genealogy of Morals, Twilight of the Idols, Ecce Homo*, and *The Antichrist*; and, finally, a generous helping from Nietzsche's uncollected writings.

The study of the "elective affinity" (Stack) of Emerson and Nietzsche pursues two major objectives in terms of cultural studies. First, it helps to deprovincialize the reading of Emerson and liberate him from the role of a mere or predominantly New England late-Romantic intellectual with strong religious leanings. Emerson's stature as a thinker of not only transatlantic but truly cosmopolitan significance (Buell, *Emerson*) and a writer of world literature in Goethe's sense of the term (Stievermann) becomes manifest in the massive presence of central aspects and tenets of his thought in Nietzsche's appropriation and in Emerson's impact on international modernism partly through Nietzsche. Second, the study of Emerson in Nietzsche, of Nietzsche's Emerson, helps to correct the prevailing myth of a predominant or even exclusive dependence of American culture on European models, as the comments on Emerson's important role in Nietzsche's presence in America in Jennifer Ratner-Rosenhagen's book *American Nietzsche* remind us. As in the case of Poe and Baudelaire or, less visible but highly important, of William James and Henri Bergson, the Emerson-Nietzsche relationship makes it clear that the transatlantic cultural and philosophical exchange or conversation is not a one-way affair.

In terms of philosophical significance, Emerson and Nietzsche mark the beginning of that major and perhaps ongoing endeavor to overcome or abandon traditional Western metaphysics. For that purpose both philosophers resuscitate and reinterpret what Emerson refers to as primary thinking (*Collected Works* 2: 204), which is manifest in the writings of the pre-Socratics, especially Heraclitus, or in symbolic Asian representatives of a premodern, nonmetaphysical vision like Zoroaster (Zarathustra). Students devoting themselves to the painstaking task of collecting and evaluating all references to Zoroaster in Emerson in the light of the function of Nietzsche's Zarathustra as prophet of a philosophy of the future will be richly rewarded. There is no more radical and profound intimation of the joint antimetaphysical project in Emerson and Nietzsche than this stunning aphoristic statement from "The American Scholar" answering the question as to what nature, reality, Being,[1] is: "There is never a beginning, there is never an end, to the inexplicable continuity of this web of God, but always circular power returning into itself" (Collected Works 1: 54). No creation, no last judgment, no origin, no telos; the web of the world creates God, God creates the world as a web of relations, there is only one event, one world; there is continuity beyond philosophical conceptualization and explication; the true being of this radically undetermined course of events is power (the *essentia* of the world) in the mode of an eternal return of the same (the formal *existentia* of reality). This Emersonian post- or a-Christian vision encapsulates the central elements of Nietzsche's ontology that were critically analyzed in great depth in Heidegger's Nietzsche studies.

Students and teachers interested in biographical and more narrowly defined cultural contexts will delight in finding parallels in Emerson's and Nietzsche's upbringing and their early careers through the final abandonment of their chosen professions, the ministry and the professorship. Biographies with detailed information abound (e.g., Parkes, Janz). The central concern and methodology of the course and of student papers, however, should follow Emerson's heuristic injunction from *Representative Men*: "Other men are lenses through which we read our own minds" (Collected Works 4: 4). Emerson read from the point of view of Nietzsche's transformative appropriation of his central visions and ideas allows the student who is overly familiar with a traditional image of Emerson to rediscover his original, radical, and unadulterated importance in the form of the "alienated majesty" (Collected Works 2: 27) of a different philosophical temperament. Furthermore, Nietzsche read from an Emersonian perspective will reveal subtleties and generosities of philosophical mood often submerged in the sometimes strident hyperbole of his devastating moral, cultural, and religious criticism.

As a starting point in the classroom, Nietzsche's comments on the importance of Emerson may create an even deeper interest and fascination with the subject of the course than the biographical approach. Under the impression of his repeated and intense readings, Nietzsche called Emerson the richest mind of the nineteenth century (Nietzsche 9: 602) and thus, by implication, more suggestive than, say, Hegel, Schelling, Carlyle, or even Schopenhauer. In the late *Twilight of the Idols* Nietzsche said about Emerson that "he simply does not know yet how old he is and how young he will yet be" (6: 120).[2] This means that, for Nietzsche, Emerson went back to and regained the original and metaphysically unadulterated vision of the primary thinkers and, at the same time, assumed the role and significance of a prophet of a philosophy of the future, the very role of Nietzsche/Zarathustra.

In a truly moving comment, Nietzsche stated that he could not praise Emerson since he was too close to him and that he, who styled himself the homeless, the unprecedented thinker par excellence, did feel at home, in his own home, in Emerson's works (9: 588). In this way Nietzsche emphasizes time and again the intimate relation, the very identity, of his and Emerson's visions of absolute intellectual self-reliance.

Re-creating and thinking through the Emerson-Nietzsche conversation in depth, the class may want to move on by assembling what I would like to call micro-level correspondences, Emersonian echoes of a significant but rather narrowly circumscribed thematic range that, cumulatively, begin to adumbrate the intensity and reach of their *hohes Geistergespräch* (their sublime intellectual, spiritual conversation). This is a very short, somewhat random, but exemplary list of such correspondences or echoes that may also serve to inspire topics for student papers:

> In "The American Scholar" Emerson presents a grim image of man under the modern social condition of the division of labor: "The state of society is one in which the members have suffered amputation, and strut about so many walking monsters,—a good finger, a neck, a stomach, an elbow, but never a man" (*Collected Works* 1: 53). Nietzsche clearly echoes this nightmare vision in his characterization of the "last men," the cripples of modern culture, in *Zarathustra II*, "On Redemption": "humans who are nothing but one big eye, or one big mouth, or a big stomach or anything big,—I call those inverted cripples. . . . Truly, my friends, I walk among men as among fragments and mere limbs of humans" (4: 178).

> Nietzsche's pervasive contempt for the masses finds an intense model of revulsion in *Representative Men*: "enormous populations, if they be beggars, are disgusting, like moving cheese, like hills of ants or fleas,— the more, the worse" (Emerson, *Collected Works* 4: 4).

> A glance at the term *slave* in Eugene F. Irey's *A Concordance to the Collected Essays of Ralph Waldo Emerson* will provide the student with numerous instances of a nonracial use of the word in the sense of Nietzsche's "slave morality," meaning totally outer-directed inauthenticity. The same can and should be done for the word *herd*.

> When Emerson speaks of intellectual independence in "The American Scholar" and decrees, "Books are for the scholar's idle times" (*Collected Works* 1: 57), Nietzsche follows his example by confessing that "in times of truly intense work you will never find a book near me" (6: 284).

> In *Zarathustra IV* Nietzsche extols the glory of the *Erdenreich*, the earthly empire that will replace the religious centrality of belief in a heavenly empire (4: 393); Emerson had provided a model in answering the desire for a world beyond, an *other world*, what Nietzsche also called a *Hinterwelt* (literally, a "meta-world"): "Other world! there is no other world" (*Complete Works* 10: 199).

> Emerson's argument against imitation and dependence on intellectual precedent in "The American Scholar" and "Self-Reliance" finds its

concise counterpart in *Zarathustra I*, where Zarathustra calls upon his
pupils to overcome the hero worship of the teacher (4: 101).

Emerson's image of the great thinker as an agent of fiery destruction in
"Circles" (*Collected Works* 2: 183) impressed Nietzsche so much that
he quoted the passage extensively at the end of the third *Untimely
Meditation*, "Schopenhauer as Educator" (1: 426), and he continued to
envision himself and his philosophy in such Emersonian terms—as a
powerfully destructive agent in the necessary processes of the revalua-
tion of tradition—when he hyperbolically asserts in *Ecce Homo*, "Why
I Am a Fate": "I am not human, I am dynamite" (6: 365).

And last, but indeed not least, the very concept of and term for the over-
man is clearly foreshadowed in Emerson's essay "Power," where he
speaks of the truly authentic and ideal future personality as *"plus* man"
(*Collected Works* 4: 31).

I have not yet properly mentioned such additional and major shared concerns of Emerson and Nietzsche as their radical questioning of institutionalized
Christianity ("The Divinity School Address," "Worship," and *Antichrist*), their
re- or transvaluing of all (cultural and moral) values ("Circles" and *The Genealogy of Morals* or *Twilight of the Idols*), or their overcoming the Aristotelian
logic of the excluded middle ("Nominalist and Realist" and Nietzsche's readings
in Heraclitus and a world of radical transitions; cf. Friedl, "1838" 248), which
might be added to the arsenal of topics for class discussion or major term papers
I have proposed thus far.

By way of deepening and concluding my survey of teaching possibilities, I
would now like to focus on one exemplary and, as I personally see it, central and
often not sufficiently appreciated common philosophical concern in Emerson
and Nietzsche: the role of time and, most prominently, the significance of the
present (cf. Stambaugh). In Emerson's "History" it is the authentic individual
existence in the now that determines the meaning of the past as a guideline
for the future. Famously and similarly, Nietzsche's second *Untimely Meditation*, "History in the Service and Disservice of Life," insists on the preeminent
importance of the present and its existential, vital demands and interests as
determining the meaning and significance both of the past and of the future.
The now as the pivot and turning point that allows human existence to abandon the burden of the past and to create the vital dimension of future action
in Emerson and Nietzsche prepares that modernist turn from antecedents to
consequences that will become prominent in both the pragmatists and modernist writers like Gertrude Stein, with her insistence on the authentic gesture of
being, writing, and thinking as a "beginning again and again" (23). Emerson's
"Circles" articulates and celebrates these endless processes of re- or transvalu-
ation by "an endless seeker with no Past at [his] back" (*Collected Works* 2: 188).
The thinker and writer becomes a seeker, an experimentalist, an essayist, someone who "essay[s] to be" (*Collected Works* 1: 103). Nietzsche saw himself cor-

respondingly as a *Versucher* (meaning both experimentalist *and* seducer, but also a writer of *essays* [in German: *Versuche*]). In *Zarathustra III* ("On Old and New Tablets"), one of many examples in Nietzsche, this foundational modernist gesture of abandonment of the old and the ecstatic projection of new meanings and laws recalls and rephrases the Emersonian vision of "Circles" (4: 246–69). One of the profoundest visualizations of the ontological depth of the now as prepared in Emerson is the great chapter "On the Vision and the Riddle" in *Zarathustra III*. The now, the moment, is experienced by Zarathustra as the meeting point of the two eternities of past and future joined now and forever in a circle, necessitating the eternal return of the same (4: 200). It is the free acceptance of this necessity ("where necessity was freedom itself" [4: 248]) that leads one, I believe, into the very center of Nietzsche's, and Emerson's, both cosmic and ontological total vision. And this makes me go back to Emerson and the essay "Fate" (Friedl, "Fate"), which Nietzsche had, with far-reaching consequences, read so early in his career, in 1862. Having, by way of preparation, discussed Nietzsche's basic intuition of the identity or continuity of fate and freedom, at some point the class should be encouraged to engage in a painstakingly close reading of "Fate" in order to identify the wealth of Emersonian foreshadowings of Nietzsche's central vision and thus put itself imaginatively in the place of young Nietzsche as reader of Emerson. One may imagine the class to collectively achieve and participate in a Nietzschean view of Emerson's thinking that, in condensed form, might be articulated as follows.

"Fate" should thus be read as one extended meditation on the moment of moments, the quintessential now of insight into the identities of freedom and fate, determination by the past and free agency, person and event. Emerson returns again and again to the central ontological and cosmological intuition: "if there be irresistible dictation, this dictation understands itself"; "in the history of the individual is always an account of his condition, and he knows himself to be a party to his present estate"; "The revelation of Thought takes man out of servitude into freedom"; "He who sees through the design, presides over it, and must will that which must be"; "Fate, then, is a name for facts not yet passed under the fire of thought;—for causes which are unpenetrated" (*Collected Works* 6: 2, 7, 14, 15, 17). In Nietzsche this moment of awareness of the identity of fate and freedom, of being determined by the burden of the past ("the spirit of heaviness" [4: 200; 241–45]) and the possibility of liberation, becomes the grand revelation of the idea of the eternal return of the same (4: 200–01). In this moment what appears to be dualistic and oppositional manifests itself as one, or as Emerson says in "Fate," "fate slides into freedom, and freedom into fate" (*Collected Works* 6: 20). Each single being, each entity, and each human being is fundamentally and radically self-conditioned: "Person makes event, and event person" (6: 21). This implies that, ultimately, there is only the continuity of becoming, the free unfolding of the will: "The one serious and formidable thing in nature is a will" (6: 16) and this sole agent of all being as becoming manifests itself as power: "this is an element with which the world is so saturated, there is no chink or crevice in which it is not lodged" (6: 28). Nietzsche will echo this thought when he exclaims and demands in the voice of Zarathustra, "To redeem the past in and of man and to change and newly create all 'it was' till the will says: 'Thus I wanted it, this way I shall will it . . .'" (4: 249). In both Emerson and Nietzsche meditating on the identity of freedom and fate, all beings, including the human being, become knowing and willing participants in the one and only event, the eternal, the ceaseless return of willing and knowing power, or as Emerson announced already in "The American Scholar": there is nothing but "circular power returning into itself." The intentional (through willing) and the intelligent (through thinking) returning into the "it was" redeems the past in its innocence of becoming for the present and the future. Karl Löwith has explicated this ontological and cosmological gesture as the ultimate translation of the human being back into the nature of all things, and he understands this as the modernist philosophical return of the oldest intuition, that of the ancient Greek *physikoi*, of Thales, of Anaximander, of Heraclitus, in the shape of the very circle of Being as thinking (192).

NOTES

[1] *Being* spelled with a capital B is used in this essay in order to distinguish it from mere beings according to Heidegger's differentiation of the two realms, which arises from and expresses the ontological difference.

[2] References to Nietzsche are from *Sämtliche Werke: Kritische Studienausgabe*, edited by Giorgio Colli and Mazzino Montinari. All translations of Nietzsche passages are those of the author.

Emerson in the East:
Perennial Philosophy as Humanistic Inquiry

John Michael Corrigan

In the following pages, I outline a pedagogy that employs Ralph Waldo Emerson's perennial philosophy as a site in which encounters between Western and Eastern conceptions of selfhood, culture, and history open themselves to critical analysis. Ideally suited for upper-level seminars, this pedagogy explores the humanistic foundations of Emerson's thought, particularly his Platonic orientalism and adaptation of the ancient wisdom narrative of the Renaissance, both of which exerted a profound influence on his interpretation of Asian religions and forms of thought. The course focuses on how his thought was born out of a sea change in the West's own self-conception and a new intercultural awareness as Europeans and Americans came into greater contact with the peoples, customs, and faiths of the lands beyond the classical world.

Since 2010 I have taught in two research universities in Taiwan. My classrooms are composed primarily of Taiwanese students, although international students constitute a strong presence in my classes. Teaching Emerson as world literature encourages my Taiwanese students to engage the texts in terms of their own Han Chinese heritage, while also allowing international students to contribute their own responses to the cross-cultural conversation. During the eighteen-week semester, the students read a number of Emerson's most famous essays—*Nature*, "History," "Circles," "The Over-Soul," "The Poet," "Experience," and "Fate"—and compare his portrayal of selfhood, consciousness, and history with the traditions he engaged: Platonic orientalism, the Vedic religious tradition (emphasizing key concepts such as Atman, reincarnation, karma, and maya), and Buddhism (samsara, dhyana, sunyata, or *kong*), including Taoist ideas such as the two modes of *wu* and *yu*.

I require my students to keep journals and guide their reading by posting two questions for each text on Moodle, an open-source learning program. Students write responses so as to engage in the assigned readings, to exercise their writing skills, and to develop their own interpretative framework for classroom discussion. This last goal is especially important. In comparison to Western students, students from Taiwan, China, Korea, and Japan are much more likely to remain silent during class. The journals play a key role in bringing them into the discussion, since they can initially report or draw from their written responses. This paradigm gradually instills a level of trust and comfort that brings the students into full dialogue. By periodically evaluating their journals, moreover, I am able to evaluate their writing and identify topics that the students can develop into larger essays.

In terms of teaching Emerson as world literature, my aim is to find not one-on-one correspondences of belief but striking resonances of Emerson's ideas with the forms of knowledge he adapted. In "History," a text we read early on in the semester, the students encounter Emerson's use of reincarnation or samsara in his depictions of "the metempsychosis of nature" or "the transmigration of souls" (*Collected Works* 2: 8, 14). For their journals, I ask the students how Emerson's descriptions of reincarnation relate to the forms of knowledge that are part of their own heritage. Are there any fundamental differences between Emerson's "transmigration of souls" and these traditions? By having them interpret Emerson in this way, I draw the students into the universalist framework of the essays themselves. "History" itself can be quite naturally interpreted in this way. Emerson opens the essay with a very decided emphasis: "There is one mind common to all individual men. Every man is an inlet to the same and to all of the same" (2: 3). I show how Emerson's universal mind can be fruitfully related to the ancient Greek notion of nous, the Vedic understanding of Atman, or the ancient Taoist idea of a celestial energy that emanates into individuation, a concept fundamental to later Confucian and Buddhist thought. Students learn to respond to Emerson's conception of reincarnation as part of a larger heritage that resonates in many traditions. More than a Hellenic idea re-formed or an appropriation of Eastern spirituality, it is part of a consistent effort on Emerson's part to embrace intercultural concepts in order to illuminate the self and its histories.

This approach allows me to place Emerson in his New England context and introduce the universalist notion of religion that was emerging at that time. I show how Emerson's life provides a microcosm of a broader shift away from a Christ-centered worldview. Even while his family background set him toward the ministry, Emerson's education propelled him from this vocation. His attraction to Asian forms of thought was preset by his father's dissemination of materials associated with it, for William Emerson was an early circulator of essays on Asian religions in the United States. In his college years, Emerson's reading of translations and colonial-tinged interpretations of India is apparent in his journals. Emerson moved beyond these colonial conceptions of Asian religions to a number of source materials as they became more accessible. By 1836 he had read the Manusmṛti (Laws of Manu), selections from the Mahabharata, and the works of Confucius—and in the coming decade, the Bhagavad Gita and Upanishads would profoundly influence his writing (Versluis 54–55).

Students benefit from learning that Emerson's view of the East as a genuine source of knowledge reflected an older belief system that was fundamental to the development of the ancient wisdom narrative of the Renaissance and the Western invention of single oriental philosophy. That Emerson did not initially understand the ancient wisdom narrative but gradually came to accept it shows something important about his reading of an earlier heritage that preset the ways in which Europeans interpreted the Far East as they gained greater access to it, first through missionary and trade relations and, later, through colonial conquest. Scholars have called this earlier heritage Renaissance Neoplatonism or Hermetic Neoplatonism. In recent years, a clearer picture of the Platonic orientalism of the Renaissance, along with its ancient wisdom narrative, has appeared. This version of the Platonic heritage stems from a form of Platonism that was considered heretical "on account of 1) its reverence for the philosophy of Plato as a kind of divine revelation; and 2) its location of earlier expressions of this divine revelation in 'the orient' or 'the East'" (Kripal 14).

In "Plato, or the Philosopher" from *Representative Men* (1850), Emerson captures the central claim of the ancient wisdom narrative. He states emphatically that the foundation of Western knowledge is to be found in the East:

> Meantime, Plato, in Egypt and in Eastern pilgrimages, imbibed the idea of one Deity, in which all things are absorbed. The unity of Asia and the detail of Europe; the infinitude of the Asiatic soul and the defining, result-loving, machine-making, surface-seeking, opera-going Europe,—Plato came to join, and, by contact, to enhance the energy of each. The excellence of Europe and Asia are in his brain. Metaphysics and natural philosophy expressed the genius of Europe; he substructs the religion of Asia, as the base.   (*Collected Works* 4: 30–31)

Emerson's Plato is a synthesizer of wisdom traditions rather than the philosopher of discursive reason enshrined in the Enlightenment. This interpretation of Plato draws from a heritage that is ancient and in the process of being rediscovered today. Indeed, a proto–Silk Road allowing full East-West contact from 1300 to 1100 BCE seeded many of the ideas that led to the development of the contemplative philosophy of the Hellenic world (McEvilley 4). In this context, Emerson's Plato can be interpreted as a refracted, even invented image from a world long since lost but whose memory of civilizational interconnectedness nonetheless persisted from the ancient world through to modern times.

I ask the students to consider that Emerson's belief in the interconnectedness of all cultures reflects this much older heritage. The Neoplatonists of late antiquity, whose writing exerted a major influence on Emerson, certainly believed they were carrying on a priestly philosophy that originated in Egypt, Persia, and the Far East. It is important that students understand that this conception of philosophy carrying on the gnosis of ancient times was also central to Suhrawardi and other major Islamic thinkers. In the twelfth century Suhrawardi "claimed to be reviving the tradition of the 'Ancients' . . . an intellectual affiliation including, in one sense or another, Hermes Trismegistus, Pythagoras, Empedocles, Socrates, Plato, Aristotle, the oriental sages of ancient Persia and India, and certain Sufis" (Walbridge 5).

Students benefit from knowing that a similar wisdom narrative flourished centuries later in the Italian Renaissance and possessed a twofold expression in the concepts of *prisca theologia* (ancient theology) and *philosophia perennis* (perennial philosophy) (Hanegraaff 67–68). The humanists gave accounts of an ancient theology that predated the modern religions. In their efforts to find the oldest and, they assumed, truest theology, the humanists believed that all traditions had a single source and expressed perennial principles that were transmitted from one region to another and developed under the auspices of certain sages or holy men. I explain to students that Emerson, writing some three hundred years after the Italian humanists, embraced aspects of this ancient wisdom narrative, especially the practice of perennial philosophy, finding in both the Platonic heritage and Asiatic traditions kindred articulations of divinely inspired insight.

Once students are aware of Emerson's reading in the ancient wisdom narrative outlined above, they can better discern the message in *Essays: First Series* that all cultures are linked together. Like the humanists, Emerson claims that "rare, extravagant spirits come by us at intervals [and] disclose to us new facts in nature. I see that men of God have, from time to time, walked among men and made their commission felt in the heart and soul of the commonest hearer." In "History," the major figures of the ancient wisdom narrative serve to unite the human being with his or her history: "How easily these old worships of Moses, of Zoroaster, of Menu, of Socrates, domesticate themselves in the mind. I cannot find any antiquity in them. They are mine as much as theirs." Emerson champions the "priestcraft of the East and West" and emphatically ties these figures to the perennial ideas expressed in Mosaic, Persian, Vedic, Confucian, and Hellenic traditions that lay the basis for our modern world (*Collected Works* 2: 16).

In Emerson's creative use of past religious traditions, students are also asked to consider the potential limitations of the Western view of the East in the early modern era. I ask students to consider to what degree Emerson follows the tendency to frame Asiatic religions as a single philosophy or make them reflect the claims of Platonic orientalism. It is important to show that one of the key Buddhist teachings, sunyata or *kong* (usually translated as "emptiness" or "void"), has a strained history in the West. The Jesuit missionaries, who were the principal arteries through which Eastern thought reached Europe, initially encountered a Zen Buddhist elite in Japan whose notion of emptiness was different from the Indian Buddhist idea of self-emptying and comparable Taoist notions like the modes of *wu* and *yu* (nonbeing and being). The Jesuits saw the Zen formulations of emptiness as a dangerous atheism that needed to be either rejected outright or contextualized in the Western invention of an oriental philosophy (App, *Cult*). I ask students therefore to think critically about the potential connections among perennial philosophy, colonial practices, and present-day globalization.

The course thus approaches students in a way that is directly accessible to them in their own traditions, yet challenges them to think about the development of civilizations from perspectives that are simultaneously more reflective of a shared past and more mindful of a common responsibility for our future. As a course grounded in Emerson, we are guided by his own sense of mission. He repeatedly called his readers to draw energy from the sacred practices of the past and to invent themselves beyond the parochial ground into which they were born. In his conclusion to "Circles," Emerson offers a complex conception of self-transformation, which echoes at once the practice of self-emptying (kenosis) in Western mystical traditions and the core Buddhist teaching of sunyata or *kong*: "The one thing we seek with insatiable desire, is to forget ourselves, to be surprised out of our propriety, to lose our sempiternal memory, and to do something without knowing how or why; in short, to draw a new circle" (*Collected Works* 2: 190). Unlike many of the colonial interpreters of Asian religions, Emerson does not champion one civilization over another, nor does he advocate withdrawing from tradition and superstition; the truth he seeks attempts to balance the mind's activity of synthesizing the world around it with the mystical willingness to let go of our own constructions of reality: "The way of life is wonderful," he affirms; "it is by abandonment" (2: 19).

NOTES ON CONTRIBUTORS

Branka Arsić is Charles and Lynn Zhang Professor of English and comparative literature at Columbia University. Her recent works include *Bird Relics: Grief and Vitalism in Thoreau* (2016), *On Leaving: A Reading in Emerson* (2010), and *The Other Emerson* (coedited with Cary Wolfe [2010]).

Dan Beachy-Quick is a poet and essayist whose most recent books include *Of Silence and Song* (essays, fragments, and poems) and *gentlessness* (poems). His work has been supported by the Lannan and Guggenheim Foundations.

Martin Bickman is professor of English and President's Teaching Scholar at the University of Colorado, Boulder. His *Minding American Education: Reclaiming the Tradition of Active Learning* won the Outstanding Book Award from the American Education Research Association. He is also the author of *American Romantic Psychology* and *Walden: Volatile Truths*.

Corinne E. Blackmer is professor of American literature and Judaic Studies at Southern Connecticut State University. She has published on Elizabeth Bishop, Ralph Waldo Emerson, Allen Ginsberg, the Hebrew Bible, Nella Larsen, and Gertrude Stein and coedited *En Travesti: Women, Gender Subversion, Opera*. She has recently finished a book, *Queering Anti-Zionism* (Wisconsin UP, forthcoming), and is coediting a volume called *Poisoning the Wells: Antisemitism in Contemporary American Culture, Politics, and Education.*

Ronald A. Bosco, distinguished professor of English and American literature and distinguished service professor at the State University of New York at Albany, served as the general editor of *The Collected Works of Ralph Waldo Emerson* and the coauthor of *The Emerson Brothers: A Fraternal Biography in Letters* (with Joel Myerson).

Michael P. Branch is professor of Literature and Environment at the University of Nevada, Reno. His recent books are *Raising Wild* (2016), *Rants from the Hill* (2017), *"The Best Read Naturalist": Nature Writings of Ralph Waldo Emerson* (coedited with Clinton Mohs, 2017), and *How to Cuss in Western* (2018).

Jean Ferguson Carr is coauthor of *Archives of Instruction: Nineteenth-Century Rhetorics, Readers, and Composition Books in the U.S.*; coeditor of the Pittsburgh Series in Composition, Literacy, and Culture; and textual coeditor of two volumes of *The Collected Works of Ralph Waldo Emerson*. She teaches at the University of Pittsburgh.

Nels Anchor Christensen teaches environmental literature at Albion College in southern Michigan. His scholarship and creative nonfiction have appeared in *ISLE: Interdisciplinary Studies in Literature and Environment*, *Gray's Sporting Journal*, *Wake: Great Lakes Thought and Culture*, and *Resilience: A Journal of the Environmental Humanities*.

John Michael Corrigan is associate professor at National Chengchi University. He is the author of *American Metempsychosis: Emerson, Whitman, and the New Poetry* (2012) and an editor for the University of Virginia's *Digital Yoknapatawpha*.

David O. Dowling is associate professor at the University of Iowa. His numerous articles and six books include *Emerson's Protégés: Mentoring and Marketing Transcendentalism's Future* (2014) and the monograph "Emerson's Newspaperman: Horace Greeley and Radical Intellectual Culture, 1836–1872" in *Journalism and Communication Monographs* (2017).

Susan L. Dunston is professor of English at New Mexico Tech, former president of the Emerson Society, and author of *Romance of Desire: Emerson's Commitment to Incompletion* and essays on Emerson's philosophy in the *Journal of Speculative Philosophy, ESQ, The Journal of American Culture, ATQ, Emerson for the Twenty-First Century, Ralph Waldo Emerson in Context,* and *Romanticism and Philosophy.*

Amy Earhart is associate professor of English at Texas A&M University. She is the author of *Traces of the Old, Uses of the New: The Emergence of Digital Literary Studies,* coeditor of *The American Literature Scholar in the Digital Age,* and the author of numerous book chapters and articles.

Leslie Elizabeth Eckel, associate professor of English at Suffolk University in Boston, is the author of *Atlantic Citizens: Nineteenth-Century American Writers at Work in the World* (2013) and the coeditor of *The Edinburgh Companion to Atlantic Literary Studies* (with Clare Elliott [2016]).

Meredith Farmer is assistant teaching professor at Wake Forest University, where her work is focused on the intersections between literature and science. Her book project, "Melville's Ontology," is under advance contract with Northwestern University Press. She is also developing a related collection, "Rethinking Ahab: Melville and the Materialist Turn."

Anne (Anita) Fountain is professor emerita of Spanish at San José State University. She has published extensively on José Martí in both English and Spanish. Her translations include Martí's poetry (*Versos sencillos*) and stories by the Cuban authors Nancy Alonso, Marilyn Bobes, Senel Paz, Leonardo Padura Fuentes, and Aida Bahr.

Herwig Friedl is professor emeritus of American literature and history of ideas at Heinrich-Heine-Universität Düsseldorf, Germany. He has published books on Henry James, women's studies as cultural studies, and spatial conceptions. His numerous essays focus on American transcendentalism, pragmatism, and the cultural exchange between America and Asia.

Len Gougeon, distinguished professor of American literature at the University of Scranton, is a former president of the Ralph Waldo Emerson Society and a recipient of the society's Distinguished Achievement Award. He is the author of *Virtue's Hero: Emerson, Antislavery, and Reform* and the coeditor of *Emerson's Antislavery Writings* (with Joel Myerson).

Jennifer Gurley is associate professor of English at Le Moyne College. Her work has appeared in *ESQ, The New England Quarterly, Philosophy and Literature,* and elsewhere. She is currently completing a study of Emerson as a religious writer and a volume of the collected poems of Ellen Sturgis Hooper.

Christoph Irmscher, provost professor of English and director of the Wells Scholars Program at Indiana University, is the author of *Max Eastman: A Life, Louis Agassiz:*

Creator of American Science, Longfellow Redux, and *The Poetics of Natural History.* He has edited Audubon for the Library of America and contributed to *The Cambridge History of American Poetry.*

Andrew Kopec is assistant professor of English at Purdue University, Fort Wayne. His recent work appears in *PMLA, ELH, Early American Literature,* and *ESQ,* as well as in *Henry David Thoreau in Context* (2017). He is currently completing a manuscript entitled "The Pace of Panic: American Romanticism and the Business Cycle."

Mark C. Long is professor of English and American studies at Keene State College, where he teaches courses in American literature, poetry, and the environmental humanities. He is coeditor of *Teaching North American Environmental Literature* (2009) and is an associate editor for the journal *Pedagogy: Critical Approaches to Teaching Literature, Language, Composition, and Culture.*

Carolyn R. Maibor is professor of English at Framingham State University, where she teaches classes on early through nineteenth-century American literature. She is the author of *Labor Pains: Emerson, Hawthorne, and Alcott on Work and the Woman Question* (2004) as well as a number of scholarly articles.

T. S. McMillin, professor of English at Oberlin College, teaches courses on American literature and environmental studies. He is the author of *The Meaning of Rivers: Flow and Reflection in American Literature* and *Our Preposterous Use of Literature: Emerson and the Nature of Reading,* along with numerous articles on transcendentalism.

Sean Ross Meehan, associate professor of English and director of writing at Washington College, is the author of *Mediating American Autobiography: Photography in Emerson, Thoreau, Douglass, and Whitman.* His recent work includes "Metonymies of Mind: Ralph Waldo Emerson, William James, and the Rhetoric of Liberal Education," published in the journal *Philosophy and Rhetoric* (2016).

Saundra Morris, professor of English at Bucknell University, is coeditor, with the late Joel Porte, of *Emerson's Prose and Poetry: A Norton Critical Edition* and *The Cambridge Companion to Ralph Waldo Emerson.* She has published essays on Emerson's poetry in nineteenth-century and current contexts and on transcendentalist poetry.

Wesley T. Mott is emeritus professor of English at Worcester Polytechnic Institute. Author of *"The Strains of Eloquence": Emerson and His Sermons* (1989) and editor of volume 4 of Emerson's *Complete Sermons* (1992) and *Ralph Waldo Emerson in Context* (2014), he organized the Ralph Waldo Emerson Society in 1989.

Todd H. Richardson is associate professor of English at the University of Texas of the Permian Basin. His work has appeared in *The New England Quarterly, The Concord Saunterer, The Oxford Handbook of Transcendentalism,* and the *Walt Whitman Quarterly Review.* He currently serves as president of the Ralph Waldo Emerson Society.

David M. Robinson, distinguished professor emeritus of American literature at Oregon State University, is a former president of the Ralph Waldo Emerson Society and the author of *Emerson and the Conduct of Life* and *Apostle of Culture: Emerson as Preacher and Lecturer.*

Ned Stuckey-French teaches at Florida State University and is the author of *The American Essay in the American Century* and the coeditor of *Essayists on the Essay: Montaigne to Our Time* (with Carl Klaus). His articles and essays have appeared in journals such as *Culturefront, Guernica, TriQuarterly,* and *American Literature.*

SURVEY PARTICIPANTS

The following scholars and teachers of Emerson's works participated in the survey that provided material for the preparation of this book:

Stephen Arch, *Michigan State University*
Peter Balaam, *Carleton College*
Mashey Bernstein, *University of California, Santa Barbara*
Martin Bickman, *University of Colorado, Boulder*
Corinne E. Blackmer, *Southern Connecticut State University*
Geoff Bouvier, *Florida State University*
Nancy Bunge, *Michigan State University*
Owen Cantrell, *Georgia State University*
Jean Ferguson Carr, *University of Pittsburgh*
Raj Chandarlapaty, *American University of Afghanistan*
Aravind Chilukuri, *ECET, India*
Patrick Chura, *University of Akron*
John Michael Corrigan, *National Chengchi University, Taiwan*
Michael Ditmore, *Pepperdine University*
Noël Dolan, *Villanova University*
David O. Dowling, *University of Iowa*
Susan Dunston, *New Mexico Institute of Mining and Technology*
Meredith Farmer, *Wake Forest University*
Anne Fountain, *San José State University*
Mark Russell Gallagher, *University of California, Los Angeles*
Barbara George, *Kent State University*
Shoji Goto, *Rikkyo University*
Jennifer Gurley, *Le Moyne College*
Martha Kennedy, *Cuyamaca College*
Mabel Khawaja, *Hampton University*
William E. Kinnison, *Bishop Hartley High School and Ohio Dominican University*
Andrew Kopec, *Indiana University–Purdue University, Fort Wayne*
Carolyn R. Maibor, *Framingham State University*
Ruth Martin, *Northwestern University*
Sharon B. Meltzer, *Richard J. Daley College, City Colleges of Chicago*
Ricardo Miguel-Alfonso, *University of Castilla–LaMancha (Spain)*
Wesley T. Mott, *Worcester Polytechnic Institute*
Marianne Noble, *American University*
Maria O'Malley, *University of Nebraska, Kearney*
Jeffrey Pusch, *University of Southern Mississippi*
Todd H. Richardson, *University of Texas of the Permian Basin*
Augusta Rohrbach, *Tufts University*
Lawrence Rosenwald, *Wellesley College*
Judith P. Saunders, *Marist College*
John Schwiebert, *Weber State University*

Jonathan Senchyne, *University of Wisconsin, Madison*
Christopher Stampone, *Southern Methodist University*
Michael Seth Stewart, *Hunter College*
Joseph Urbas, *Université Bordeaux Montaigne*
Michael West, *University of Pittsburgh*
Robert A. Wilson, *Cedar Crest College*
Michael Ziser, *University of California, Davis*

WORKS CITED

Alcott, [Amos] Bronson. "Fuller, Thoreau, Emerson: Estimate by Bronson Alcott: The Substance of a 'Conversation.'" *Boston Commonwealth*, 6 May 1871, pp. 1–2.

———. *Ralph Waldo Emerson: An Estimate of His Character and Genius in Prose and Verse*. A. Williams, 1882.

Alcott, Louisa May. *The Journals of Louisa May Alcott*. Edited by Joel Myerson et al., Little, Brown, 1989.

Allen, Gay Wilson. *Waldo Emerson: A Biography*. Viking, 1981.

American Verse Project. University of Michigan Humanities Text Initiative, U of Michigan Library, quod.lib.umich.edu/a/amverse/project.html.

Anders, George. "That 'Useless' Liberal Arts Degree Has Become Tech's Hottest Ticket." *Forbes*, 29 July 2015, www.forbes.com/sites/georgeanders/2015/07/29/liberal-arts-degree-tech/#6ba950425a75.

Anderson, Quentin. *The Imperial Self: An Essay in American Literary and Cultural History*. Knopf, 1971.

Angelou, Maya. *The Complete Poetry*. Random House, 2015.

App, Urs. *The Cult of Emptiness: The Western Discovery of Buddhist Thought and the Invention of Oriental Philosophy*. UniversityMedia, 2012.

Arsić, Branka. "Brain Walks: Emerson on Thinking." *The Other Emerson*, edited by Branka Arsić and Cary Wolfe, U of Minnesota P, 2010, pp. 59–97.

———. *On Leaving: A Reading in Emerson*. Harvard UP, 2010.

Arsić, Branka, and Cary Wolfe, editors. *The Other Emerson*. U of Minnesota P, 2010.

Atkinson, Brooks, editor. *The Essential Writings of Ralph Waldo Emerson*. Modern Library, 2000.

Auden, W. H. *The Complete Works of W. H. Auden: Prose: Volume II, 1939–1948*. Edited by Edward Mendelson, Princeton UP, 2002.

Bacevich, Andrew J. *The Limits of Power: The End of American Exceptionalism*. Holt, 2008.

Ballón, José C. *Autonomía Cultural Americana: Emerson y Martí*. Editorial Pliegos, 1986.

Baumgarten, Eduard. "Mitteilungen und Bemerkungen über den Einfluss Emersons auf Nietzsche." *Jahrbuch für Amerikastudien*, vol. 1, 1956, pp. 93–152.

Baym, Nina, et al., editors. *The Norton Anthology of American Literature*. 8th ed., vol. B, W. W. Norton, 2012.

Beardsley, David A., director. *Emerson: The Ideal in America*. Ralph Waldo Emerson Institute, 2007.

Bellah, Robert N., et al. *Habits of the Heart: Individualism and Commitment in American Life*. U of California P, 1985.

Bennett, Jane. *Vibrant Matter: A Political Ecology of Things*. Duke UP, 2010.

Bercovitch, Sacvan. *The Puritan Origins of the American Self*. Yale UP, 1975.

Berthoff, Ann E. *The Making of Meaning: Metaphors, Models, and Maxims for Writing Teachers.* Boynton/Cook, 1981.

Bérubé, Michael. "The Humanities, Declining? Not According to the Numbers." *The Chronicle of Higher Education,* 1 July 2013, chronicle.com/article/ The-Humanities-Declining-Not/140093.

Bickman, Martin. *Minding American Education: Reclaiming the Tradition of Active Learning.* Teachers College P, 2003.

———. "Seeing What I Say: Emerson, Berthoff, and the Dialectical Notebook." *Reader: Essays in Reader-Oriented Theory, Criticism, and Pedagogy,* no. 51, Fall 2004, pp. 22–31.

Bishop, Jonathan. *Emerson on the Soul.* Harvard UP, 1964.

Bloom, Harold. *A Map of Misreading.* Oxford UP, 1975.

———, editor. *Ralph Waldo Emerson.* Updated ed., Chelsea House, 2006.

Bloom, Harold, and Paul Kane, editors. *Emerson: Collected Poems and Translations.* Penguin, 1994. Library of America 70.

Bloom, Lynn Z. "The Essay Canon." *College English,* vol. 61, no. 4, Mar. 1999, pp. 401–30.

———. "Once More to the Essay: The Essay Canon and Textbook Anthologies." *symploke,* vol. 8, nos. 1–2, 2000, pp. 20–35.

Boller, Paul F. *American Transcendentalism, 1830–1860: An Intellectual Inquiry.* G. P. Putnam's Sons, 1974.

"Books by Emerson, Ralph Waldo." *Project Gutenberg,* www.gutenberg.org/ebooks/ author/1071.

Bosco, Ronald A. *"His Lectures Were Poetry, His Teaching the Music of the Spheres": Annie Adams Fields and Francis Greenwood Peabody on Emerson's "Natural History of the Intellect" University Lectures at Harvard in 1870.* Special issue of *Harvard Library Bulletin,* vol. 8, no. 2, Summer 1997.

———. Introduction. *Nature's Panorama: Thoreau on the Seasons.* U of Massachusetts P, 2005, pp. xiii–xxvii.

Bosco, Ronald A., and Joel Myerson. *The Emerson Brothers: A Fraternal Biography in Letters.* Oxford UP, 2005.

———, editors. *Emerson in His Own Time: A Biographical Chronicle of His Life, Drawn from Recollections, Interviews, and Memoirs by Family, Friends, and Associates.* U of Iowa P, 2003.

Branch, Michael P., and Clinton Mohs, editors. *"The Best Read Naturalist": Nature Writings of Ralph Waldo Emerson.* U of Virginia P, 2017.

Brown, Lee Rust. "The Emerson Museum." Special issue of *Representations,* no. 40, Autumn 1992, pp. 57–80.

———. *The Emerson Museum: Practical Romanticism and the Pursuit of the Whole.* Harvard UP, 1997.

Brownson, Orestes. *The Spirit of Gain; or, The Fall of Babylon, a Discourse on the Times.* 1837. *Nineteenth Century Collections Online,* tinyurl.galegroup.com/ tinyurl/5oXDC1. Accessed 10 June 2015.

Buell, Lawrence. *Emerson.* Belknap-Harvard UP, 2003.

———. "Postcolonial Anxiety in Classic U.S. Literature." *Postcolonial Theory and the United States: Race, Ethnicity, and Literature*, edited by Amritjit Singh and Peter Schmidt. U of Mississippi P, 2000, pp. 196–219.

———, editor. *Ralph Waldo Emerson: A Collection of Critical Essays*. Prentice Hall, 1993.

Bulkeley, Peter. *The Gospel-Covenant; or, The Covenant of Grace Opened*. 2nd ed., London, 1651.

Burkholder, Robert E., and Joel Myerson. *Emerson: An Annotated Secondary Bibliography*. U of Pittsburgh P, 1985.

Cabot, James Elliot. *A Memoir of Ralph Waldo Emerson*. Houghton Mifflin, 1887. 2 vols.

Cadava, Eduardo. *Emerson and the Climates of History*. Stanford UP, 1997.

Callero, Peter L. *The Myth of Individualism: How Social Forces Shape Our Lives*. Rowman and Littlefield, 2009.

Cameron, Kenneth Walter. *The Emerson Tertiary Bibliography with Researcher's Index*. Transcendental Books, 1986.

———. *Transcendental Log: Fresh Discoveries in Newspapers Concerning Emerson, Thoreau, Alcott and Others of the American Literary Renaissance, Arranged Annually for Half a Century from 1832*. Transcendental Books, 1973.

Carpenter, Frederic Ives. *Emerson Handbook*. Hendricks House, 1953.

Carr, Nicholas. *The Shallows: What the Internet Is Doing to Our Brains*. W. W. Norton, 2011.

Casselman, Ben, and Marcus Walker. "Wanted: Jobs for the New 'Lost' Generation." *The Wall Street Journal*, 14 Sept. 2013, www.wsj.com/articles/SB1000142412788 7323893004579057063223739696.

Cavell, Stanley. *Conditions Handsome and Unhandsome: The Constitution of Emersonian Perfectionism*. U of Chicago P, 1990.

———. *Emerson's Transcendental Etudes*. Edited by David Justin Hodge, Stanford UP, 2003.

———. *Philosophical Passages: Wittgenstein, Emerson, Austin, Derrida*. Blackwell, 1995.

———. *This New Yet Unapproachable America: Lectures after Emerson after Wittgenstein*. Living Batch Press, 1989.

———. "What's the Use of Calling Emerson a Pragmatist?" *Emerson's Transcendental Etudes*, edited by David Justin Hodge, Stanford UP, 2003, pp. 215–23.

Chace, William M. "The Decline of the English Department: How It Happened and What Could Be Done to Reverse It." *The American Scholar*, 1 Sept. 2009, theamericanscholar.org/the-decline-of-the-english-department/#. Vq4kTBgrJRZ.

Chai, Leon. *The Romantic Foundations of the American Renaissance*. Cornell UP, 1987.

Channing, William Henry. "Emerson's Phi Beta Kappa Oration." *Estimating Emerson: An Anthology of Criticism from Carlyle to Cavell*, edited by David LaRocca, Bloomsbury, 2013, pp. 74–81.

Chiasson, Dan. "Ecstasy of Influence: Ralph Waldo Emerson's American Poetry." *The New Yorker*, 7 Sept. 2015, pp. 85–87.

Coates, Ta-Nehisi. "The Case for Reparations." *The Atlantic*, June 2014, pp. 56–71.

Connors, Robert J. *Composition-Rhetoric: Backgrounds, Theory, and Pedagogy*. U of Pittsburgh P, 1997.

Conway, Moncure. "The Transcendentalists of Concord." *Fraser's Magazine*, Aug. 1864, p. 247.

Cooke, George Willis. *Ralph Waldo Emerson: His Life, Writings, and Philosophy*. James R. Osgood, 1881.

Cooper, Thomas W. *Fast Media / Media Fast: How to Clear Your Mind and Invigorate Your Life in an Age of Media Overload*. AuthorHouse / Gaeta, 2011.

Cramer, Jeffrey S., editor. *The Portable Emerson*. Penguin, 2014.

D'Agata, John, editor. *The Lost Origins of the Essay*. Graywolf, 2009.

———, editor. *The Making of the American Essay*. Graywolf, 2016.

———, editor. *The Next American Essay*. Graywolf, 2003.

Daston, Lorraine J., and Peter Galison. *Objectivity*. Zone, 2007.

Davies, Edward. *The Mythology and Rites of the British Druids*. London, 1809.

Dennison, George. *The Lives of Children: The Story of the First Street School*. Addison-Wesley, 1969.

Dickinson, Emily. *The Poems of Emily Dickinson: Reading Edition*. Edited by R. W. Franklin. Belknap-Harvard UP, 1999.

Dimock, Wai Chee. "Deep Time: American Literature and World History." *American Literary History*, vol. 13, no. 4, 2001, pp. 755–75.

———. "Scarcity, Subjectivity, and Emerson." *Boundary 2*, vol. 17, no. 1, Spring 1990, pp. 83–99.

———. *Through Other Continents: American Literature across Deep Time*. Princeton UP, 2006.

Dolan, Neal. *Emerson's Liberalism*. U of Wisconsin P, 2009.

Douglass, Frederick. *Narrative of the Life of Frederick Douglass, an American Slave, Written by Himself*. Boston, 1845.

Early, Gerald, editor. *Speech and Power: The African-American Essay and Its Cultural Content, from Polemics to Pulpit*. Ecco, 1992–93. 2 vols.

Eckel, Leslie Elizabeth. *Atlantic Citizens: Nineteenth-Century American Writers at Work in the World*. Edinburgh UP, 2013.

Elder, John. Introduction. Nature/"*Walking*." Beacon, 1994, pp. vii–xviii.

Elder, John, and Robert Finch, editors. *The Norton Book of Nature Writing*. Norton, 2002.

Ellison, Julie K. *Emerson's Romantic Style*. Princeton UP, 1984.

"Emerson and the Examined Life." Philosophy Foundation, 28 June 2003, Faneuil Hall, Boston. C-SPAN, www.c-span.org/video/?156135-1/emerson-examined -life.

Emerson, Ralph Waldo. *The Collected Works of Ralph Waldo Emerson*. Edited by Alfred R. Ferguson et al., Harvard UP, 1971–2013. 10 vols.

———. *The Complete Sermons of Ralph Waldo Emerson*. Chief editor, Albert J. von Frank, U of Missouri P, 1989–92. 4 vols.

———. *The Complete Works of Ralph Waldo Emerson*. Edited by Edward Waldo Emerson, Houghton Mifflin, 1903–04. 12 vols.

———. *The Complete Works of Ralph Waldo Emerson*. Digital Collections, U of Michigan Library, quod.lib.umich.edu/e/emerson.

———. *The Correspondence of Emerson and Carlyle*. Edited by Joseph Slater, Columbia UP, 1964.

———. *The Early Lectures of Ralph Waldo Emerson*. Edited by Stephen E. Whicher et al., Harvard UP, 1959–72. 3 vols.

———. *Emerson's Antislavery Writings*. Edited by Len Gougeon and Joel Myerson, Yale UP, 1995.

———. *Emerson's Complete Works*. Edited by James Elliot Cabot, Houghton Mifflin, 1883–93. 12 vols.

———. English Traits, Representative Men, *and Other Essays*. Edited by Ernest Rhys, J. M. Dent, 1910, archive.org/details/englishtraitsrepr00emeruoft. Accessed 2 July 2017.

———. "Experience." *Quotidiana*, edited by Patrick Madden, 2005, essays.quotidiana .org/emerson/experience/.

———. "Illusions." *Quotidiana*, edited by Patrick Madden, 2005, essays.quotidiana .org/emerson/illusions/.

———. *The Journals and Miscellaneous Notebooks of Ralph Waldo Emerson*. Edited by William H. Gilman and Ralph H. Orth, Belknap-Harvard UP, 1960–82. 16 vols.

———. *The Later Lectures of Ralph Waldo Emerson, 1843–1871*. Edited by Ronald A. Bosco and Joel Myerson, U of Georgia P, 2001. 2 vols.

———. *The Letters of Ralph Waldo Emerson*. Edited by Ralph L. Rusk and Eleanor M. Tilton, Columbia UP, 1939, 1990–95. 10 vols.

———. "New England Reformers." *Emerson Central*, edited by Jone Johnson Lewis, emersoncentral.com/texts/essays-second-series/new-england-reformers/. Accessed 5 June 2017.

———. *The Poetry Notebooks of Ralph Waldo Emerson*. Edited by Ralph H. Orth et al., U of Missouri P, 1986.

———. *Ralph Waldo Emerson: The Major Poetry*. Edited by Albert J. von Frank, Belknap-Harvard UP, 2015.

———. *Ralph Waldo Emerson: The Major Prose*. Edited by Ronald A. Bosco and Joel Myerson, Belknap-Harvard UP, 2015.

———. *Representative Men. Hypertexts*, American Studies at the University of Virginia, 1994–2005, xroads.virginia.edu/~HYPER/EMERSON/repmen.

———. *The Selected Lectures of Ralph Waldo Emerson*. Edited by Ronald A. Bosco and Joel Myerson, U of Georgia P, 2005.

———. *The Selected Letters of Ralph Waldo Emerson*. Edited by Joel Myerson, Columbia UP, 1997.

————. *The Topical Notebooks of Ralph Waldo Emerson*. Chief editor, Ralph H. Orth, U of Missouri P, 1990–94. 3 vols.

Emerson, Ralph Waldo, and Henry David Thoreau. Nature/"*Walking*." Introduction by John Elder. Beacon, 1991.

Emerson, Ralph Waldo, et al., editors. *Memoirs of Margaret Fuller Ossoli*. Phillips, Sampson, 1852. 2 vols.

"Emerson Society Papers." *The Ralph Waldo Emerson Society*, 15 Apr. 2003, emersonsociety.org/emerson-society-papers/.

Englekirk, John E. "El epistolario Pombo Longfellow." *Boletín del Instituto Caro y Cuervo*, vol. 10, nos. 1–3, Jan.–Dec. 1954, pp. 1–58.

Everton, Michael J. *The Grand Chorus of Complaint: Authors and the Business Ethics of American Publishing*. Oxford UP, 2011.

Fabian, Ann. "Speculation on Distress: The Popular Discourse of the Panics of 1837 and 1857." *The Yale Journal of Criticism*, vol. 3, no. 1, Fall 1989, pp. 127–42.

Fern, Fanny. *Rose Clark*. New York, 1856.

Field, Peter S. *Ralph Waldo Emerson: The Making of a Democratic Intellectual*. Rowman and Littlefield, 2003.

Foucault, Michel. *Fearless Speech*. Edited by Joseph Pearson, Semiotext(e), 2001.

Fountain, Anne. *José Martí and U.S. Writers*. UP of Florida, 2003.

Friedl, Herwig. "1838, July 15: 'The Divinity School Address.'" *A New Literary History of America*, edited by Greil Marcus and Werner Sollors, Belknap-Harvard UP, 2009, pp. 244–49.

————. "Emerson and Nietzsche: 1862–1874." *Religion and Philosophy in the United States of America*, edited by Peter Freese, vol. 1, Die Blaue Eule, 1987, pp. 267–88.

————. "Fate, Power, and History in Emerson and Nietzsche." *ESQ*, vol. 43, 1997, pp. 267–93.

Fuller, Margaret. *The Letters of Margaret Fuller*. Edited by Robert N. Hudspeth, Cornell UP, 1983–94. 6 vols.

————. *Margaret Fuller, Critic: Writings from the* New-York Tribune, *1844–1846*. Edited by Judith Mattson Bean and Joel Myerson, Columbia UP, 2000.

————. *Papers on Literature and Art*. Wiley and Putnam, 1846. 2 vols.

————. *Woman in the Nineteenth Century*. Greeley and McElrath, 1845.

Fyfe, Paul. "Digital Pedagogy Unplugged." *Digital Humanities Quarterly*, vol. 5, no. 3, 2011, digitalhumanities.org/dhq/vol/5/3/000106/000106.html.

Gailey, Amanda. "Teaching Attentive Reading and Motivated Writing through Digital Editing." *The CEA Critic*, vol. 76, no. 2, July 2014, pp. 191–99.

Garvey, T. Gregory, editor. *The Emerson Dilemma: Essays on Emerson and Social Reform*. U of Georgia P, 2001.

Gass, William H. "Emerson and the Essay." *Habitations of the Word*, Simon and Schuster, 1985, pp. 9–49.

————. *Fiction and the Figures of Life*. Vintage Books, 1972.

Giles, Paul. *Atlantic Republic: The American Tradition in English Literature.* Oxford UP, 2006.

Gilligan, Carol. "In a Different Voice: Women's Conceptions of Self and of Morality." *Harvard Educational Review*, vol. 47, no. 4, 1977, pp. 481–517.

Gitelman, Lisa. *Always Already New: Media, History, and the Data of Culture.* MIT P, 2006.

Goodman, Russell, editor. *Pragmatism: A Contemporary Reader.* Routledge, 1995.

———. "Ralph Waldo Emerson." *The Stanford Encyclopedia of Philosophy*, edited by Edward N. Zalta, plato.stanford.edu/entries/emerson.

Gougeon, Len. *Virtue's Hero: Emerson, Antislavery, and Reform.* U of Georgia P, 1990.

Greeley, Horace. *Hints toward Reform.* Harper and Brothers, 1850.

———. *Recollections of a Busy Life.* New York, 1868.

Greenham, David. *Emerson's Transatlantic Romanticism.* Palgrave, 2012.

Grimké, Charlotte Forten. *The Journals of Charlotte Forten Grimké.* Edited by Brenda Stevenson, Oxford UP, 1988.

Grimstad, Paul. *Experience and Experimental Writing: Literary Pragmatism from Emerson to the Jameses.* Oxford UP, 2013.

Gross, John, editor. *The Oxford Book of Essays.* Oxford UP, 1991.

Gruesz, Kirsten Silva. *Ambassadors of Culture: The Transamerican Origins of Latino Writing.* Princeton UP, 2002.

"Guide to Writing Programs." *Association of Writers and Writing Programs*, www .awpwriter.org/guide/guide_writing_programs.

Guignon, Charles, editor. *The Good Life.* Hackett, 1999.

Gurley, Jennifer. "Reading." *Ralph Waldo Emerson in Context*, edited by Wesley T. Mott, Cambridge UP, 2013, pp. 59–66.

Habich, Robert D. *Building Their Own Waldos: Emerson's First Biographers and the Politics of Life-Writing in the Gilded Age.* U of Iowa P, 2011.

———. "Emerson, Thoreau, Fuller, and Transcendentalism." *American Literary Scholarship*, vol. 2014, no. 1, 2016, pp. 3–20.

———, editor. *Selected Writings of Ralph Waldo Emerson.* Broadview, 2017.

Hanegraaff, Wouter J. *Esotericism and the Academy: Rejected Knowledge in Western Culture.* Cambridge UP, 2013.

Hanlon, Christopher. *America's England: Antebellum Literature and Atlantic Sectionalism.* Oxford UP, 2013.

Harding, Walter. *Emerson's Library.* UP of Virginia, 1967.

Harvey, Samantha C. *Transatlantic Transcendentalism: Coleridge, Emerson, and Nature.* Edinburgh UP, 2013.

Hawkins, Ann R. "Making the Leap: Incorporating Digital Humanities into the English Classroom." *The CEA Critic*, vol. 76, no. 2, July 2014, pp. 137–39.

Hawthorne, Nathaniel. Letter to William D. Ticknor. 19 Jan. 1855. *Letters of Hawthorne to William D. Ticknor, 1851–1864*, vol. 1, Carteret Book Club, 1910, pp. 73–75.

The Hĕĕtōpădēs of Vĕĕshnŏŏ-Sărmā, in a Series of Connected Fables, Interspersed with Moral, Prudential, and Political Maxims, translated by Charles Wilkens, Bath, 1787.

Heidegger, Martin. *Nietzsche I, II.* Gesamtausgabe vols. 6.1 and 6.2, Vittorio Klostermann, 1996–97.

Herder, Johann Gottfried. *Gott: Einige Gespräche.* Ettinger, 1787.

Hesse, Douglas. "The Place of Creative Nonfiction." *College English,* vol. 65, no. 3, Jan. 2003, pp. 237–41.

Hollander, John, editor. *American Poetry: The Nineteenth Century.* Library of America, 1996.

Holmes, Oliver Wendell. *Ralph Waldo Emerson.* Houghton Mifflin, 1886.

Holzer, Elie. *A Philosophy of Havruta: Understanding and Teaching the Art of Text Study in Pairs.* Academic Studies Press, 2014.

hooks, bell. *Teaching to Transgress: Education as the Practice of Freedom.* Routledge, 1994.

Hooper, Ellen Sturgis. *Poems.* Caroline Sturgis Tappan papers, MS Am 1221, Houghton Library, Harvard University, AC8.H7663.872P, MH-H.

Howe, Daniel Walker. *Making the American Self: Jonathan Edwards to Abraham Lincoln.* Harvard UP, 1997.

———. *What Hath God Wrought: The Transformation of America, 1815–1848.* Oxford UP, 2007.

Hubbard, Stanley. *Nietzsche und Emerson.* Verlag für Recht und Gesellschaft, 1958.

Hudspeth, Robert N. Review of *The Collected Works of Ralph Waldo Emerson. Nineteenth-Century Prose,* vol. 40, no. 2, 2013, pp. 1–104.

Hutchinson, Thomas. *The History of the Province of Massachusetts Bay, from the Settlement Thereof in 1628 until the Year 1750.* 3rd ed., Boston, 1795. 2 vols.

"Images of Emerson." *The Ralph Waldo Emerson Society,* 15 Apr. 2003, ralphwaldoemersonimages.wordpress.com.

I Remain: A Digital Archive of Letters, Manuscripts, and Ephemera. Lehigh U Digital Library, digital.lib.lehigh.edu/remain/index.html.

Irey, Eugene F., compiler. *A Concordance to the Collected Essays of Ralph Waldo Emerson.* Dec. 2005, concordlibrary.org/scollect/EmersonConcordance.

Irmscher, Christoph. "Linen Shreds and Melons in a Field: Emerson and His Contemporaries." *The Cambridge History of American Poetry,* edited by Alfred Bendixen and Stephen Burt, Cambridge UP, 2015.

Irving, Washington. *The Sketch Book of Geoffrey Crayon, Gent.* Edited by Haskell Springer, Twayne, 1978.

Jacobs, Jerry A. "American Studies: A Case Study of Interdisciplinarity." Population Studies Center, PSC Working Paper Series, 13-08. *University of Pennsylvania ScholarlyCommons,* Oct. 2013, repository.upenn.edu/cgi/viewcontent.cgi? article=1049&context=psc_working_papers.

Jacobson, David. *Emerson's Pragmatic Vision: The Dance of the Eye.* Pennsylvania State UP, 1993.

James, William. "Address at the Centenary of Ralph Waldo Emerson." *Pragmatism and Other Writings*, edited by Giles Gunn, Penguin, 2000, pp. 307–13.

Janz, Curt Paul. *Friedrich Nietzsche*. Carl Hanser, 1979. 3 vols.

Johnson, Edward. *Wonder-Working Providence of Sions Saviour in New England*. London, 1654.

Josselyn, John. *An Account of Two Voyages to New-England, Made during the Years 1638, 1663. Collections of the Massachusetts Historical Society*. 3rd series, vol. 3., Cambridge, MA, 1833, pp. 211–354.

Jowett, Benjamin, editor. *The Dialogues of Plato*. Clarendon, 1871.

Kateb, George. *Emerson and Self-Reliance*. 1995. Rowman and Littlefield, 2002.

———. *The Inner Ocean: Individualism and Democratic Culture*. Cornell UP, 1992.

Kazin, Alfred. *An American Procession: Major American Writers from 1830 to 1930*. Knopf, 1984.

Kent, Orit. "A Theory of *Havruta* Learning." *Journal of Jewish Education*, vol. 76, no. 3, July–Sept. 2010, pp. 215–45.

Kirkland, Caroline M. (Mary Clavers). *A New Home—Who'll Follow? or, Glimpses of Western Life*. New York, 1841.

Kirschenbaum, Matthew, and Sarah Werner. "Digital Scholarship and Digital Studies: The State of the Discipline." *Book History*, vol. 17, 2014, pp. 406–58.

Klaus, Carl H., and Ned Stuckey-French, editors. *Essayists on the Essay: Montaigne to Our Time*. U of Iowa P, 2012.

Klein, Lauren F. "The 'Emerson Museum' and the Darwin Exhibit: Observation, Classification and Display in the Early Works of Ralph Waldo Emerson and Charles Darwin." *Victorian Network*, vol. 2, no. 1, Summer 2010, pp. 7–26.

Koch, Daniel. *Ralph Waldo Emerson in Europe: Class, Race, and Revolution in the Making of an American Thinker*. Tauris, 2012.

Konvitz, Milton R., and Stephen E. Whicher, editors. *Emerson: A Collection of Critical Essays*. Greenwood Press, 1978.

Kripal, Jeffrey J. *Comparing Religions: Coming to Terms*. Wiley and Sons, 2014.

LaRocca, David. *Emerson's English Traits and the Natural History of Metaphor*. Bloomsbury, 2013.

———, editor. *Estimating Emerson: An Anthology of Criticism from Carlyle to Cavell*. Bloomsbury, 2013.

LaRocca, David, and Ricardo Miguel-Alfonso, editors. *A Power to Translate the World: New Essays on Emerson and International Culture*. Dartmouth College P, 2015.

Larson, John Lauritz. *The Market Revolution in America: Liberty, Ambition, and the Eclipse of the Common Good*. Cambridge UP, 2009.

Larson, Kerry C. Review of *The Emerson Museum: Practical Romanticism and the Pursuit of the Whole*, by Lee Rust Brown. *Configurations*, vol. 6, no. 3, Fall 1998, pp. 395–97.

Lauter, Paul, et al., editors. *The Heath Anthology of American Literature*. 7th ed., vol. B, Cengage, 2013.

Lawrence, Roderick J. "Deciphering Interdisciplinary and Transdisciplinary Contributions." *Transdisciplinary Journal of Engineering and Science*, vol. 1, no. 1, Dec. 2010, pp. 125–30.

Levin, Jonathan. *The Poetics of Transition: Emerson, Pragmatism, and American Literary Modernism*. Duke UP, 1999.

Levine, Alan M. and Daniel S. Malachuk, editors. *A Political Companion to Ralph Waldo Emerson*. UP of Kentucky, 2011.

Lewis, Jone Johnson, editor. "Ralph Waldo Emerson Texts." *Emerson Central*, 1996–2018, www.emersoncentral.com.

Lipset, Seymour Martin. *American Exceptionalism: A Double-Edged Sword*. W. W. Norton, 1997.

Ljungquist, Kent P. "Lectures and the Lyceum Movement." Myerson et al., pp. 330–47.

Lopate, Phillip, editor. *The Art of the Personal Essay: An Anthology from the Classical Era to the Present*. Doubleday, 1994.

———. "Foreword: The Undisguised Emerson." *The Annotated Emerson*, edited by David Mikics, Belknap-Harvard UP, 2012, pp. ix–xxi. Originally published as "Between Insanity and Fat Dullness: How I Became an Emersonian" in *Harper's*, Jan. 2011, pp. 67–73.

Lorde, Audre. *Sister Outsider: Essays and Speeches*. Crossing Press, 1984.

[Lowell, James Russell.] Review of *Letters to Various Persons*, by Henry David Thoreau. *The North American Review*, vol. 101, no. 209, Oct. 1865, pp. 597–608. *JSTOR*, www.jstor.org/stable/25107873. Accessed 25 Mar. 2015.

Löwith, Karl. *Nietzsches Philosophie der ewigen Wiederkehr des Gleichen*. 3rd ed., Felix Meiner Verlag, 1978.

Lysaker, John T., and William Rossi, editors. *Emerson and Thoreau: Figures of Friendship*. Indiana UP, 2010.

Maibor, Carolyn R. *Labor Pains: Emerson, Hawthorne, and Alcott on Work and the Woman Question*. Routledge, 2004.

Malin, Brenton. *Feeling Mediated: A History of Media Technology and Emotion in America*. New York UP, 2014.

Malloy, Charles. *A Study of Emerson's Major Poems*. Edited by Kenneth Walter Cameron, Transcendental Books, 1973.

Marr, David. *American Worlds since Emerson*. U of Massachusetts P, 1988.

Marshall, Megan. *Margaret Fuller: A New American Life*. Houghton Mifflin, 2013.

Martí, José. *Obras completas*. Editorial Nacional de Cuba / Instituto Cubano del Libro, 1963–73. 28 vols.

———. *Selected Writings*. Edited and translated by Esther Allen, introduction by Roberto González Echevarría, Penguin, 2002.

———. *Versos sencillos*, translated by Anne Fountain, foreword by Pete Seeger, McFarland, 2005.

Matthiessen, F. O. *American Renaissance: Art and Expression in the Age of Emerson and Whitman*. Oxford UP, 1941.

McAleer, John. *Ralph Waldo Emerson: Days of Encounter*. Little, Brown, 1984.

McEvilley, Thomas C. *The Shape of Ancient Thought: Comparative Studies in Greek and Indian Philosophy*. Allworth Press, 2002.

McGann, Jerome. "To the Nines." *Association of Research Libraries*, October 2005, old.arl.org/arldocs/events/fallforum/forum05/mcgann.html.

McGurl, Mark. *The Program Era: Postwar Fiction and the Rise of Creative Writing*. Harvard UP, 2009.

McKay, Claude. *Complete Poems*. Edited by William J. Maxwell, U of Illinois P, 2004.

Meehan, Sean Ross. "Education after an Earthquake: Emerson's Lessons in Panic and Pedagogy." *Pedagogy*, vol. 11, no. 2, Spring 2011, pp. 247–55.

Michael, John. *Emerson and Skepticism: The Cipher of the World*. Johns Hopkins UP, 1988.

Mihesuah, Devon A. *Cultivating the Rosebuds: The Education of Women at the Cherokee Female Seminary, 1851–1909*. U of Illinois P, 1993.

Mikics, David, editor. *The Annotated Emerson*. Belknap-Harvard UP, 2012.

Miller, Perry. *The Life of the Mind in America, from the Revolution to the Civil War*. Harcourt, Brace and World, 1965.

Mitchell, Charles E. *Individualism and Its Discontents: Appropriations of Emerson, 1880–1950*. U of Massachusetts P, 1997.

Montaigne, Michel de. *The Complete Essays of Montaigne*. Translated by Donald M. Frame, Stanford UP, 1958.

Montero, Oscar. *José Martí: An Introduction*. Palgrave Macmillan, 2004.

Montgomery, Georgina M., and Mark A. Largent, editors. *A Companion to the History of American Science*. John Wiley and Sons, 2015.

Morris, Saundra. "Whim upon the Lintel: Emerson's Poetry and a Politically Ethical Aesthetic." *Nineteenth-Century Prose*, vol. 40, no. 2, Fall 2013, pp. 189–216.

Mott, Wesley T. "'The Age of the First Person Singular': Emerson and Individualism." *A Historical Guide to Ralph Waldo Emerson*, edited by Joel Myerson, Oxford UP, 2000, pp. 61–100.

———. "'Monarch of All I Survey': Thoreau among Engineering Students." *Approaches to Teaching Thoreau's* Walden *and Other Works*, edited by Richard J. Schneider, Modern Language Association, 1996, pp. 187–91.

———, editor. *Ralph Waldo Emerson in Context*. Cambridge UP, 2013.

———. "*The Strains of Eloquence": Emerson and His Sermons*. Pennsylvania State UP, 1989.

Mott, Wesley T., and Robert E. Burkholder, editors. *Emersonian Circles: Essays in Honor of Joel Myerson*. U of Rochester P, 1997.

Mozoomdar, Protap Chunder. "Emerson as Seen from India." *The Genius and Character of Emerson: Lectures at the Concord School of Philosophy*, edited by F. B. Sanborn, James R. Osgood, 1885, pp. 365–71.

Myerson, Joel, editor. *Emerson and Thoreau: The Contemporary Reviews*. Cambridge UP, 2009.

———, editor. *Emerson Centenary Essays*. Southern Illinois UP, 1982.

———, editor. *A Historical Guide to Ralph Waldo Emerson*. Oxford UP, 2000.

————, editor. *Transcendentalism: A Reader.* Oxford UP, 2000.

Myerson, Joel, et al., editors. *The Oxford Handbook of Transcendentalism.* Oxford UP, 2010.

Myerson, Joel, and Leslie Perrin Wilson. *Picturing Emerson: An Iconography.* Special issue of *Harvard Library Bulletin*, vol. 27, nos. 1–2, Spring-Summer 2016.

Neal, Daniel. *History of New-England.* London, 1747. 2 vols.

Newfield, Christopher. *The Emerson Effect: Individualism and Submission in America.* U of Chicago P, 1996.

Nietzsche, Friedrich. *Sämtliche Werke: Kritische Studienausgabe.* Edited by Giorgio Colli and Mazzino Montinari, Deutscher Taschenbuch Verlag / de Gruyter, 1980. 15 vols.

Norton, Andrews. *A Discourse on the Latest Form of Infidelity.* Cambridge, MA, 1839. *Google Books*, books.google.com/books?id=2NQQAAAAYAAJ. Accessed 18 Mar. 2016.

Oates, Joyce Carol, and Robert Atwan, editors. *The Best American Essays of the Century.* Houghton Mifflin, 2000.

"The Oracles of Zoroaster." *The Phenix: A Collection of Old and Rare Fragments: Viz . . . the Oracles of Zoroaster. . . .* New York, 1835, pp. 125–76.

O'Sullivan, John L. "The Great Nation of Futurity." *The United States Magazine and Democratic Review*, vol. 6, no. 23, Nov. 1839, pp. 426–30.

Pace, Joel. "'Lifted to Genius'?: Wordsworth in Emerson's Nurture and *Nature*." *Symbiosis*, vol. 2.2, Oct. 1998, pp. 125–40.

Packer, Barbara L. *Emerson's Fall: A New Interpretation of the Major Essays.* Continuum, 1982.

Parkes, Graham. *Composing the Soul: Reaches of Nietzsche's Psychology.* U of Chicago P, 1994.

Paul, Sherman. *Emerson's Angle of Vision: Man and Nature in American Experience.* Harvard UP, 1952.

Perry, Bliss. "Emerson's Savings Bank." *Nation*, 24 Sept. 1914, pp. 371–73.

————. *Emerson Today.* Princeton UP, 1931.

Phelps, Elizabeth Stuart. *Chapters from a Life.* Boston, 1897.

Plato. *Opera: Volume II: Parmenides, Philebus, Symposium, Phaedrus, Alcibiades I and II, Hipparchus, Amatores.* Edited by J. Burnet, 2nd ed., Clarendon, 1922. Oxford Classical Texts.

Poirier, Richard. *Poetry and Pragmatism.* Harvard UP, 1992.

————. *The Renewal of Literature: Emersonian Reflections.* Random House, 1987.

Pombo, Rafael. *Fábulas y verdades.* Panamericana Editorial, 2000.

Porte, Joel, editor. *Emerson: Essays and Lectures.* Library of America, 1983.

————, editor. *Emerson in His Journals.* Belknap-Harvard UP, 1982.

————, editor. *Essays: First and Second Series.* Library of America, 1990.

————. "The Problem of Emerson." *Uses of Literature*, edited by Monroe Engel, Harvard UP, 1973, pp. 85–114. Harvard English Studies 4.

Porte, Joel, and Saundra Morris, editors. *The Cambridge Companion to Ralph Waldo Emerson*. Cambridge UP, 1999.

———, editors. *Emerson's Prose and Poetry: Authoritative Texts, Contexts, Criticism.* W. W. Norton, 2001.

Porter, David T. *Emerson and Literary Change.* Harvard UP, 1978.

Posner, Miriam. "Very Basic Strategies for Interpreting Results from the Topic Modeling Tool." *Miriam Posner's Blog*, 29 Oct. 2012, miriamposner.com/blog/very-basic-strategies-for-interpreting-results-from-the-topic-modeling-tool.

Quesada y Miranda, Gonzalo de. *Facetas de Martí.* Editorial Trópico, 1939.

"Ralph Waldo Emerson (1803–1882)." *The Web of American Transcendentalism*, June 2002, transcendentalism.tamu.edu/emerson.

Ratner-Rosenhagen, Jennifer. *American Nietzsche: A History of an Icon and His Ideas.* U of Chicago P, 2012.

"Related Sites." *The Ralph Waldo Emerson Society*, 15 Apr. 2003, emersonsociety.org/related-sites/.

Reuben, Paul P. "Ralph Waldo Emerson." *Perspectives in American Literature: An Ongoing Research and Reference Guide*, California State U–Stanislaus, www.paulreuben.website/pal/chap4/emerson.html.

Reynolds, David S. "'A Chaos-Deep Soil': Emerson, Thoreau, and Popular Literature." *Transient and Permanent: The Transcendentalist Movement and Its Contexts*, edited by Charles Capper and Conrad Edick Wright, Massachusetts Historical Society, 1999, pp. 282–309.

———. *John Brown, Abolitionist: The Man Who Killed Slavery, Sparked the Civil War, and Seeded Civil Rights.* Vintage, 2006.

Rezek, Joseph. "What Are the Standard Novels? Thoughts on Richard Bentley's Transatlantic Editions." History of the Book / American Literature and Culture Seminar, 25 Mar. 2015, Mahindra Humanities Center, Harvard U, Cambridge, MA. Lecture.

Richards, Leonard L. *"Gentlemen of Property and Standing": Anti-Abolition Mobs in Jacksonian America.* Oxford UP, 1971.

Richardson, Joan. *A Natural History of Pragmatism: The Fact of Feeling from Jonathan Edwards to Gertrude Stein.* Cambridge UP, 2006.

Richardson, Robert D., Jr. *Emerson: The Mind on Fire.* U of California P, 1995.

———. *First We Read, Then We Write: Emerson on the Creative Process.* U of Iowa P, 2009.

Riordan, Rick. *The Battle of the Labyrinth.* Hyperion, 2008. Percy Jackson and the Olympians 4.

Roberson, Susan L. *Emerson in His Sermons: A Man-Made Self.* U of Missouri P, 1995.

Robinson, David M. *Apostle of Culture: Emerson as Preacher and Lecturer.* U of Pennsylvania P, 1982.

———. *Emerson and the Conduct of Life: Pragmatism and Ethical Purpose in the Later Work.* Cambridge UP, 1993.

———. "Poetry, Personality, and the Divinity School Address." *Harvard Theological Review*, vol. 82, no. 2, Apr. 1989, pp. 185–99.

———. *The Unitarians and the Universalists.* Greenwood, 1985.

Rosenwald, Lawrence. *Emerson and the Art of the Diary.* Oxford UP, 1988.

———, editor. *Emerson: Selected Journals, 1820–1842.* Library of America, 2010.

———, editor. *Emerson: Selected Journals, 1841–1877.* Library of America, 2010.

Rusk, Ralph L. *The Life of Ralph Waldo Emerson.* Charles Scribner's Sons, 1949.

Sacks, Kenneth S. *Understanding Emerson: "The American Scholar" and His Struggle for Self-Reliance.* Princeton UP, 2003.

Sanders, Scott Russell. *Staying Put: Making a Home in a Restless World.* Beacon, 1993.

Sarmiento, Domingo Faustino. "Emerson." *Obras de D. F. Sarmiento*, vol. 45, Buenos Aires, 1900, pp. 374–76.

Schiller, F. C. S. "Relevance." *Mind*, vol. 21, no. 82, Apr. 1912, pp. 153–66.

Sealts, Merton M., Jr. *Emerson on the Scholar.* U of Missouri P, 1992.

Sealts, Merton M., Jr., and Alfred R. Ferguson, editors. *Emerson's Nature: Origin, Growth, Meaning.* 1969. 2nd ed., Southern Illinois UP, 1979.

Shillingsburg, Peter. "From Physical to Digital Textuality: Loss and Gain in Literary Projects." *The CEA Critic*, vol. 76, no. 2, July 2014, pp. 158–68.

Simmons, W. Michele. "Adapting: Online Learning Environments, Visual Pedagogy, and Active Learners." *Innovations*, special issue of *Romantic Pedagogy Commons*, Dec. 2004, www.rc.umd.edu/pedagogies/commons/innovations/simmons.html.

Smith, Robert. "Emerson as Reader or Critic and What It Means for Emerson Studies." Final paper, English 351, Indiana U, 2010.

Smith, Sydney. Review of *Statistical Annals of the United States of America*, by Adam Seybert. *The Edinburgh Review*, vol. 33, no. 65, Jan. 1820, pp. 69–80.

Sowder, William J. *Emerson's Impact on the British Isles and Canada.* UP of Virginia, 1966.

———. *Emerson's Reviewers and Commentators: A Biographical and Bibliographical Analysis of Nineteenth-Century Periodical Criticism with a Detailed Index.* Transcendental Books, 1968.

Stack, George J. *Nietzsche and Emerson: An Elective Affinity.* Ohio UP, 1992.

Stambaugh, Joan. *The Problem of Time in Nietzsche.* Translated by John F. Humphrey, Bucknell UP, 1987.

Stearns, Mary. *John Brown Album. Emancipation Evening, 1863.* American Literature Mss., The Lilly Library, Indiana U, Bloomington.

Stein, Gertrude. "Composition as Explanation." *Look at Me Now and Here I Am: Writings and Lectures 1909–45*, edited by Patricia Meyerowitz, Penguin, 1971, pp. 21–30.

Stievermann, Jan. "'We want men . . . who can open their eyes wider than to a nationality': Ralph Waldo Emerson's Vision of an American World Literature." *Emerson for the Twenty-First Century*, edited by Barry Tharaud, U of Delaware P, 2010, pp. 165–215.

St. John, Bayle. *Montaigne the Essayist: A Biography.* 2 Vols. London, 1858.

Tanner, Tony. *City of Words: American Fiction, 1950–1970.* Harper and Row, 1971.

Taylor, Anne-Marie. *Young Charles Sumner and the Legacy of the American Enlightenment, 1811–1851.* U of Massachusetts P, 2001.

Tharaud, Barry, editor. *Emerson for the Twenty-First Century: Global Perspectives on an American Icon.* U of Delaware P, 2010.

Thompson, Roger. *Emerson and the History of Rhetoric.* Southern Illinois UP, 2017.

Thoreau, Henry David. "The Best Criticism." 1840. Autograph Fragment. American Literature Mss., The Lilly Library, Indiana U, Bloomington.

———. *Journal.* Edited by Elizabeth Witherell, Princeton UP, 1981. 8 vols.

———. "Let such pure hate still underprop." *Collected Poems,* edited by Carl Bode, Johns Hopkins UP, 1964, pp. 71–73.

———. *Walden.* Edited by J. Lyndon Shanley, Princeton UP, 1971.

Toadvine, Ted. "Six Myths of Interdisciplinarity." *Thinking Nature,* vol. 1, 2011, pp. 1–7, thinkingnaturejournal.files.wordpress.com/2011/06/six-mythsbyted toadvine.pdf.

Tocqueville, Alexis de. *Democracy in America.* Translated by Arthur Goldhammer, Library of America, 2004.

United Nations. Universal Declaration of Human Rights. 1948, www.un.org/en/ universal-declaration-human-rights.

Van Cromphout, Gustaaf. *Emerson's Ethics.* U of Missouri P, 1999.

Van Leer, David. *Emerson's Epistemology: The Argument of the Essays.* Cambridge UP, 1986.

Venuti, Lawrence. *Translation Changes Everything: Theory and Practice.* Routledge, 2013.

Versluis, Arthur. *American Transcendentalism and Asian Religions.* Oxford UP, 1993.

von Frank, Albert J. *An Emerson Chronology.* 1994. 2nd ed., CreateSpace, 2016. 2 vols.

———. *The Trials of Anthony Burns: Freedom and Slavery in Emerson's Boston.* Harvard UP, 1998.

von Hammer, Joseph, translator. *Der Diwan von Mohammed Schemsed-din Hafis.* Stuttgart / Tübingen, 1812–13. 2 vols.

———. *Geschichte der schönen redekünste Persiens, mit einer Blüthenlese aus zweyhundert persischen Dichtern.* Wien, 1818.

Waite, Stacey. *Butch Geography: Poems.* Tupelo Press, 2013.

———. "Embracing the Contradictions: Stacey Waite on Gender, Poetry, and Infinite Possibility." Interview by Jennifer Perrine. *Pilot Light,* Dec. 2011, www.pilot lightjournal.org/2/7/1.

———. *The Transcendentalists.* U of Georgia P, 2007.

Walbridge, John. *The Leaven of the Ancients: Suhrawardi and the Heritage of the Greeks.* State U of New York P, 1999.

Walls, Laura Dassow. *Emerson's Life in Science: The Culture of Truth.* Cornell UP, 2003.

Wayne, Tiffany K. *Critical Companion to Ralph Waldo Emerson: A Literary Reference to His Life and Work*. Infobase, 2010.

Weisbuch, Robert. "Post-Colonial Emerson and the Erasure of Europe." Porte and Morris, *Cambridge Companion*, pp. 192–217.

Welch, James. *Riding the Earthboy 40: Poems*. Harper and Row, 1976.

West, Cornel. *The American Evasion of Philosophy: A Genealogy of Pragmatism*. U of Wisconsin P, 1989.

Whicher, Stephen E. *Freedom and Fate: An Inner Life of Ralph Waldo Emerson*. U of Pennsylvania P, 1953.

Whitman, Walt. *Leaves of Grass*. 1855. *The Walt Whitman Archive*, edited by Ed Folsom and Kenneth M. Price, Center for Digital Research in the Humanities, U of Nebraska at Lincoln, whitmanarchive.org.

Wider, Sarah Ann. *The Critical Reception of Emerson: Unsettling All Things*. Camden House, 2000.

Williford, Lex, and Michael Martone, editors. *Touchstone Anthology of Contemporary Creative Nonfiction: Work from 1970 to the Present*. Simon and Schuster, 2007.

Wilson, Harriet. *Our Nig; or, Sketches from the Life of a Free Black*. Boston, 1859.

Woodruff, Paul. *Reverence: Renewing a Forgotten Virtue*. Oxford UP, 2001.

Wright, Conrad. "Emerson, Barzillai Frost, and the Divinity School Address." *Harvard Theological Review*, vol. 49, no. 1, Jan. 1956, pp. 19–43.

———. "Soul Is Good, but Body Is Good Too." *Journal of Unitarian Universalist History*, vol. 37, 2013–14, pp. 1–20.

"Writings by Emerson." *The Ralph Waldo Emerson Society*, emersonsociety.org/writings/writings-by-emerson/.

York, Maurice, and Rick Spaulding, editors. *Natural History of the Intellect: The Last Lectures of Ralph Waldo Emerson*. Wrightwood, 2008.

INDEX